SALT LAKE CITY

The Place Which God Prepared

SALT LAKE CITY

◎

The Place Which God Prepared

EDITED BY

SCOTT C. ESPLIN and
KENNETH L. ALFORD

Regional Studies in
Latter-day Saint Church History

RELIGIOUS STUDIES CENTER
BRIGHAM YOUNG UNIVERSITY

DESERET
BOOK

Published by the Religious Studies Center, Brigham Young University, Provo, Utah, in cooperation with Deseret Book Company, Salt Lake City

http://rsc.byu.edu

Interior design and layout by Art Morrill.

US $23.99
ISBN 978-0-8425-2799-6

Library of Congress Cataloging-in-Publication Data

Salt Lake City : the place which God prepared.
  pages cm — (Regional studies in Latter-day Saint Church history)
Includes bibliographical references and index.
ISBN 978-0-8425-2799-6 (hard cover : alk. paper)
1. Salt Lake City (Utah)—History. 2. Church of Jesus Christ of Latter-day Saints—History.
I. Esplin, Scott C. (Scott Clair), 1974– editor. II. Alford, Kenneth L., 1955– editor. III. Series:
Regional studies in LDS Church history.
F834.S257S25 2011
979.2'258—dc23
                                                                                    2011026686

Contents

Introduction

In 1829, almost a full year before the Church was organized, the Lord challenged the Prophet Joseph Smith and his associates to "seek to bring forth and establish the cause of Zion" (D&C 6:6; 11:6; 12:6). Though he vigorously pursued the cause of Zion throughout the remainder of his life, the Prophet's death left fully establishing Zion as a goal for others to accomplish. Within a few short years after his martyrdom, Joseph Smith's vision regarding Zion was transported more than 1,200 miles west when Brigham Young and his faithful followers established the City of the Great Salt Lake. Much of the history of Salt Lake City is grounded in the revelations, visions, and plans of the Prophet Joseph regarding Zion, and many of the commandments in the Doctrine and Covenants find their fulfillment in the development of Salt Lake City as the headquarters of the Church. Indeed, in Salt Lake City, "Zion [has] flourish[ed] upon the hills and rejoice[d] upon the mountains" as the Saints have "assembled together unto the place which [God has] appointed" (D&C 49:25).

In 2010, the Department of Church History and Doctrine at Brigham Young University focused its biennial Regional Studies in Latter-day Saint Church History on Salt Lake City. Faculty researched the history of the Church in Salt Lake—its pioneer founding, early growth, and development, as well as its bright present and future. With significant cooperation from several Church departments, the Regional Studies Committee (Craig J. Ostler as chair, along with John P. Livingstone, Scott C. Esplin, and Kenneth L. Alford) led the faculty on a focused overview of the Church's headquarters. The fruits of that experience are reflected here.

This publication begins appropriately with remarks delivered by Elder Marlin K. Jensen, Church Historian and Recorder, at the dedication of the new Church History Library in 2009. Elder Jensen outlines both the history of the Church Historian's office and its purpose in preserving the sacred history of the Church. His text serves as a prelude to chapters focused on the common mission of recognizing "the hand of God in the history of this Church and in our own lives."[1] Subsequent chapters outline how that history has unfolded in Salt Lake.

Craig James Ostler analyzes how revelations in the Doctrine and Covenants seem to have guided Church leaders as a pattern for the development of Salt Lake City. Early commands to build a temple, a house for the presidency, a print shop, and a boarding house for strangers see their fulfillment in structures erected in and around Salt Lake's Temple Square. Next Dennis A. Wright and Rebekah E. Westrup focus on Ensign Peak's role in laying out the pattern for Salt Lake City. They discuss the historical significance of the peak to early city settlers, address questions regarding its use, and outline its modern transformation.

This volume then turns its attention to historic structures erected by city founders. Richard O. Cowan discusses designing and building Salt Lake City's crown jewel, the world-famed Salt Lake Temple. Cowan notes several unique aspects of the building's construction as well as its importance both as a building project for the early Saints and now as the spiritual symbol for worldwide Church membership. Addressing the Temple's iconic neighbor, Scott C. Esplin turns the reader's attention to the Salt Lake Tabernacle, the oldest standing structure on Temple Square and the "grand old dame of pioneer Utah."[2] Esplin discusses the Tabernacle's witness to Church history, highlighting how both the building itself as well as its use have changed over its lifetime. Kenneth L. Alford and Robert C. Freeman move away from Temple Square to shine a spotlight on the Salt Lake Theatre, "Brigham's Playhouse." Alford and Freeman discuss the theatre's construction and operation, the support it received from Church leadership, its eventual demise, and the legacy of dramatic tradition it left among the Saints. Susan Easton Black concludes the building section, analyzing the visual influence of the Book of Mormon on the settling of Salt Lake. Her article focuses on the use of images of the beehive and of Deseret, prominent in the famed Beehive House but also common in less-familiar aspects of the city's history.

Moving from structures to individuals, this volume shifts to the stories of early settlers. Fred E. Woods shares his expertise of Mormon migration, chronicling the gathering places throughout the valley for nineteenth-century emigrants while highlighting how they were received by and assimilated into their "City of Zion." Arnold K. Garr draws attention to the numerous and significant contributions of Thomas Bullock. "The Lord's Clerk," Bullock participated in many of the historic details regarding the founding of Salt Lake City, preserving the legacy for future posterity. Bidding farewell to the city's founding fathers, David F. Boone captures the little-known story of Salt Lake's pioneer burial grounds. Boone highlights the beautiful Salt Lake City Cemetery, final resting place to numerous pioneers and Church leaders, and the private cemeteries, including the Brigham Young, Heber C. Kimball, Newel K. Whitney, Willard Richards, and John Smith family burial plots. The final chapter on Salt Lake's citizens centers on the relationship between the Saints and the federal government in telling the story of Camp Douglas. Kenneth L. Alford weaves a narrative of conflict between the two parties, highlighted by the actions of the chief antagonists, President Brigham Young and Colonel Patrick Edward Connor.

The final section of the book focuses on various Church departments and organizations that, because of Salt Lake's role as the world headquarters of the Church, leave a mark on the city's rich history. Matthew O. Richardson begins with the most prominent of the city's Church organizations, the First Presidency, and the history of the Church Administration Building. His chapter chronicles the construction of Salt Lake's version of "a house for the presidency" (D&C 94:3) as well as its symbolic significance for the entire Church. Michael A. Goodman continues analysis of the twentieth-century Church, discussing the development of correlation, a program centered in Salt Lake but also, through its influence on programs and publications, extends worldwide. Similarly, John P. Livingstone narrates the growth and development of LDS Family Services, another Salt Lake-based organization charged to provide spiritual and temporal aid to God's children across the globe. While programs like correlation and LDS Family Services take Salt Lake and the mission of the Church internationally, other significant Church efforts like family history research invite the world to Salt Lake. Kip Sperry's article highlights how the Church's mission to provide salvation for all of God's children, living and dead, has transformed Salt Lake City into the international center for family history research. One of the city's most famous organizations, the Mormon Tabernacle Choir, through its television and radio show *Music and the Spoken Word*, has in many ways similarly connected Salt Lake with the world. Lloyd D. Newell traces the history of the Choir's eight-decade long impact, highlighting how its weekly messages transport Salt Lake City and the Church into millions of homes worldwide. Finally, Craig J. Ostler concludes this volume, connecting early Saints' zeal to create Zion with its modern establishment in Salt Lake City. Looking forward to millennial glory, Ostler discusses Salt Lake's past in anticipation of a destined future.

Throughout this volume, the authors echo the message that reverberated with our pioneer forefathers during their westward trek. We invite readers, as they did, to "Come, Come, Ye Saints" and learn about the history of the Church in Salt Lake City—a city that has been, and continues to be, "the place which God for us prepared."[3]

Scott C. Esplin
Kenneth L. Alford
Editors

Notes

1. Marlin K. Jensen, "Dedication of the Church History Library."
2. Ronald W. Walker, "The Salt Lake Tabernacle in the Nineteenth Century: A Glimpse of Early Mormonism," *Journal of Mormon History* 32, no. 3 (Fall 2005): 198.
3. William Clayton, "Come, Come, Ye Saints," *Hymns of The Church of Jesus Christ of Latter-day Saints* (Salt Lake City: Deseret Book, 1985), no. 30.

Elder Marlin K. Jensen of the First Quorum of the Seventy, Church Historian and Recorder.
(© Intellectual Reserve, Inc.)

Chapter 1

Remarks at the Dedication of the Church History Library

Elder Marlin K. Jensen

Remarks at the dedication of the Church History Library in Salt Lake City on June 20, 2009.

Days of dedication are almost always days of celebration and occasions for expressions of gratitude. This is definitely a great day in the history of Church history!

This magnificent new Church History Library has taken fifteen years to plan and nearly four years to build. It will protect the Church's priceless historical collections—books, pamphlets, periodicals, journals, manuscripts, records, and photographs—against fire, theft, and forces of nature. It provides an open and welcoming gathering place for all who want access to those collections. Many heads, hearts, and hands have been involved in this accomplishment. We express sincere appreciation to all who have assisted in any way.

Elder Marlin K. Jensen is Church Historian and Recorder of The Church of Jesus Christ of Latter-day Saints.

View (ca. 1865) of the building on South Temple Street that housed the Church Historian's Office from 1856 to 1917. (© Intellectual Reserve, Inc.)

The available facilities for housing the Church's historical enterprise have not always been as grand as the home provided by this new library. During the Church's early years, record keeping was done in a variety of locations, including the Prophet Joseph Smith's home, his smokehouse where meat was cured, the Kirtland Printing Office and Temple, an upper room in the red brick store in Nauvoo, and a room in the Nauvoo Temple.

When the Saints were driven from Nauvoo in 1846, the Church historian and recorder of that day, Willard Richards, supervised the packing of existing Church records into two large boxes for the trip west. Once he reached the Salt Lake Valley, it appears that Brother Richards pursued his work in several temporary locations, including the Church office, his own home, the Council House, and the tithing storehouse. Eventually, in 1855, President Brigham Young decided that a new Historian's Office, combined with a private residence for Brother Richards's successor, Apostle George A. Smith, would be built on the south side of South Temple Street, opposite the Lion House. On September 15, 1856, in the presence of a handful of clerks then working in the Church Historian's Office, assistant Church historian and recorder Wilford Woodruff offered a prayer of dedication for that newly completed structure. His words that day are relevant still:

> And, by virtue of the Holy Priesthood vested in us, in the name of Jesus Christ, we do dedicate it and consecrate it unto the Lord our God, and we set it apart that it may contain the holy records of the Church and kingdom of God, and we ask in the name of Jesus Christ that it may be sanctified and holy unto thy name and we pray that we may be inspired by the gift and power of the Holy Ghost, while acting as Historians, or clerks for the Church; and may we keep a true and faithful record and history of thy Church and kingdom, and thy servants, and may it be kept in that way and manner that it may be acceptable unto thee, O Lord, and unto thy servants the presidency of thy Church.[1]

Following its dedication, the Historian's Office served as the location for the work of Church history from 1856 to 1917, a period of sixty-one years.

By 1917, a new Church office building, now named the Church Administration Building, had been built in Salt Lake City at an address that has since become very well known: 47 East South Temple. The work and collections of the Historian's Office had expanded by that time to justify turning the entire third floor of the building over to Church historian Anthon H. Lund and his staff. That location remained the center of Church history operations until once again, in 1972, a move was made to the east wing of the newly constructed Church Office Building at 50 East North Temple. The Church Historical Department did its business in that venue for thirty-seven years, ending with its recent move to this new facility a few weeks ago. Much like the ark of the covenant, which was temporarily housed in the tabernacle during Israel's wanderings and finally found a more

Church Historian's Office staff, February 1917. Left to right: John Powell (custodian), A. William Lund, Laurinda Pratt Weihe, President Anthon H. Lund (Church Historian), Harold Jenson, Andrew Jenson, and Alvin Olsen. (© Intellectual Reserve, Inc.)

permanent home in Solomon's Temple, the treasures of Church history have now found a welcome resting place here.

This brief chronology of what we may call the "homes" of Church history has more than mere historical value. Near the end of his life, the Prophet Joseph Smith foresaw dissensions within the Church and knew that apostates would lead many astray. At that time he told the Saints, "I will give you a key by which you may never be deceived, if you will observe these facts: Where the true Church is, there will always be a majority of the Saints, and the records and history of the Church also."[2] Those records and history now reside safely within the walls of this beautiful facility.

However, far more important than considerations of buildings and facilities is the purpose for which the Lord, at the Church's founding, commanded that a record be kept. In a word, God wants us to *remember*. It is a vital part of our worship of Him and His divine Son. This new Church History Library will play a vital role in helping us remember.

To this destination, the mecca of Latter-day Saint history, will flow the stories of the people, places, and events that make up that history. Here historical information will be catalogued, preserved, and shared with a local as well as a worldwide audience. Technology will enable historical information to flow in and out, reaching to and from the remotest corners of the world.

In this process, the hope of all of us charged with keeping the record is as expressed in 1904 by President Joseph F. Smith: That we may "see in every hour and in every moment of the existence of the Church, from its beginning until now, the overruling, almighty hand of Him who sent His only Begotten Son to the world."[3] That we may indeed come to know and remember the hand of God in the history of this Church and in our own lives is my prayer.

Exterior view of the Church History Library. (© Intellectual Reserve, Inc.)

Notes

1. Wilford Woodruff, in Journal History of The Church of Jesus Christ of Latter-day Saints, September 15, 1856, 3, Church History Library, The Church of Jesus Christ of Latter-day Saints, Salt Lake City. Spelling and punctuation have been standardized.

2. In Andrew Jenson and Edward Stevenson, *Infancy of the Church: A Series of Letters Written by Elders Andrew Jenson and Edward Stevenson* (Salt Lake City: n.p., 1889), 5.

3. Joseph F. Smith, in Conference Report, April 1904, 2.

Chapter 2

Salt Lake City: Founded upon the Doctrine and Covenants

Craig James Ostler

Salt Lake City is a unique city, due in part to the influence of revelations received by the Prophet Joseph Smith as recorded in the Doctrine and Covenants. As the headquarters of The Church of Jesus Christ of Latter-day Saints, the influence of the Lord's directives recorded in the Doctrine and Covenants is evident in the buildings at the heart of the city—the world-renowned Salt Lake Temple, the elliptical-domed Tabernacle, the ten-acre Conference Center, the regal Joseph Smith Memorial Building, and the high-rise Church Office Building; all ornamented with beautiful gardens and fountains. In addition, local residents and visitors alike may tour Welfare Square and the Church's Humanitarian Center, located away from the downtown area, to learn about efforts to provide for the poor and needy around the world.

One might ask, "Why did the early Mormon pioneers and those who have followed them build up Salt Lake City as they have?"

Craig James Ostler is a professor of Church history and doctrine at Brigham Young University.

Although no available records specifically state that Brigham Young and succeeding leaders of the Church searched the Doctrine and Covenants as the pattern to establish the city, there is ample indication that such was and is the case. Francis M. Gibbons noted that "after the Prophet [Joseph Smith]'s death, the whole object of Brigham's ministry seemed to represent a deliberate effort to execute, in the most minute detail, the plans and programs of his predecessor."[1] The Lord revealed to Brigham Young and the Saints that he called upon Joseph Smith "to bring forth my work; which foundation he did lay, and was faithful" (D&C 136:37–38). Those who accepted Joseph Smith as a prophet saw themselves as building upon the foundation that he laid. Indeed, Brigham Young openly declared, "Brother Joseph, the Prophet, has laid the foundation for a great work, and we will build upon it."[2] At a later time Brigham exclaimed, "I feel like shouting hallelujah, all the time, when I think that I ever knew Joseph Smith, the Prophet whom the Lord raised up and ordained, and to whom he gave keys and power to build up the Kingdom of God on earth and sustain it. These keys are committed to this people, and we have power to continue the work that Joseph commenced, until everything is prepared for the coming of the Son of Man. This is the business of the Latter-day Saints, and it is all the business we have at hand."[3] Further, the correlation between the instructions the Lord gave as recorded in the Doctrine and Covenants and the Church buildings erected in Salt Lake City strongly suggests that such a connection between the two should be considered.

Most of the revelations in the Doctrine and Covenants were received in the 1830s and 1840s. Over the ensuing years, their instructions have served as the foundation of the Lord's work wherever the Saints have gathered. Initially, the Lord addressed the community-building efforts of the Saints in upstate New York, Ohio, Missouri, and Illinois—all areas in which the main body of Saints remained for less than ten years. In each case, the Saints did not have time to fully carry out the Lord's commands. In contrast, Salt Lake City has been the headquarters of the Church for more than 160 years. Thus, as one might expect, the implementation of the revelations in the Doctrine and Covenants is most evident in the work of the Church in Salt Lake City.

As recorded in the Doctrine and Covenants, the Lord revealed that several specific stewardships and structures are integral to building his kingdom. The stewardships or responsibilities the Lord gave to the Church are connected to the buildings that provide a space to fulfill the Lord's commands to build up Zion. Several buildings pivotal to establishing Zion have been built in Salt Lake City, with the attendant responsibilities of the stewardships given. The influence of the revelations in the Doctrine and Covenants may be seen in the building of the Salt Lake Temple, the Church Administration Building, the Bishops' Central Storehouse, Welfare Square, the Humanitarian Center, Church Printing Services, the Church Office Building, the Church History Library, the Tabernacle and Conference Center, the remodeled Joseph Smith Memorial Building, various Church-owned businesses, and more. The genesis for each of these buildings may be traced to the revelations of the Doctrine and Covenants. That which follows is intended as an overview of the relationship between the Doctrine and Covenants and selected buildings in Salt Lake City. Further research regarding each of the buildings, as well as their purposes and history, will continue to reveal a rich story illustrating the influence of the revelations in the Doctrine and Covenants.

Temples: Houses of the Lord

In the Doctrine and Covenants, the chief edifice God commanded to be built was a temple—the house of the Lord. The Lord commanded temples to be built wherever the Saints have gathered in sufficient numbers to accomplish his work.[4] In 1831, he initially commanded that his house be built in Independence, Missouri (D&C 57:3). Subsequently, in 1833, he commanded that the Saints "establish a house, even a house of prayer, a house of fasting, a house of faith, a house of learning, a house of glory, a house of order, a house of God" (D&C 88:119) for the building up of "the city of the stake of Zion . . . in the land of Kirtland, [Ohio]" (D&C 94:1). In 1838, after the Saints gathered to Far West, Missouri, the Lord declared, "Let the city, Far West, be a holy and consecrated land unto me. . . . Therefore, I command you to build a house unto me, for the gathering together of my saints, that they may worship me" (D&C 115:7–8). Later, the Lord commanded the Saints in Nauvoo, Illinois, to "build a house to my name, for the Most High to dwell therein" (D&C 124:27).

In 1847, after announcing that the Salt Lake Valley was the site the Lord wished the Saints to settle, one of the first matters of business for Brigham Young and other Church leaders was to identify a location for the temple. Indeed, the plat for Salt Lake City was organized around the block for Temple Square.[5] Efforts were soon begun to prepare a foundation for the temple on the center block of the city. Today the majestic, six-spired Salt Lake Temple is one of the most recognized symbols of the Latter-day Saints.

The Doctrine and Covenants also contains directions about the purposes of those temples. These directions expand the concept of temples to places of worship and instruction, as well as places to perform ordinances. For example, the Lord's instructions regarding the structural pattern of the Kirtland Temple focused on providing space for worship meetings and for education. By revelation to the Prophet Joseph Smith, the Lord directed that sacred space on the first floor of the Kirtland Temple be provided "for your sacrament offering, and for your preaching, and your fasting, and your praying" (D&C 95:16). Further, he instructed that the upper court be used "for the school of mine apostles" (D&C 95:17). Earlier, the Lord had designated an upper room of the Newel K. Whitney store in Kirtland as "the house of God" in which the Saints were to hold the "school of the prophets" (see D&C 88:136–37). The Lord commanded that those attending the school "be instructed more perfectly in theory, in principle, in doctrine, in the law of the gospel, in all things that pertain unto the kingdom of God, that are expedient for you to understand" (D&C 88:78).

In Salt Lake City, the revelations regarding locations for the instruction and education of the Saints have resulted in buildings such as the Tabernacle, the Assembly Hall, and the spacious Conference Center, which occupies the entire block north of Temple Square. In addition, numerous Church buildings throughout the city follow the revealed pattern for the Kirtland Temple, with chapels set aside as places for worship and partaking of the sacrament, and classrooms for instructing young children, youth, and adults in the Primary, Sunday School, Young Women, Relief Society, and priesthood organizations and quorums.

The Lord's revealed purposes for the Nauvoo Temple added distinct purposes to those for the temple in Kirtland. For example, the Lord instructed the Saints to build a baptismal font for performing baptisms for the dead in the Nauvoo Temple (see D&C 124:29–36). In addition, the Lord indicated that within the Nauvoo Temple the Saints should receive the ordinances of washings, anointings, conversations, statutes, and judgments (see D&C 124:37–41). Later the Lord commanded that the Saints enter into and seal their marriage covenants by the authority of the priesthood within the walls of his house.[6] In accordance with those revelations, sacred ordinances are performed within the Salt Lake Temple such as baptisms for the dead, washings, anointings, endowments, and sealings for the living and the dead.[7]

A House for the Presidency

After instructing the Saints to build temples in Kirtland, Ohio, and in Independence, Missouri, the Lord commanded the Saints to build "a house for the presidency, for the work of the presidency, in obtaining revelations; and for the work of the ministry of the presidency, in all things pertaining to the church and the kingdom" (D&C 94:3).

In Salt Lake City, the house for the presidency began modestly as an annex between Brigham Young's homes—the Lion House and the Beehive House. In 1917, the Church Administration Building became

11

the house for the First Presidency, the Quorum of the Twelve, and other Church officers.[8]

Bishops' Storehouse

The Lord commanded that a bishops' storehouse be established as one of the first Church buildings in Kirtland and later in Independence, "to administer to the poor and the needy" (D&C 42:34; see also 58:24). Originally the bishops' storehouse in Salt Lake City was located on lots overseen by President Brigham Young and Bishop Newel K. Whitney on the southwest corner of the block east of Temple Square. Currently, there are 141 bishops' storehouses around the world.[9] The largest bishops'

View of the granary at Welfare Square, part of the bishops' storehouse system. (Courtesy of Craig James Ostler.)

storehouse, which serves as the flagship for the welfare system, is located on Welfare Square in Salt Lake City.[10] In the revelations of the Doctrine and Covenants, a tithing and contributions office was added to the bishops' responsibility and stewardship (see D&C 72:5–6; 119:1–5) and was to be presided over by the First Presidency and the Quorum of the Twelve (see D&C 120). Consequently, in Salt Lake City, the President's Office in the annex between President Brigham Young's residences included an early tithing office. In addition, a separate building was erected on that same block, directly east of Temple Square and occupying the same lot as the Bishops' Central Storehouse, with yards for livestock and buildings for other donations in kind. Today the Council for the Disposition of the Tithes (see D&C 120), which oversees the use of sacred funds used in providing for the poor and needy through bishops' storehouses, operates from two locations on the block east of Temple Square. The First Presidency and the Quorum of the Twelve Apostles are housed in the Church Administration Building, and those working in the office of the Presiding Bishopric occupy space in the high-rise Church Office Building.

Printing Office

Among the first buildings the Lord connected with Zion were Church-owned printing establishments. In July 1831, he commanded, "Let my servant William W. Phelps be planted in this place [Independence], and be established as a printer unto the church" (D&C 57:11). In addition, the Lord revealed that "there should be lands purchased in Independence, for . . . the house of the printing" (D&C 58:37). Likewise, in Kirtland, the Lord directed that "the second lot on the south [of the temple] shall be dedicated unto me for the building of a house unto me, for the work of the printing of the translation of my scriptures, and all things whatsoever I shall command you" (D&C 94:10). The Lord appointed six brethren—Joseph Smith Jr., Martin Harris, Oliver Cowdery, John Whitmer, Sidney

The Church's Printing Divsion building in Salt Lake City. (Courtesy of Craig James Ostler.)

Rigdon, and William W. Phelps (see D&C 70:1)—as stewards to oversee the publishing of "the revelations and commandments which I have given unto them, and which I shall hereafter give unto them" (D&C 70:3). This council of brethren, known as the Literary Firm, prepared manuscripts of revelations and began to print the Book of Commandments before mobs in Missouri destroyed the printing establishment and printed pages. At the dissolution of the firm in Kirtland, the Lord appointed that "my servants Frederick G. Williams and Oliver Cowdery have the printing office and all things that pertain unto it" as their stewardship (D&C 104:29).

In accordance with the Lord's commandments in the revelations of the Doctrine and Covenants, Church leaders in Salt Lake City established the printing office of the Church in the Deseret News Building, which faced South Temple, where the Joseph Smith Memorial Building stands today. As the Church has grown, the needs for larger facilities have repeatedly arisen. The Church Printing Service building[11] currently occupies about 335,411 square feet of building space—roughly the size of six football fields.[12] Modern presses roll six days a week, twenty-four hours a day, printing over twenty thousand Church publications. Church periodicals such as the *Ensign, New Era, Friend,* and the international magazine the *Liahona,* as well as manuals, pamphlets, paintings reproduced for meetinghouses and temples, and most importantly, scriptures, are printed and made ready for distribution there.

Translation of Sacred Texts and Church Publications

In order to send the word of the Lord to every kindred, tongue, and people, the Lord instructed that the Saints have a place for translation of the scriptures. The revelatory foundation and history of the Lord's latter-day work regarding translation is rich and unremitting. During the process of bringing forth the Book of Mormon, the Prophet Joseph Smith sought a place to translate the plates in peace. In December 1827, he moved from Manchester, New York, to Harmony, Pennsylvania, with the financial help of Martin Harris.[13] In June 1829, approximately two months after Oliver Cowdery arrived in Harmony to serve as Joseph's scribe, David Whitmer transported the plates to his father's home in Fayette, New York, where Joseph and Oliver completed the translation.[14] Within two months after the Church was organized in the Whitmer home on April 6, 1830, the Lord directed the Prophet Joseph Smith to begin a revelatory and inspired translation of the Bible.[15] After Joseph and Emma moved to Kirtland, the Lord revealed, "It is meet that my servant Joseph Smith, Jun., should have a house built, in which to live and translate" (D&C 41:7). In Kirtland, the Lord commanded the "printing of the translation of my scriptures, and all things whatsoever I shall command you" (D&C 94:10).

Today the Church's Translation Department is centered in the Church Office Building, with satellite locations around the world that are coordinated through Church headquarters in Salt Lake City. Thus far, the Book of Mormon has been translated into eighty-seven languages, and selections of the Book of Mormon into twenty-five additional languages.[16] In 2009, the first Latter-day Saint Spanish edition of the Bible, based on the 1909 edition of the Reina-Valera Spanish Bible, was published with excerpts from the Joseph Smith Translation of the Bible, new chapter headings, footnotes, and cross-references to all scriptures used by The Church of Jesus Christ of Latter-day Saints. The duty of the President of the Church is "to be a seer, a revelator, a translator, and a prophet" (D&C 107:92; see also D&C 21:1). Thus he directs the translations of sacred texts, such as scriptures and temple ordinances, into new languages. Employees and volunteers within the Translation Department act under the direction of the President of the Church.[17]

Church History and Church Records

From the earliest days of the Church, the Lord gave the Saints a command to keep a history. The first revelation given to members of the newly organized Church of Christ began, "Behold, there shall be a record kept among you" (D&C 21:1). Initially, Oliver Cowdery served as the Church historian and recorder.[18] Later, the Lord called John Whitmer "to keep the church record and history continually; for Oliver Cowdery I have appointed to another office" (D&C 47:3). In November 1831, the Lord reemphasized the importance of John Whitmer's calling to "continue in writing and making a history of all the important things which he shall observe and know concerning my church" (D&C 69:3). Further, the Lord added that John was to "travel many times from place to place, . . . writing, copying, selecting, and obtaining all things which shall be for the good of the Church, and for the rising generations" (D&C 69:7–8). Underscoring the importance given to keeping and preserving the history of the Lord's people, the Prophet Joseph Smith explained, "I will give you a key by which you may never be deceived, if you will observe these facts: Where the true Church is, there will always be a majority of the Saints, and the records and history of the Church also."[19]

After the Saints began to settle in Salt Lake City, the records of the Church were located in various temporary homes and buildings until 1856, when a modest building was constructed on South Temple across the street from Brigham Young's homes and offices. That building served as the Historian's Office until 1917, when the office and records were moved to the new Church Administration Building. Today the central locations fulfilling the divine command to keep records are the spacious Church History Library located on the corner of North Temple and Main Street and in the Church membership department in the Church Office Building.[20] Underscoring the influence of the Doctrine and Covenants upon the building of the Church History Library, the words "Behold, there shall be a record kept among you" (D&C 21:1) are inscribed over the entrance to the library.

Declare the Lord's Word to All the World

When the Prophet Joseph Smith first arrived in Independence, the Lord commanded that "the sound [of the gospel] must go forth from this place into all the world, and unto the uttermost parts of the earth" (D&C 58:64). In 1833, mobs drove the Saints from Jackson County, Missouri, before this command could be fulfilled. Nonetheless, from other locations the Saints have sent forth the word of the Lord in preaching the gospel.

Prophets have taught that obedience to this command includes sending missionaries to teach the gospel in every nation, wherever they are permitted to enter. For decades, thousands of missionaries came to Salt Lake City to receive instructions, be endowed in the temple, and receive training before embarking to their fields of labor. Today missionaries do not gather to Salt Lake City but attend classes in Missionary Training Centers in various locations throughout the world. However, calls to serve continue to originate from Salt Lake City, making it the center for gospel preaching within the Church. In addition, the sound of the gospel has literally gone forth from Salt Lake City to the entire world in other ways. General conferences of the Church, wherein the First Presidency, Quorum of the Twelve Apostles, and others preach the gospel, have been held in Salt Lake City for more than 150 years. Through the blessings of radio, television, satellites, and the Internet, conference proceedings are transmitted around the world. For most of that time, the sound of the gospel was sent forth from the famed Tabernacle. Since April 2000, the Church has broadcast most conferences and general meetings from the Conference Center.

A massive interpretation center, in which proceedings are rendered into many languages and broadcast around the world, is located in the basement of the Conference Center. Satellite centers, which are connected to the computers and a broadcast hub in the Conference Center, are found in various locations around the world. The author met with the directors for interpretation and broadcasts, who emphasized that in their work they were fulfilling the commandments in the Doctrine and Covenants. They cited such passages as, "For, verily, the sound must go forth from this place into all the world, and unto the utmost parts of the earth . . ." (D&C 58:64). Although this command was originally given in Independence, Missouri, in 1831, the interpreters felt that it was also their mandate for the work they are doing in Salt Lake City.

Peace for the Visitor to Zion

The Lord instructed the Saints settling Nauvoo to build a place where the traveler to Zion "may come from afar to lodge therein, . . . that the weary traveler may find health and safety while he shall contemplate the word of the Lord; and the corner-stone I have appointed for Zion" (D&C 124:23), "which shall be polished with the refinement which is after the similitude of a palace" (D&C 124:2). The

Saints carried out this command by beginning the construction of the Nauvoo House, located not far from the banks of the Mississippi River, from which visitors were received to Nauvoo. Unfortunately, the Saints were forced to leave Nauvoo before the Nauvoo House could be completed.

In Salt Lake City, the Saints erected the majestic Hotel Utah east of Temple Square. The hotel was completed in 1911, with protest from some Church members that the building "was a useless expenditure and the money should have been put to better use."[21] Addressing those critics, President Smith took a moment in his closing remarks at the October 1911 general conference: "We have helped to build one of the most magnificent hotels that exists on the continent of America, or in the old continent either. I am told that it is equal to any in the world, for convenience and comfort of its guests, for sanitation, for its situation, and architectural beauty, and in many other ways. Well, some of our people have thought that we were extravagant. I would like you to turn to the book of Doctrine and Covenants and read the commandment of the Lord to the Prophet Joseph Smith in the city of Nauvoo (D&C 124:22–24). The people were requested to contribute of their means to take stock in this building [the Nauvoo House]. . . , for it was intended for the beauty of the city, for the glory of that stake of Zion, and to accommodate the stranger from afar who came to contemplate the doctrines of the Church and the work of the Lord."[22] Today the original Hotel Utah has been renovated and serves as the Joseph Smith Memorial Building. Although lodging is no longer provided to the weary traveler, the Joseph Smith Memorial Building provides a place of respite in the midst of the city in a magnificent but tastefully adorned setting. Keeping with the original intent of providing for the visitor to Salt Lake City, three of the four Temple Square Hospitality restaurants are located within the building.[23] In addition, the large-screened Legacy Theater, a centerpiece of the building, is dedicated to showing films portraying the truths of the Restoration of the gospel, allowing visitors to contemplate the word of the Lord in latter days.

Church-Owned Businesses

The Lord directed that the Church manage for-profit businesses, often as stewardships, in which goods were to be sold "without fraud . . . [to] obtain money to buy lands for the good of the saints" (D&C 57:8). In Kirtland, the Lord commanded that those who oversaw Church properties such as the tannery, the printing office, the mercantile establishment, and the ashery place their profits in a treasury that could be drawn upon for "improving upon the properties which I have appointed unto you, in houses, or in lands, or in cattle" (D&C 104:68; see also vv. 19–39). In addition to the earlier Hotel Utah and current Joseph Smith Memorial Building, the Church has made selected investments in other properties. During the administration of President Joseph F. Smith (1901–18), "the Church maintained or acquired control of the *Deseret News,* Zion's Savings Bank and Trust Company, Utah-Idaho Sugar, and the Beneficial Life Insurance Company. It also purchased about 25 percent of the ZCMI stock. In 1919, the Deseret Sunday School Union Bookstore and the Deseret News Bookstore combined to form the Church operated Deseret Book Company."[24] Today the Deseret Management Corporation, organized in 1966, is the holding company of the Church. Several of the companies overseen by Deseret Management Corporation are headquartered in Salt Lake City, including Deseret Media Companies, Beneficial Financial Group, and Temple Square Hospitality.

Deseret Media Companies include Bonneville International Corporation, a major broadcasting group of television and radio stations, satellite communications, web broadcasting, and more; and the aforementioned Deseret Book Company, which since 1866 has been the market leader in the publishing, distribution, and retailing of faith-based books, music, and art.[25]

In 1905, the Church established Beneficial Financial Group "in direct response to Heber J. Grant's recognition of a community's responsibility to protect its widows and orphans." Then on June 16, 2009, after considering that other businesses met the needs of providing life insurance and other services, "Beneficial and its parent company, Deseret Management Corporation (DMC), made a strategic decision to discontinue issuing new life insurance policies and annuities and no longer accept applications for these products after August 31, 2009."[26] However, they continue to provide services for all those that had contracted with them before that time.

Temple Square Hospitality includes three restaurants in the Joseph Smith Memorial Building as well as the Lion House Pantry in Brigham Young's historic home. All of these restaurants provide banquet services and are favorite locations for wedding breakfasts, luncheons, dinners, and receptions.

Prominently located south of Temple Square and extending east and west are Church-owned buildings leased to various private businesses. The most prominent for-profit business venture is the current City Creek project, which envisions redeveloping downtown by providing the area near Temple Square with resident housing and attendant food, clothing, and other stores. The Church's business arm has

View of Temple Square. (© Intellectual Reserve, Inc.)

invested hundreds of millions of dollars into the City Creek project to make housing available to a community that lives in the area continuously. By revitalizing this block with upscale housing and business buildings, the Church is working to prevent the downtown decay that is evident in many other large cities. The Lord directed that the Presiding Bishopric shoulder the responsibility for temporal needs in his kingdom. Thus, often the Presiding Bishopric and those working under their direction have carried out those duties under the watchful eye and guidance of the First Presidency of the Church.[27]

Conclusion

From the Salt Lake Temple to the Church Administration Building to the Church Office Building and the Church History Library, the structures in Salt Lake City vividly illustrate the details for buildings in the Lord's kingdom, which are recorded in the pages of the Doctrine and Covenants. Church leaders and employees take great care to adhere to the guidance and direction given in the revelations of the Doctrine and Covenants. Following scriptural mandates, many Church departments have crafted mission statements that connect their work to the revelations of the Restoration. As the world headquarters of the Church, Salt Lake City serves as an excellent reminder of the foundational revelations in the Doctrine and Covenants and the Lord's constant and continuing hand in the work of the Restoration.

Notes

1. Francis M. Gibbons, *Brigham Young: Modern Moses, Prophet of God* (Salt Lake City: Deseret Book, 1981), 22.

2. *History of the Church of Jesus Christ of Latter-day Saints*, ed. B. H. Roberts, 2nd ed. rev. (Salt Lake City: Deseret Book, 1973), 7:234. (Hereafter *History of the Church*.)

3. Brigham Young, in *Journal of Discourses* (London: Latter-day Saints' Book Depot, 1854–86), 3:51.

4. *History of the Church*, 5:424, 427.

5. President Brigham Young assigned Orson Pratt to design the future city by drawing upon Joseph Smith's plan for the city of Zion. Orson went to work immediately, drawing the city plat with wide streets and large lots. By August 2, 1847, the base and meridian were established as the southeast corner of what became Temple Square. From there, he and Henry Sherwood began to survey the plat for Salt Lake City; streets were identified by the number of blocks east, west, north, or south of the meridian marker.

6. There is no specific revelation stating that the covenant of eternal marriage is to be performed only in temples. The Lord indicated that he wanted a house built unto his name in Nauvoo, "for there is not a place found on earth that he may come to restore again that which was lost unto you, or which he hath taken away, even the fulness of the priesthood" (D&C 124:28). If "the fulness of the priesthood" includes eternal marriage, then there is a direct connection to the revelations of the Doctrine and Covenants. Over the last century, on the other hand, prophets and apostles have taught that eternal marriages are authorized only within the walls of a temple. Yet ample evidence might be cited that eternal marriages performed by proper authority have occurred outside the temple over the history of the Restoration. For example, see Charles C. Rich, in *Journal of Discourses*, 19:164. It is evident from Doctrine and Covenants 132:7 that the one man who holds the keys to this power, the President of the high priesthood and of the Church (see D&C 107:65–66, 91), directs the work of performing the eternal marriage covenants. Those individuals have emphatically taught that the covenants of eternal marriage and of temple marriage are one and the same. Marriages for eternity were performed in the Nauvoo Temple in 1846. It also appears that the restricting of authorized eternal marriages to the temple occurred during the administration of President Joseph F. Smith. The restricting of eternal marriages to the temple is spelled out in James E. Talmage, *The Articles of Faith*, 12th ed. (Salt Lake City: The Church of Jesus Christ of Latter-day Saints, 1924), 458. He repeated that explanation in his volume *The House of the Lord* (Salt Lake City: Bookcraft, 1962), 57. Further research beyond the scope and intent of this article is needed to provide specifics that answer the questions of when and why eternal marriages may only be performed in temples today.

7. See Richard O. Cowan's chapter in this volume.

8. See Matthew O. Richardson's chapter in this volume.

9. "Welfare Service Fact Sheet," 2009.

10. Welfare Square is located at 751 West 700 South, Salt Lake City. The author has toured the facilities on several occasions as a guest of the directors of Welfare Square. These directors emphasized that the work at Welfare Square finds its foundation in the revelations of the Doctrine and Covenants and the Lord's inspiration to Church leaders that have clarified and built upon those revelations.

11. The Church Printing Building is located at 1980 Industrial Circle (about 2000 South and 2000 East) in Salt Lake City.

12. Author's conversation with Craig Sedgwick, director of Printing Division, LDS Church, June 14, 2011.

13. *History of the Church*, 1:19.

14. *History of the Church*, 1:48–49.

15. Robert J. Matthews, *"A Plainer Translation," Joseph Smith's Translation of the Bible: A History and Commentary* (Provo, UT: Brigham Young University Press, 1975), 3–4, 26–28.

16. "News of the Church: Book of Mormon Published in Guarani," *Ensign*, August 2009, 80.

17. The introduction in the Latter-day Saint edition of the Santa Biblia includes the explanation that the Bible was prepared under the direction of the First Presidency and the Quorum of the Twelve Apostles as a revision of the Reina-Valera 1909 edition of the Bible. See also author's notes from a presentation by Todd Harris of the Church Translation Department to professors and spouses from the Brigham Young University Department of Church History and Doctrine, July 14, 2010. Brother Harris emphasized the importance of the revelations in the Doctrine and Covenants—especially those addressing the translation of the Book of Mormon and the Joseph Smith Translation of the Bible—as the foundation for the Church's work of translation.

18. *History of the Church*, 1:166n.

19. Joseph Smith, in Andrew Jenson and Edward Stevenson, *Infancy of the Church* (Salt Lake City: n.p., 1889), 5.

20. See Elder Marlin K. Jensen's chapter in this volume.

21. Joseph Fielding Smith, *The Life of Joseph F. Smith* (Salt Lake City: Deseret Book, 1938), 425.

22. Joseph F. Smith, "Closing Remarks," in Conference Report, October 1911, 129–30.

23. On the main floor is the Nauvoo Café, which offers a variety of menu selections throughout the day. On the top floor are the Garden and the Roof, offering fine dining with incredible views overlooking Temple Square.

24. Richard O. Cowan, *The Latter-day Saint Century, 1901–2000* (Salt Lake City: Bookcraft, 1999), 38.

25. http://www.deseretmediacompanies.com/content/view/48.

26. http://www.deseretmanagement.com/?nid=19.

27. Author's minutes from meetings held with Gary Porter, secretary to the Presiding Bishopric, on July 13, 2010, and Dale Bills with City Creek Reserve, Inc. (CCRI) on July 16, 2010.

A view of Ensign Peak from the south. (Courtesy of David M. Whitchurch.)

Chapter 3

Ensign Peak:
A Historical Review

Dennis A. Wright
and Rebekah E. Westrup

From the time the pioneers first entered the Salt Lake Valley until the present, Ensign Peak has received recognition beyond its geological importance. The peak is an undistinguished hill, rising over a thousand feet from the northern edge of the Salt Lake Valley, approximately one mile north of the Utah State Capitol Building.[1] While unremarkable in most ways, the peak has received attention from community and religious leaders because of its historical importance. This discussion summarizes selected events in the history of Ensign Peak, from 1843 to the present, to help readers better understand and appreciate its significance.

The pioneer history of the peak began three years before the arrival of the Mormons in the Salt Lake Valley in July 1847. George A. Smith, a counselor to President Brigham Young, described how President

Dennis A. Wright is a professor of Church history and doctrine at Brigham Young University. Rebekah E. Westrup is a humanities major at Brigham Young University who participated in this project as a mentored research assistant.

Young first saw Ensign Peak while seeking divine guidance following the 1844 death of the Prophet Joseph Smith: "After the death of Joseph Smith, when it seemed as if every trouble and calamity had come upon the Saints, Brigham Young, who was President of the Twelve, then the presiding Quorum of the Church, sought the Lord to know what they should do, and where they should lead the people for safety, and while they were fasting and praying daily on this subject, President Young had a vision of Joseph Smith, who showed him the mountain that we now call Ensign Peak, immediately north of Salt Lake City, and there was an ensign fell upon that peak, and Joseph said, 'Build under the point where the colors fall and you will prosper and have peace.'"[2] Young understood that he was to lead the Church members west and that the peak he saw in vision would be a sign that they had reached their appointed destination.

On July 24, 1847, Brigham Young arrived at an overlook for his first view of the Salt Lake Valley. "While gazing upon the scene, . . . he was enwrapped in vision for several minutes. He had seen the valley before in vision and upon this occasion he saw the future glory of Zion and of Israel, as they would be, planted in the valleys of these mountains. When the vision had passed, he said: 'It is enough. This is the right place. Drive on.'"[3]

Because the pioneers had no firsthand knowledge of the territory, they relied on their prophet to determine the place of settlement in the West.[4] This happened when President Young viewed the valley for the first time and recognized Ensign Peak, which he had seen in vision. In an 1866 interview with a visitor to Salt Lake City, Brigham reflected on this experience. The interviewer recorded the following: "When coming over the mountains, in search of a new home for his people, he [Brigham Young] saw in a vision of the night, an angel standing on a conical hill, pointing to a spot of ground on which the new temple must be built. Coming down into this basin of Salt Lake, he first sought for the cone which he had seen in his dream; and when he had found it, he noticed a stream of fresh hill-water flowing at its base, which he called City Creek."[5] Because of his prior vision, Ensign Peak played an important role in helping the prophet recognize the place appointed as a home for the Saints.

Soon after entering the valley, President Young pointed at Ensign Peak and said, "I want to go there." He suggested that the peak "was a proper place to raise an ensign to the nations," and so it was named Ensign Peak.[6] On July 26, 1847, a party consisting of Brigham Young, Heber C. Kimball, Willard Richards, Ezra T. Benson, George A. Smith, Wilford Woodruff, Albert Carrington, William Clayton, Lorenzo Dow Young, and perhaps Parley P. Pratt climbed to the top of the hill. Of the event, Wilford Woodruff recorded that the group "went North of the camp about five miles and we all went onto the top of a high peak in the edge of the mountain which we considered a good place to raise an ensign upon which we named Ensign Peak or Hill. I was the first person that ascended this hill. Brother Young was very weary in climbing the peak, he being feeble."[7] While on the peak, the group surveyed the valley below with Heber Kimball's telescope to confirm their earlier judgment of the valley. "They appeared delighted with the view of the surrounding country," said one of the settlers who heard the explorers' report later in the day.[8] From this experience, the group gained the perspective necessary to begin planning the settlement. At this time, President Young apparently also determined the location of the temple, which he announced two days later, on July 28, by planting his walking stick at the site selected for the temple and saying, "Here we will build the temple of our God."[9]

A Flag on Ensign Peak

Did the Brigham Young party of pioneers raise a flag on Ensign Peak that July day in 1847? Throughout the years, many accepted that President Young had flown an American flag from the peak on July 26, while claiming the land as US territory. Because that is highly unlikely, did the pioneers fly another type of flag that day on Ensign Peak?

As early as June 1844, the Prophet Joseph Smith had suggested the creation of an ensign or flag that could be flown by the Saints.[10] He proposed a sixteen-foot flag of a unique design and construction, but it was never completed. However, while at Winter Quarters, Brigham Young remembered that he had seen in vision a flag flying on Ensign Peak.[11] Therefore, he commissioned the purchase of material suitable for a flag. Young desired that the colors of red, white, and blue be used along with a purple and scarlet insignia. Because the exact design of the flag was unknown, Heber C. Kimball suggested the Church leaders dream about it. The resulting flag became known as one of a group of flags known by the title "mammoth flag."[12] While this flag may have been publicly displayed during pioneer times, there is no evidence that this flag or others constructed by the Saints were flown publicly from Ensign Peak on July 26.

Many Saints, including Wilford Woodruff, fully expected to see a literal "Standard of Liberty reared up as an ensign to the nations."[13] In 1847, he spoke of "the standard and ensign that would be reared in Zion" and even made a sketch of a possible flag that he believed would serve as a standard to the nations. His version of the flag had distinctive Mormon symbols such as the sun, moon, and stars, as well as the symbolic use of the number twelve. It is clear that Woodruff believed that a flag such as this could be flown from the peak.[14] However, no evidence exists that this took place.

While it is possible that a group of pioneers did fly an American flag from Ensign Peak in 1847, there is also no evidence to support the community belief that President Young flew an American flag on Ensign Peak, July 26, while claiming the region for the United States. Regardless of the lack of historical details, Salt Lake City newspapers regularly referred to the raising of an American flag as a political act. For example, an 1884 news article referred to such an event in an article written to promote American patriotism.[15] Another news article in 1886 quoted a judge who described the Mormons as good citizens and cited as evidence their hoisting of an American flag on the peak upon their arrival in 1847.[16] Such reports persisted into the new century, as observed in an article written in 1901 that stated that Brigham Young had raised a flag on Ensign Peak and claimed the land in the name of the United States.[17] Stimulus for this belief continued into the twentieth century and was fueled by Susa Young Gates, a daughter of Brigham Young. Anxious to demonstrate the loyalty of the Mormons to the United States, she declared that her father and others had flown the American flag on Ensign Peak at the time they first climbed to its summit. Later, when writing her father's biography, she softened her claim regarding the American flag.[18] The origins of these beliefs appear to be more politically motivated than historically accurate. In 1921, Elder B. H. Roberts, a Church historian, wrote the following to quell the myth of the American flag on Ensign Peak:

> There has been one error promulgated in respect to the United States flag and Mormon history that I think, for the sake of accuracy in our history, ought to be corrected. This is the quite generally accepted idea or understanding that on the 26th day of July, when what is now called Ensign Peak was first visited by President Young and a group of pioneers, they there and then raised a United States flag and named the mount Ensign Peak. There is no evidence that they raised any flag on that mount at that time, or that they referred to the flag of the United States, when speaking of an "Ensign" in relation to that "hill" in the side of the mountain. They were merely out exploring the Salt Lake Valley northward, and extended their short journey as far as the Hot Springs, during which they climbed the hill we now call Ensign Peak. Had such an event as raising the United States flag taken place at that time, it certainly would have been recorded in the journal of some of the men present. Brigham Young gave the mountain its name, and makes an entry of that fact in his journal, but says nothing of any flag incident. Neither does Wilford Woodruff who related the events of the naming of Ensign Peak at length.[19]

Rather than any flag being flown on Ensign Peak upon the Saints' arrival in the valley, it appears likely that the brethren waved a large yellow bandana at the peak's summit. In support of this view, the *Salt Lake Tribune* quoted William A. C. Smoot, an early Church pioneer, as saying, "While they were up there looking around they went through some motions that we could not see from where we were, nor know what they meant. They formed a circle, seven or eight of them. But I could not tell what they were doing. . . . They hoisted a sort of flag on Ensign Peak. Not a flag, but a handkerchief belonging to Heber C. Kimball, one of those yellow bandanna kind."[20] While this appears to be the truth of the matter, the controversy was not fully resolved. In the years that followed, many continued to believe that some type of flag unique to the Saints had flown or that Brigham Young had flown an American flag as part of an effort to claim Utah for the United States, an act which, in that time frame, would not have been legally feasible.

Pioneer Uses of Ensign Peak

During the latter part of the nineteenth century, the Church and community found a variety of uses for Ensign Peak. At that time, Addison Pratt received the temple endowment ordinance there in preparation for his mission to the South Seas. Of this event, Brigham Young recorded, "Addison Pratt received his endowments on Ensign Hill on the July 21, 1849, the place being consecrated for the purpose. Myself and Elders Isaac Morley, P. P. Pratt, L. Snow, E. Snow, C. C. Rich and F. D. Richards, Levi W. Hancock, Henry Harriman and J. M. Grant being present. President H. C. Kimball, Bishop N. K. Whitney and Elder John Taylor came after the ordinances were attended to. Elders C. C. Rich and Addison Pratt were blessed by all, President Kimball being mouth."[21] While there may have been other such events on Ensign Peak, direct evidence is lacking.

Another use of the peak occurred during the Utah War (1857–58), when Church leaders stationed watchmen on the summit to watch for signals that indicated troop movements toward Salt Lake City. Smoke signals were used during the day, and fires provided the signals at night. When the watchmen saw these signals, they sent notices from Ensign Peak to the militia stationed in the city.[22]

Some years later, in 1899, the Army Signal Corps climbed the peak to demonstrate the effectiveness of their mirror signal techniques. In August of that year, they raised an American flag and then signaled the state governor, Herbert Manning Wells, that they had hoisted the flag in honor of the Utah volunteers in the Spanish-American War. Governor Wells then signaled back, "Hurrah for the signal corps! Let the flag float for the boys who have fought and bled and died for us."[23]

In 1897, the *Salt Lake Tribune*, a local newspaper, erected a wooden flagpole on Ensign Peak to celebrate the fiftieth anniversary of the arrival of the pioneers in the Salt Lake Valley.[24] The wooden flagpole stood until 1947, when another one was erected as part of the pioneer centennial celebration.[25]

During the latter part of the nineteenth century, the peak served as a popular gathering place for public speeches and events hosted by Church and community groups. It was also common for individuals and groups to hike to the summit for a variety of purposes. Boy Scouts, Church groups, and other parties regularly climbed the peak to commemorate special dates or achievements. Many of these expeditions took place on July 24 as part of local Pioneer Day celebrations. So popular was the peak as a gathering place that many hoped that a formal park or memorial might be constructed at the summit.

Ensign Peak in the Twentieth Century

Early in the twentieth century, interest in a public park prompted Lon J. Haddock, a leader in the Salt Lake City Manufacturers and Merchants Association, to propose constructing a park on the peak that would attract tourists. The project was to be privately funded and managed for commercial purposes.[26] Utah senator Reed Smoot added his support to the effort, as did the local newspapers. However, the years passed with little progress being made in developing a park on Ensign Peak.

Nevertheless, efforts to use the peak for commercial purposes continued. One of the more interesting exploits of the peak came in 1910, when the first automobile was driven to its summit.[27] Not to be outdone, other automobile dealers and enthusiasts drove cars and motorcycles up the peak. The ventures proved to be excellent advertising for dealerships seeking increased sales. Given the local historical significance of the peak, such spectacles attracted considerable public interest.

In 1916, the public debated a plan to place a cross at the summit of Ensign Peak. Surprisingly enough, Charles W. Nibley, Presiding Bishop of the Church, suggested placing a large concrete cross on the peak.[28] Bishop Nibley announced that the Church would provide leadership and funding for the project, which was designed to achieve two objectives. The first was to provide a visible reminder to the city below of the sacrifices made by the pioneers of 1847. Secondly, a visible cross would stand as a symbol to visitors who were not members of the Church that the Latter-day Saints were indeed a Christian people.[29] Many groups in the community objected to the plan, including members of the Church and various other religious organizations. This growing opposition within the community and Church prompted Bishop Nibley to abandon the plan.[30]

One year later, another proposal came to the attention of the city council. A monument to the Mormon Battalion was proposed for the summit of the peak. The plan called for a granite structure with four sides containing plaques listing the names of the members of the battalion and a brief account of their contribution to pioneer history.[31] Like previously proposed plans, this one never materialized.

Throughout the years, Ensign Peak remained a popular place to celebrate Pioneer Day; the Church's Ensign Stake provided leadership for many of these events. Typical of these special affairs was a Boy Scout program conducted on the summit in July 1916. On that occasion, B. H. Roberts spoke to the gathering about pioneer history; his talk was followed by the raising of an American flag and the lighting of a huge bonfire.[32]

One of the most unusual events at Ensign Peak in the early twentieth century involved the Ku Klux Klan. During the 1920s this organization expanded into the western states. In the fall of 1924 they concentrated their efforts in Salt Lake County. By the end of the year, they had succeeded in establishing a statewide administrative structure that touched most of the communities within the state. In 1925, the rapid expansion of the Klan created a public backlash in Utah and throughout much of the nation. The Klan responded with a series of public demonstrations to regain their momentum. Marches were held in Washington, DC; Salt Lake City; and other major cities. In February 1925, the Klan launched their Utah offensive with a parade through the business district of Salt Lake City. They followed up with a second demonstration on April 6, during the Church's semiannual general conference. Defying increasing community opposition, members of the Klan marched up Ensign Peak and burned several large crosses at the summit. To ensure the success of this effort, hooded Klansmen blocked access to the summit. This resulted in a public assembly at the foot of Ensign Peak that numbered in the thousands; some of those gathered were members of the Klan, and others were simply onlookers who were curious over the actions of this controversial group. While the Klan considered the event a success, it frightened the community, causing the Klan to continue to lose influence in Utah.[33]

Organized Efforts to Develop Ensign Peak

A few years later, community groups began another organized effort to develop the peak. Foremost among these groups was the newly organized Utah Pioneer Trails and Landmarks Association. Elder George Albert Smith initiated the organization of this group in September 1930 for the purpose of creating permanent markers

35

to identify key pioneer historical sites. The members of the group desired to commemorate and preserve pioneer history for generations to come.[34] To achieve their objectives, they encouraged Church groups to host dinners and other fund-raising events to meet the costs of the markers. Others in the community also lent financial support, because the group planned to place markers at non-Mormon pioneer sites as well as at those associated with Church history. In the years that followed, the association placed numbered markers at key pioneer historical sites, starting at Nauvoo and stretching across the west to the end of what they considered the Mormon Trail in San Diego. The group remained active for years to come, placing 125 markers throughout the West.

Significant to these endeavors, in 1934 the Utah Pioneer Trails and Landmarks Association became part of the effort of the Ensign Stake to construct a monument and marker on Ensign Peak. Arza Hinckley, president of the Ensign Stake, commissioned architect George Cannon Young to design a monument commemorating the arrival of the pioneers in the Salt Lake Valley. Church members and others contributed time and resources to construct the monument. The elaborate plans required that the monument be constructed of stones gathered from the Mormon Pioneer Trail and from different Church historical sites, including the Sacred Grove and the temple site in Independence, Missouri.

On July 26, 1934, a gathering of several hundred viewed the unveiling of the eighteen-foot monument as part of a ceremony that included addresses from community and Church leaders. President Heber J. Grant and other Church leaders climbed to the top of the peak to participate in the event. George Albert Smith, president of the Utah Pioneer Trails and Landmarks Association, served as the master of ceremonies. The keynote speaker was Reverend John Edward Carver of Ogden. Music for this occasion was provided by the 145th Field Artillery Band and the Orpheus Club Male Chorus. Young women who were direct descendants of the pioneers who first climbed the peak unveiled the monument.[35]

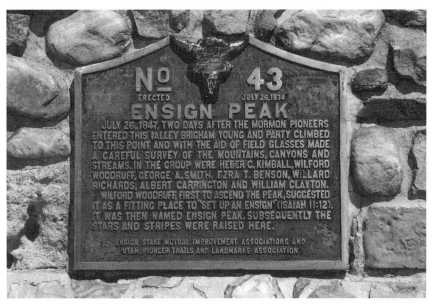

Historical plaque placed on Ensign Peak in 1934. (Courtesy of David M. Whitchurch.)

The Utah Pioneer Trails and Landmarks Association placed their forty-third marker on the monument, which provided an account of the naming of the mount on July 26, 1847. However, the information on the plaque concluded with the lines, "It was then named Ensign Peak. Subsequently the stars and stripes were raised here," thus contributing to the myth that Brigham Young had raised an American flag there in 1847.

In the years that followed, the peak remained undeveloped, in spite of proposals to use it for advertising, real estate development, agriculture, or other commercial uses. Groups such as the Sons of Utah Pioneers staunchly defended the peak from such commercial ventures. During these years of discussion regarding the future of the peak, the City of Salt Lake continued to maintain the stance that their long-range goal envisioned the creation of a city park on Ensign Peak. Despite this claim, in 1952 the city renewed its efforts to commercially develop the land surrounding the peak when they proposed the sale of land at the base of the peak for a housing development.[36] This proposal was met with stiff opposition. The Utah Pioneer Trails and Landmarks Association joined the Sons of Utah Pioneers, the Daughters of Utah Pioneers, and the Utah Historical Society to meet with the City Parks and Public Property Department to oppose the matter. Nevertheless, the project proceeded with a master plan that initially provided for eighty residential lots.[37] The housing development continued to expand around the base of the peak during the ensuing years.

Several years later, in 1961, the city responded to renewed attempts to develop a public park on Ensign Peak.[38] One proposal included the construction of a lookout on the summit and an outdoor amphitheater below the peak, suitable for performances by groups such as the Tabernacle Choir and the Utah Symphony. Another proposal suggested a park similar to that at the "This Is the Place" monument east of the city. Unfortunately, such efforts as these were met with little community support.

In the meantime, developers proposed the construction of a hundred-mile parkway from Fort Douglas, across the north bench of Salt Lake City, and around Ensign Peak, connecting Salt Lake and Davis counties.[39] The city determined that projected costs made this project unworkable. However, the idea of a parkway received renewed attention when others proposed the construction of a tunnel through Ensign Peak connecting Salt Lake City with Bountiful. Again the difficulty and cost of such a project led to its rejection.[40] Later, a road construction plan was revisited as part of a proposed scenic two-lane highway between Salt Lake City and Layton. The proposed drive would have a thirty-mile-an-hour speed limit as it wound around Ensign Peak and traveled north. Careful review of the plan, however, revealed that it would be inadequate for existing traffic demands between the cities.[41] In the following years, efforts to gain approval for a road around Ensign Peak that would connect Salt Lake City and Bountiful continued to prove unsuccessful.

Nevertheless, in spite of many unsuccessful proposals, interest in a public park on Ensign Peak did not diminish. In 1981, the city received a proposal for a smaller park than previously suggested. The proposal involved a land swap between the city and the Ensign Downs housing developer. Crowds gathered at the city council chambers to oppose this plan and support the development of a wilderness park on the peak. They feared that an expansion of the housing development that already surrounded much of the peak posed a further threat of encroachment on the peak itself.[42]

Recent Developments

By the end of the 1980s, time had taken a toll on Ensign Peak. Deep four-wheel-drive ruts ran across its face, the flagpole at the summit was rusted, and the monument had been defaced. Yet many groups remained interested in the potential of the site. Because the original historical marker placed on Ensign Peak in 1934 had been removed by vandals, the Sons of Utah Pioneers prepared a new one for placement adjacent to the peak in July 1989.[43] Gordon B. Hinckley, then counselor in the First Presidency of the Church, dedicated the marker. Later, the original marker was found in an old chicken coop by a scrap metal dealer, who gave it to the Daughters of Utah Pioneers organization. Although vandals had shot at the marker, leaving impressions in the metal face, it was otherwise in good condition.[44]

In 1990, the Salt Lake City Council approved ordinances that would enable the development of a 150-acre nature park around Ensign Peak. Included in the plans for the nature park was a proposal for a six-acre community park and a trail to the summit of the peak.[45] The development would also include an attractive entrance plaza with information markers, a viewpoint, and a trail leading to the summit. Throughout this process, a community organization known as Ensign Peak Foundation provided the leadership for the public-private venture.[46] President Hinckley also remained interested and involved in the development, even personally leading hikes to the summit, where he addressed participants.[47] On one such occasion, Elder Robert L. Backman observed, "We have not kept very good track of it [Ensign Peak]." He then quoted President Hinckley as saying, "We've neglected that peak too long."[48] Interest in completing the development of Ensign Peak in time for the 1996 Utah State Centennial and the 1997 sesquicentennial of the arrival of the pioneers continued to gain momentum.

Following the groundbreaking ceremony on April 17, 1996, work began with the reseeding of the slopes and the construction of a permanent nature park and hiking trail.[49] On July 26, President Hinckley formally dedicated the Ensign Peak Historic Site and Nature Park. He reminded those gathered of the joy felt by the group that had first climbed Ensign Peak for a view of the valley below. "They had done a great thing. They had traveled all the way from a river to this valley. . . . They had reason to feel exultant and uplifted and positive and affirmative. . . . In Brigham Young's mind, there was a fruition of the visions which he had had of this valley."[50] As part of the service, Governor Michael O. Leavitt proffered a pioneer tribute, after which leaders of the Ensign Peak Foundation presented the completed park to the City of Salt Lake. In addition to their leadership and vision, this foundation had raised almost five hundred thousand dollars in support of the peak's development. Without their dedicated efforts, the project would not have succeeded as it did. As a fitting conclusion to the dedication ceremony, the organizers released hundreds of helium balloons and waved large flags from the summit as a chorus sang the hymn "High on the Mountain Top."[51]

The completed park features an entrance plaza with ten informational plaques and the refurbished 1934 marker. A trail beginning at the plaza leads to a viewpoint located halfway up the summit. The trail then continues to the summit, with stations along the way marked by benches and informational signs. From the summit, visitors can view the Salt Lake Valley, as did Brigham Young and his associates on July 26, 1847.[52]

During 1997, the Church constructed a memorial garden on land it owned near the base of the mount.[53] The garden features benches, trees, and a walkway with informational panels relating the history and significance of Ensign Peak. This final project completed, correlated, and reinforced the efforts of the Ensign Peak Foundation, the Church, and the City of Salt Lake in developing Ensign Peak as a historical site. It now stands as a witness of the inspiration that guided the Saints westward to their new home. From the visionary experience during which the Prophet Joseph Smith showed Brigham Young Ensign Peak to the experience of the first pioneer group who waved a yellow bandana on its summit to the thousands who have climbed to its summit in the years that followed, Ensign Peak remains a witness to the Lord's hand in guiding his children and establishing the kingdom of God on the earth.

Afterword

Recently, Ensign Peak received renewed attention when the newly sustained Young Women general presidency climbed to its summit. Before her call as the Young Women general president, Elaine S. Dalton had climbed Ensign Peak with a group of youth. At that time she participated in a discussion related to the sacrifices required to establish the gospel and build the kingdom of God. At the conclusion of the meeting, each of the participants waved a symbolic banner on which they had written what they wanted to stand for in their lives. All those present then sang "High on the Mountain Top" and cheered in unison, "Hurrah for Israel."[54]

When Sister Dalton became the general president of the Young Women in 2008, she led her counselors on a hike to the top of Ensign Peak. Upon reaching the summit, they gazed over the valley below and saw the statue of the angel Moroni atop the Salt Lake Temple. The impression was clear: their mission was to "help prepare each young woman to be worthy to make and keep sacred covenants and receive the ordinances of the temple."[55] Like the first pioneers to climb the peak, they also waved a banner of their own. They considered their banner, made of a gold Peruvian shawl, to be an ensign to all nations, a symbolic call for a return to virtue.[56]

The experience of the Young Women general presidency and others has fulfilled in part the request made by President Hinckley in his dedicatory prayer: "We pray that through the years to come, many thousands of people of all faiths and all denominations, people of this nation and of other nations, may come here to reflect on the history and the efforts of those who pioneered this area. May this be a place of pondering, a place of remembrance, a place of thoughtful gratitude, a place of purposeful resolution."[57]

Recent experiences such as these confirm the importance of the historic symbolism related to the peak. When Brigham Young and others stood on the summit, they envisioned the scope and direction of their call to build a grand city and temple to the Lord. Today, as Sister Dalton and others climb the peak, they view the great legacy left by the pioneers and the realization of their vision. Climbing the peak continues to provide the means of connecting the past with the present in order to better envision the future. And while some aspects of Ensign Peak have changed, it remains a place where Saints can gather to rejoice in the Restoration of the gospel, unfurling banners that "wave to all the world."

Notes

In writing this article, the authors express appreciation for the definitive work of Ronald W. Walker. See Ronald W. Walker, "A Banner Is Unfurled," Dialogue 26, no. 4 (1993): 71–91, and Ronald W. Walker, "A Gauge of the Times: Ensign Peak in the Twentieth Century," Utah Historical Quarterly 62, no. 1 (1994): 4–25.

1. Coordinates 40°47′40″N 111°53′27″W / 40.7944°N 111.8907°W.

2. George A. Smith, in *Journal of Discourses* (London: Latter-day Saints' Book Depot, 1854–86), 13:85.

3. Wilford Woodruff, "The Pioneers," *Contributor*, August 1880, 252–53.

4. Erastus Snow, in *Journal of Discourses*, 16:207.

5. British author and critic William Hepworth Dixon interviewed Brigham Young in 1866 and reported his statement concerning Ensign Peak. William Hepworth, Dixon, *New America* (New York: AMS, 1972), 133–134.

6. Smith, in *Journal of Discourses*, 16:207; Woodruff, "The Pioneers," 253.

7. *Wilford Woodruff's Journal* (Salt Lake City: Kraut's Pioneer Press, 1982), 3:236.

8. Howard Egan, *Pioneering the West, 1846 to 1847*, ed. William M. Egan (Richmond, UT: Howard R. Egan Estate, 1917), 108.

9. Susa Young Gates and Leah D. Widstoe, *The Life Story of Brigham Young* (New York: Macmillan, 1931), 104.

10. Council Meeting, February 26, 1847, Thomas Bullock minutes, in Walker, "Banner," 75.

11. Smith, in *Journal of Discourses*, 13:86.

12. In Walker, "Banner," 75–76.

13. In Walker, "Banner," 77.

14. D. Michael Quinn, "The Flag of the Kingdom of God," *BYU Studies* 14, no. 1 (1973): 106–8.

15. "The Mormons Defended," *Deseret News*, June 25, 1884, 14.

16. "Polygamy and the Common Law," *Deseret News*, March 10, 1886, 6.

17. "The 'Mormon' Creed and Its 'Exponents,'" *Deseret News*, October 26, 1901, 23.

18. Walker, "Gauge," 9–10.

19. B. H. Roberts, "The 'Mormons' and the United States Flag," *Improvement Era*, January 1921, 3.

20. William C. A. Smoot, "Remarks at the American Party Banquet–Ensign Peak Flag Incident," *Salt Lake Tribune*, March 18, 1910, 2, in Walker, "Banner," 82. President Hinckley, an avid student of Church history, accepts this account as evidenced by his reference to the bandana flown by Wilford Woodruff from Ensign Peak on July 26, 1847. Gordon B. Hinckley, "An Ensign to the Nations," *Ensign*, November 1989, 51.

21. *Manuscript History of Brigham Young*, ed. William S. Harwell (Salt Lake City: Collier's, 1997), 224–25.

22. B. H. Roberts, *A Comprehensive History of the Church of Jesus Christ of Latter-day Saints* (Salt Lake City: Deseret News, 1912), 4:507.

23. H. M. Wells, "Message from Ensign Peak," *Deseret Evening News*, August 19, 1899, 2.

24. Walker, "Gauge," 5.

25. "Utah Pioneers Will Receive Special Medals," *Deseret Evening News*, March 14, 1947, 15. Eight years later, another flagpole was erected on Ensign Peak. The flagpole weighed over seven hundred pounds and was carried to the summit by hand. "New Flagpole Installed on Peak," *Deseret News*, November 8, 1955, 2B.

26. "Ensign Peak," *Deseret Evening News*, August 8, 1908, 4.

27. "Velie Automobile Climbs Ensign Peak," *Salt Lake Tribune*, March 10, 1910, 4.

28. "To Erect Cross on Ensign Peak," *Deseret Evening News*, May 5, 1916, 2.

29. "To Erect Cross on Ensign Peak," 2.

30. For a thorough treatment of the proposed cross, see Walker, "Gauge," 13–16.

31. A. Ad. Ramseyer, "Suggests Monument for Mormon Battalion," *Deseret News,* February 5, 1917, 16.

32. "Details Arranged for Boy Scout Program at Top of Ensign Peak," *Deseret News*, July 26, 1916, 12.

33. For a more complete treatment of the Klan in Utah, see Larry R. Gerlach, *Blazing Crosses in Zion: The Ku Klux Klan in Utah* (Logan: Utah State University Press, 1982), 105–110.

34. "President Smith Realizes Dream at Dedication," *Deseret News*, July 24, 1947, 1, 8.

35. "Ensign Peak Monument to Be Unveiled," *Deseret News*, July 24, 1934, 9.

36. "SUP Protests Sale of City-Owned Ensign Peak Region," *Deseret News*, May 12, 1952, 6; "Pioneer Unit Sets Meet on Land Sale," *Deseret News*, November 12, 1952, 18A.

37. "Ensign Downs Firm Completes Master Building Plan for Area," *Deseret News*, August 28, 1953, B1, B7.

38. "Development Proposed for Ensign Peak Area," *Deseret News*, December 28, 1961, 12A.

39. Clarence Barker, "S.L. Road's Price Tag: $101.5 Million," *Deseret News*, February 1, 1964, B1, B8.

40. "Revises 'Peak' Tunnel Plan," *Deseret News,* March 14, 1974, 2B.

41. Wanda Lund, "Scenic Route Termed Impractical Now," *Deseret News,* April 18, 1975, 4B.

42. "Ensign Peak Plans Studied," *Deseret News,* September 26, 1981, 2B.

43. Scott Lloyd, "Sons of Utah Pioneers Unveil Maker to Honor the Naming of Ensign Peak," *Deseret News*, July 22, 1989, B3.

44. Jay Evensen, "Stolen Historic Marker Found in Old Chicken Coop," *Deseret News*, September 27, 1992, B4. The original marker is now located in the plaza at the base of Ensign Peak.

45. Joel Campbell, "Council OKs Plans Clearing Way for Zoning Change, Land Trade," *Deseret News*, October 17, 1990, B3.

46. After leading a successful effort to restore Ensign Peak, the Ensign Peak Foundation was reorganized in 1992 as the Mormon Historic Sites Foundation. Using the expertise they gained in the peak project, they expanded their work to include other historic sites. To date, they have proven to be one of the most successful groups in identifying and preserving Church historic sites.

47. "Pres. Hinckley Will Keynote Hike to Ensign Peak," *Deseret News*, July 15, 1993, B6; Jerry Spangler, "Ceremony on Ensign Peak Hails Vision and Courage of 8 Pioneers," *Deseret News,* July 27, 1993, B3.

48. R. Scott Lloyd, "Ensign Peak Hike Recalls Prophecy," *Deseret News*, August 6, 1994, Z9.

49. Douglas Palmer, "Work Begins to Turn Ensign Peak into a Park," *Deseret News*, March 21, 1996, B11.

50. Melissa Karren, "Modern-day Pioneers Blaze an Old Trail," *Deseret News*, July 27, 1996, B3.

51. R. Scott Lloyd, "Park at Ensign Peak Dedicated," *Deseret News*, August 3, 1996, 3, 13.

52. "Plazas, Information Plaques Entrance Hike to the Peak," *Church News,* August 3, 1996, 3, 13. Currently the plaza has three flagpoles. These include one for the Utah state flag, one for the American flag, and the third for the blue and white pioneer flag first displayed during President Young's administration.

53. R. Scott Lloyd, "New Garden Graces Ensign Peak," *Deseret News*, August 2, 1997, Z6.

54. Elaine S. Dalton, "It Shows in Your Face," *Ensign*, May 2006, 111.

55. First Presidency letter, September 25, 1996, in Elaine S. Dalton, "A Return to Virtue," *Ensign*, November 2009, 78.

56. Sarah Jane Weaver, "New Value: Virtue," *Church News,* December 16, 2009, 3.

57. Lloyd, "Park at Ensign Peak Dedicated," 3, 13.

Chapter 4

The Design, Construction, and Role of the Salt Lake Temple

Richard O. Cowan

Within days of President Brigham Young's arrival in the Salt Lake Valley in July 1847, he designated the site for the future temple. As he and a few others were walking across the area that one day would be Temple Square, he stopped between the two forks of City Creek, struck the ground with his cane, and declared, "Here will be the Temple of our God." Wilford Woodruff placed a stake in the ground to mark the spot that would become the center of the future building.[1]

Building a Temple in the Desert

As early as December 23, 1847, an official circular letter from the Twelve invited the Saints to gather and bring precious metals and other materials "for the exaltation . . . of the living and the dead,"

Richard O. Cowan is a professor of Church history and doctrine at Brigham Young University.

for the time had come to build the Lord's house "upon the tops of the mountains."[2] Soon afterward, President Young named Truman O. Angell Sr. as temple architect, a post he would hold until his death in 1887. His previous work as a wood joiner on both the Kirtland and Nauvoo Temples provided useful background for his new assignment. He would have an able assistant, William Ward, who received his architectural training in England and was skilled in stone construction. (Angell's experience was primarily with wooden structures.) A skilled draftsman, Ward prepared drawings for the Salt Lake Temple under Angell's direction.[3]

In 1852, men were put to work building a fourteen-foot wall of sandstone and adobe around the temple block. This not only provided security for the construction site but, like other projects sponsored by the Church's Public Works Department, also created worthwhile employment for men who otherwise would have been idle.[4]

At the general conference of October 1852, President Heber C. Kimball, first counselor in the First Presidency, asked the Saints whether they should build the temple of sandstone, of adobe, or of "the best stone we can find in these mountains." The congregation unanimously voted that "we build a temple of the best materials that can be furnished in the mountains of North America, and that the Presidency dictate where the stone and other materials shall be obtained."[5] In the mid-1850s, when deposits of granite were discovered in Little Cottonwood Canyon twenty miles southeast of Salt Lake City, President Young determined that the temple should be built of this material. Its permanence would be a fitting symbol of the eternal covenants to be entered into there.

The Salt Lake Temple site was dedicated on February 14, 1853. During the next several weeks, excavation for the temple proceeded. Cornerstones were laid on April 6, the twenty-third anniversary of the Church's organization. Large stones, measuring approximately two by three by five feet, had been placed in convenient positions ahead of time. They were of firestone brought from nearby Red Butte Canyon.[6]

On this beautiful spring day in the valley, general conference convened in the old adobe tabernacle on the southwest corner of the temple block. Accompanied by military honor guards and the music of three bands, a procession headed by Church leaders marched to the spot where the First Presidency and the Patriarch to the Church laid the southeast cornerstone.[7] President Young then spoke, explaining that the temple had to be built in order that the Lord "may have a place where he can lay his head, and not only spend a night or a day, but find a place of peace."[8] The Presiding Bishopric, representing the lesser priesthood, laid the southwest cornerstone. The presidency of the high priests, the stake presidency, and the high council then placed the northwest cornerstone. Finally, the northeast cornerstone was laid by the Twelve and representatives of the seventies and the elders. The laying of each stone was accompanied by special music, speeches, and a prayer.

After a one-hour break, the conference resumed in the old tabernacle. Concerning the future temple, President Young declared:

I scarcely ever say much about revelations, or visions, but suffice it to say, five years ago last July [1847] I was here, and saw in the Spirit the Temple not ten feet from where we have laid the Chief Corner Stone. I have not inquired what kind of a Temple we should build. Why? Because it was represented before me. I have never looked upon that ground, but the vision of it was there. I see it as plainly as if it was in reality before me. Wait until it is done. I will say, however, that it will have six towers, to begin with, instead of one. Now do not any of you apostatize because it will have six towers, and Joseph only built one. It is easier for us to build sixteen, than it was for him to build one. The time will come when there will be one in the centre of Temples we shall build, and on the top, groves and fish ponds. But we shall not see them here, at present.[9]

Some temples built in the twentieth century, including Hawaii, Idaho Falls, Los Angeles, and Oakland, would fulfill elements of President Young's prophecy. Even though the Conference Center across the street is not a temple, some have thought of its rooftop gardens as at least a partial fulfillment of this prophecy.

William Ward later described the source of the temple's basic design: "Brigham Young drew upon a slate in the architect's office a sketch, and said to Truman O. Angell: 'There will be three towers on the east, representing the President and his two counselors; also three similar towers on the west representing the Presiding Bishop and his two counselors; the towers on the east the Melchisedek priesthood, those on the west the Aaronic preisthood. The center towers will be higher than those on the sides, and the west towers a little lower than those on the east end. The body of the building will be between these.'"[10]

Because the great temple would not be completed for forty years, temporary facilities needed to be provided where the Saints could receive temple blessings. During the pioneers' early years in the Salt Lake Valley, these blessings had been given in various places, including the top of Ensign Peak and Brigham Young's office. By 1852, endowments were being given in the Council House, located on the southwest corner of what are now South Temple and Main Streets. This facility also accommodated a variety of other ecclesiastical and civic functions, so a separate place was needed where the sacred temple ordinances could be given. The Endowment House, a two-story adobe structure dedicated in 1855, was located in the northwest corner of Temple Square. It continued to bless the Saints until it was torn down in 1889 after other temples were finished in the region and as the Salt Lake Temple itself neared completion.[11]

Meanwhile, the Saints maintained their interest in constructing the temple. In the spring of 1856, Brigham Young sent Truman Angell on a special mission to Europe. Specifically, President Young instructed him to make sketches of important architectural works to become better qualified to continue his work on the temple and other buildings.[12]

On July 24, 1857, as the Latter-day Saints were celebrating the tenth anniversary of their entrance into Salt Lake Valley, they received the latest disturbing news that a potentially hostile United States army was approaching Utah. Not knowing the army's intentions, Brigham Young had the temple foundation covered with dirt as a precaution. When the army arrived the following year, Temple Square looked like a freshly plowed field, and there was no visible evidence of the temple's construction. As it turned out, the army marched through Salt Lake City without harming any property and set up its camp some thirty miles to the southwest, near Utah Lake. Even during the years when the army was in Utah, draftsmen in the architect's office were busy planning the exact size and shape for each of the thousands of stones that would be needed for the temple. With the outbreak of the American Civil War in 1861, the army was needed elsewhere, and it departed from Utah by December of that year. The foundation was uncovered in preparation for work that would resume the following spring.[13]

At this time, President Young examined the newly uncovered foundation and became aware that it was defective. He and his associates noticed large cracks and concluded that its small stones held together with mortar could not carry the massive weight of the temple.[14] On January 1, 1862, he announced that the inadequate foundation would be removed and replaced by one made entirely of granite. The footings would be sixteen feet thick. "I want to see the Temple built in a manner that it will endure through the Millennium," he later declared.[15] The work of rebuilding the foundation moved slowly, and the walls did not reach ground level until the end of the construction season in 1867, fourteen years after the original cornerstones had been laid.

Transporting the granite by wagon to Temple Square posed a major challenge to which the coming of the railroad provided a solution. When the transcontinental railroad was completed in 1869, a more efficient method of transportation became available. During the early 1870s, tracks of the Utah Southern (later part of the Union Pacific) pushed southward toward Utah Valley. Rather than following a direct route, they were swung to the southeast in order to pass closer to the temple quarry. (Over 125 years later, this exact route would be followed by the Trax light rail system.) A connection with downtown streetcar tracks provided direct access to Temple Square. Still, at the time of President Young's death in 1877, the temple walls were only twenty feet high, just above the level of the first floor. Thus most of the temple's construction was yet to be accomplished, even though twenty-four years of the forty-year building period had already passed. During the next few years, however, with the problems of transportation resolved, the pace would accelerate considerably.

Because the builders recalled President Young's desire for this temple to stand through time, the structure was very solid. Even at their tops, the walls were six feet thick, and the granite blocks were individually and skillfully shaped to fit snugly together. Nearly a century

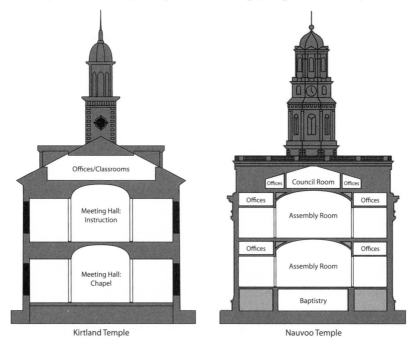

Fig. 1. Cross sections of the Kirtland and Nauvoo temples. (Image previously published in Temples to Dot the Earth *[Springville, UT: Cedar Fort, 1997]. Used with permission.)*

later, Elder Mark E. Petersen attested to the soundness of the temple's construction. He was in the temple when a rather severe earthquake hit, damaging several buildings around the Salt Lake Valley. "As I sat there in that temple I could feel the sway of the quake and that the whole building groaned." Afterward, he recalled, the engineers "could not find one semblance of damage" anywhere in the temple.[16]

Before his death in 1868, President Heber C. Kimball had prophesied that "when the walls reached the square, the powers of evil would rage and the Saints would suffer persecution."[17] This point was reached in 1885, when the main walls of the temple, excluding the towers, were completed.

This was a time of bitter anti-Mormon persecution, and Temple Square was temporarily confiscated by hostile government officials. Thus the stage was set for the anti-Mormon crusade that raged during the 1880s. The Saints' enemies boasted that the Mormons would never be allowed to finish the temple but that the "Gentiles" would complete the building for their own purposes.[18] Following the abandonment of plural marriage, relationships between Mormons and Gentiles improved. Confiscated properties were returned, and Utah finally became a state in 1896.

The Temple's Interior

The temple's exterior walls were nearing completion in the mid-1880s when the architects proposed significant changes for the yet-unconstructed interior. The original plan called for the Salt Lake Temple to follow the basic pattern of earlier temples. The Kirtland Temple had consisted primarily of two large assembly rooms, one above the other. The Nauvoo Temple expanded on this plan by adding a row of small rooms along each side of the elliptical ceiling of the two main auditoriums (see fig. 1). The large rooms were illuminated by tall windows, while the small side rooms had round windows. This pattern reflected the pattern used in the Nauvoo Temple.

With the dedication of the Logan Temple in 1884, Truman O. Angell Jr. turned his attention to assisting his elderly father in completing drawings for the Salt Lake Temple. Early the following year, he proposed that rather than having two large assembly rooms with elliptical ceilings, as had been the case in Nauvoo, the Salt Lake Temple should follow the pattern that Presidents Young and John Taylor had already approved for Logan and Manti. There would be only one assembly room (on the upper floor) and it would have balconies under the elliptical windows along each side. The temple's main floor would contain spacious rooms for presenting the endowment, while an intermediate floor would provide smaller council rooms for the use of various priesthood groups (see fig. 2). This plan would accommodate three hundred persons in the endowment sessions—more than twice the number that could be served in the basement under the original arrangement. These changes were consistent with President Young's 1860 instructions that the temple would not be designed for general meetings, but rather it would "be for the endowments—for the organization and instruction of the Priesthood."[19] Thus the design of the Salt Lake Temple reflected the Saints' unfolding understanding of temple functions.

Truman O. Angell Sr., however, urged President Taylor to finish the temple according to the original plans. No final decision was made before President Taylor's death in July of 1887. Although the general features of the younger Angell's proposal were eventually adopted, none of his plans were followed exactly. The final plans for the temple appear to have been drawn under President Wilford Woodruff's direction by Joseph Don Carlos Young, who became Church architect in 1890—just three years before the temple's completion.[20] It is evident, therefore, that most of the work on the temple's interior must have been accomplished during only these last few years of construction.

Some have suggested that in the Salt Lake Temple, shafts were provided for elevators and spaces left throughout the building for

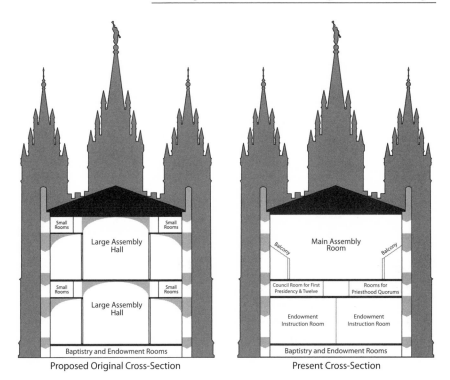

Fig. 2. Cross section of the Salt Lake Temple showing the original and final designs of the temple's interior. (Image previously published in Temples to Dot the Earth. *Used with permission.)*

electric conduits and heating ducts even before these technologies were known. Angell Sr., however, certainly would have learned about elevators, which were just coming into use at the time of his 1856 visit to Europe. By the early 1860s, electricity was already being used in Utah for the Deseret Telegraph system. Hence, most of the temple's interior was designed and built long after these technologies emerged. Although the west center tower proved to be a convenient location for the two main elevators, there is no evidence to suggest that their shafts were planned when there was no knowledge of this technology.[21]

Symbolism of the Temple's Exterior

As had been the case in ancient times, the temple's physical arrangement was calculated to teach important lessons. The intent of the temple's design, one architectural historian observed, was "to aid man in his quest to gain entrance back into the presence of God from whence he came."[22]

As with the Nauvoo Temple, special ornamental stones were an important feature of the Salt Lake Temple's exterior. An earthstone formed the base of each of the temple's fifty buttresses. These were the largest stones in the temple, weighing over six thousand pounds and having on their face a representation of the globe, four feet in diameter. These stones served as a reminder, architect Angell explained, that the gospel message had to go to all the earth.[23] Each buttress had a moonstone about halfway up and a sunstone near its top. Because the earth is presently in a telestial condition, the three ornamental stones on each buttress might represent the three degrees of glory in ascending order—telestial, terrestrial, and celestial. These, together with the starstones on the temple's towers, also reminded Latter-day Saints of these kingdoms. One scholar has suggested another possible interpretation. Referring to Abraham 3:5, he pointed out that "as we move upward into the heavens, the time sequences become longer. Likewise, the temple stones that communicate time begin with a short period of time, the day, and move toward the eternal present, where time almost ceases to move." The earthstones at the temple's base represent our planet, which rotates once every day. Stones about halfway up the building depict the moon's monthly cycle. Sunstones near the top symbolize yet a longer period of time—the year. The depiction of stars even higher on the building suggests yet longer periods of revolution.[24]

The constellation of Ursa Major (the Big Dipper), depicted on the west center tower, is positioned so that the two "pointer stars" at the end of the dipper are literally aligned with Polaris (the North Star) in the heavens. This star appears to be a fixed point in the sky around which other stars revolve; hence, it might be thought of as representing eternity, or the absence of time. Angell suggested another message to be gained from this constellation on the temple—"the lost may find themselves by the Priesthood."[25] In more recent years, President Harold B. Lee referred to this statement in conjunction with the introduction of family home evenings and other priesthood-centered programs and likened it to the increasingly important role being given to the priesthood.[26]

An interesting feature on the moonstones is often overlooked. Proceeding from right to left, they successively represent the moon's new, first-quarter, full, and third-quarter phases. Since the fifty buttresses cannot be divided evenly by these four phases, "the specific reason for fifty moon-stones," one student of the Salt Lake Temple's architecture has concluded, "was to create a sequential break to establish the beginning point of the lunar cycle."[27] This break occurs on the north wall. If the date of January 1 is assigned to the new moon immediately after this break, dates can also be assigned to each of the succeeding phases.

Fig. 3. Architectural detail on the exterior of the Salt Lake Temple showing a moon motif. (© Intellectual Reserve, Inc.)

The right buttress on the face of the temple's main east center tower would thus represent April 6, regarded by some Latter-day Saints as the date of the Savior's birth.[28] Gilded letters on this same tower identify April 6 as the date of the temple's commencement and completion (see fig. 3).[29] The left buttress on this tower includes a representation of the full moon. Because Easter is celebrated on the Sunday following the first full moon after the beginning of spring, this moonstone may remind us of the Savior's atoning sacrifice, which was completed with his Resurrection on that first glorious Easter morning. A plan for the temple drafted in 1878 carefully plotted each moonstone according to lunar phase and month of year.[30]

The buttresses of the east center tower also include cloudstones, which show rays of sunlight penetrating through the clouds. These are representations of the gospel light piercing the dark clouds of superstition and error (see Isaiah 60:2–3). They also recall how a cloud of glory filled the ancient temple (see 1 Kings 8:10) and will rest upon the latter-day temple in the New Jerusalem (see D&C 84:5). On the same tower, the keystone at the top of the lower large window depicts clasped hands. These are reminders of the power that comes from brotherly love and fellowship and of the unity that must exist among those who would build Zion (see Galatians 2:9; Moses 7:18; D&C 38:24–27; 88:133). The hands also suggest the importance of honoring sacred commitments. President Gordon B. Hinckley declared that the temple is "a house of covenants. Here we promise, solemnly and sacredly, to live the gospel of Jesus Christ in its finest expression. We covenant with God our Eternal Father to live those principles which are the bedrock of all true religion."[31] The keystone above the east center tower's upper window depicts God's "all-seeing eye," which watches over both the righteous and the wicked (see 1 Kings 9:3; Psalm 33:13–14, 18–19; Proverbs 15:3).[32]

The Angel Moroni

On April 6, 1892, as a band played "The Capstone March," the Saints gathered south of the temple. An estimated forty thousand crowded into Temple Square, while an additional ten thousand filled the surrounding streets or watched from windows and the roofs of adjacent buildings. To that date, this was the largest group of Saints to meet in one place. Promptly at high noon, President Wilford Woodruff stepped to the podium, raised "both hands to heaven," and proclaimed in a loud voice: "Attention, all ye house of Israel and all ye nations of the earth. We will now lay the top stone of the Temple of our God."[33] The official capstone was the upper half of the round ball atop the east center spire. It had been hollowed out to accommodate scriptures, selected books, and other historical mementos, including music, coins, photographs, and "a polished brass plaque inscribed with historical information."[34] President Woodruff pressed a button on the stand, and an electrically operated device lowered the capstone slowly and securely. As the stone descended into place, Elder Lorenzo Snow led the Hosanna Shout, with thousands of white handkerchiefs waving in unison. From high up on the temple, architect Joseph Don Carlos Young called out that the capstone was duly laid. With great emotion, the huge throng sang "The Spirit of God."[35]

Later that afternoon the statue of the angel Moroni was hoisted to its position on top of the capstone. The twelve-and-a-half-foot, hammered-copper figure had been prepared in Salem, Ohio, from a model by Utah sculptor Cyrus E. Dallin. Even though Dallin was not a Latter-day Saint, he later professed, "My 'Angel Moroni' brought me nearer to God than anything I ever did. It seemed to me that I came to know what it means to commune with angels from heaven."[36] Unveiled at a ceremony at 3:00 p.m., its gold-leafed surface gleamed in the sun. The statue depicted a heavenly herald sounding his trumpet, representing the latter-day fulfillment of John's prophecy of an angel bringing "the everlasting gospel to preach unto them that dwell on the earth, and to every nation, and kindred, and tongue, and people" (Revelation 14:6).

Not all temples have had statues of Moroni. Only one of the Church's previous five temples had an angel on its tower. The Nauvoo Temple featured a weathervane depicting an angel flying in a horizontal position. This was a common decoration on churches of the time, so whether or not it was specifically intended to represent Moroni is a matter of conjecture. Thus the Salt Lake Temple was the first to include the familiar vertical figure, which eventually would become a well-known feature of Latter-day Saint temples.

By 1980, the Church would dedicate fourteen more temples, with only the two largest—Los Angeles and Washington DC—having the familiar herald angel on their towers. Since that time, even smaller temples have included statues of Moroni. Other artists have sculpted these statues, and interestingly, the angel on the Atlanta Georgia Temple was a smaller replica of Cyrus Dallin's original Moroni. Many, but not all, of these angels face east, suggesting their watching for and heralding the Second Coming of Christ, which has been compared to the dawning of a new day (see Joseph Smith—Matthew 1:26).

The Temple Completed and Dedicated

At the capstone-laying ceremonies on April 6, 1892, Elder Francis M. Lyman of the Quorum of the Twelve issued a challenge to the vast multitude of Saints assembled for the occasion. He spoke of President Woodruff's desire and dream to live long enough to dedicate the temple.[37] Lyman proposed a resolution that those present pledge to provide the funds necessary to complete the building so that it might be dedicated just one year later—the fortieth anniversary of the cornerstone laying. This proposition was adopted unanimously.[38]

When this goal was set, most believed that the remaining work would take at least three more years. In fact, as late as March 1893, many still wondered if the temple could be finished by the following month. Nevertheless, those working on the temple made a special effort to complete the project on time.[39]

The temple was completed and ready for dedication by noon on April 5, 1893, just a few hours ahead of the deadline. Between three and five o'clock that afternoon, the temple was opened for visits by prominent community leaders and members of other faiths. Some six hundred responded to the invitation, including the clergy, business leaders, federal officials, and their families. They were permitted to pass through every room in the temple from the basement to the roof and to examine any portion of the interior they desired. Qualified guides escorted them and answered their questions. Many expressed appreciation to the Church for this hospitable gesture. This inaugurated the custom of conducting a public open house prior to temple dedications.[40]

At last the long-anticipated day was at hand—the dedication of the great temple at Salt Lake City following a forty-year period of construction.[41] Of those who had helped lay the cornerstone in 1853, only a few were still living. The temple's original architect, Truman O. Angell, had died in 1887. The supervising architect at the time of dedication, Joseph Don Carlos Young, had been born in 1855, two years after construction had begun.[42] During this period, more than a generation had passed away.

The first dedicatory session was on Thursday morning, April 6, 1893. "A terrible storm arose that day. Rain fell in torrents, and the wind blew with savage fury. It was as if the forces of evil were lashing out in violent protest against this act of consecration," President Hinckley reflected a century later. "But all was peace and quiet within the thick granite walls."[43]

The temple's dedication was a spiritual highlight for those who attended. In the initial session, the dedicatory prayer was offered by President Woodruff, followed by the unique Hosanna Shout, led by President Snow. Thirty-one dedicatory sessions continued over the next three weeks. They were held in the large upper assembly room, which could accommodate about 2,250 persons, and included the dedicatory prayer and Hosanna Shout. As the choirs sang the "Hosanna Anthem," composed by Evan Stephens especially for this occasion, the congregation joined at the appropriate point with the traditional singing of "The Spirit of God."

Later Reconstruction of Adjacent Facilities

An annex stood about one hundred feet north of the temple proper. Designed by Joseph Don Carlos Young, its architecture was described as Byzantine or Moorish. It was built of cream-colored oolite stone from the Manti quarry. Thus the architecture and material of the annex were different from the temple itself. Construction on this facility started in 1892, and it was dedicated the following year at the same time as the temple itself. The annex included a large entry area where patrons presented their temple recommends and where the recorder noted and distributed names of persons for whom ordinances were to be performed. It also included an assembly room seating three hundred, where meetings were held for those preparing to enter the temple.[44]

Seven decades later, this structure was razed to make way for a new annex. In August 1962, the Salt Lake Temple closed. A temporary annex was constructed in the nearly completed North Visitors' Center, and beginning in March 1963 patrons could access the temple via an underground passage while construction on the new facilities moved forward. These included a new addition on the north side of the temple, which provided several new sealing rooms. The new temple annex, entered through a doorway in the north wall of Temple Square, included a four hundred-seat chapel, subterranean dressing rooms with four thousand lockers, and large waiting rooms for those attending temple marriages. Both the annex and the addition were faced with granite from the original canyon quarry and were designed to match the architecture of the temple.[45] These new facilities, which opened in March 1966, greatly expanded the temple's capacity. On October 22, 1967, after the North Visitors' Center had gone into service, the new facilities were dedicated by President Hugh B. Brown in a service attended by General Authorities and temple workers.

The Temple's Continuing Key Role

The Salt Lake Temple as well as the angelic figure atop its highest tower are two of the most widely recognized iconic symbols of The Church of Jesus Christ of Latter-day Saints. Additionally, for the Church itself, marvelous spiritual experiences have been linked with this temple over the years. Perhaps the most outstanding example was

Daytime view of the south side of the Salt Lake Temple. (© Intellectual Reserve, Inc.)

the appearance of the Savior to President Snow in the large corridor just outside the celestial room. President Snow later described what happened: "It was right here that the Lord Jesus Christ appeared to me at the time of the death of President Woodruff. He instructed me to go right ahead and reorganize the First Presidency of the Church at once and not wait as had been done after the death of the previous presidents, and that I was to succeed President Woodruff. . . . He stood right here, about three feet above the floor. It looked as though He stood on a plate of solid gold."[46]

For many years (until the Missionary Training Center was established in Provo), this temple was where most outgoing missionaries received their endowments as part of their weeklong orientation. A disproportionately large number of Church members have chosen this temple for their eternal marriages. For example, in contrast to the roughly 5 percent of Churchwide endowments for the dead that were performed in Salt Lake during the early 1990s, 15 percent of all celestial marriages were performed there.[47]

Because of its location at Church headquarters, the Salt Lake Temple plays a unique and significant role in Church governance. Key decisions are reached following prayerful consideration by the Council of the First Presidency and Quorum of the Twelve Apostles, who meet weekly in their council room within the temple. These decisions include such matters as ordaining and setting apart new Presidents of the Church, appointing other General Authorities, creating new missions and stakes, and approving Church programs. Notable examples have included the 1952 decision to build temples overseas, the determination in 1976 to add what we now know as sections 137 and 138 to the standard works, and the 1978 revelation extending the priesthood to all worthy males (Official Declaration 2). Reflecting on these weekly meetings in the temple, Elder Spencer W. Kimball affirmed that those who could witness the prophet's wisdom in reaching decisions would surely believe he was inspired. "To hear him conclude important new developments with such solemn expressions as 'the Lord is pleased'; 'that move is right'; 'our Heavenly Father has spoken,' is to know positively."[48] Thus the Salt Lake Temple not only teaches gospel truths through its richly symbolic exterior and provides saving ordinances for the living and the dead, but also continues to play a key part as God's kingdom rolls forth to fill the whole earth.

Notes

1. Matthias F. Cowley, *Wilford Woodruff: History of His Life and Labors* (Salt Lake City: Bookcraft, 1964), 619–20; B. H. Roberts, *Comprehensive History of the Church of Jesus Christ of Latter-day Saints* (Provo, UT: Brigham Young University Press, 1965), 3:279–80. After reviewing various diary entries, Randall Dixon believes that this event took place on July 26, 1847 (statement to the author, May 6, 2010).

2. James R. Clark, comp., *Messages of the First Presidency* (Salt Lake City: Bookcraft, 1965), 1:333.

3. C. Mark Hamilton, *The Salt Lake Temple: A Monument to a People* (Salt Lake City: University Services, 1983), 51–53.

4. Arnold K. Garr, Richard O. Cowan, and Donald Q. Cannon, eds., *Encyclopedia of Latter-day Saint History* (Salt Lake City: Deseret Book, 2000), 966–67.

5. Heber C. Kimball, in *Journal of Discourses* (London: Latter-day Saints' Book Depot, 1854), 1:160, 162.

6. Firestone was a variety of sandstone found in the mountains adjacent to Temple Square. Although it was used widely in buildings, it was prone to cracking because its porous nature allowed water to permeate the rock and freeze. Therefore, it was not as suitable as granite to support a large building such as the temple.

7. The office of Patriarch to the Church was included among the General Authorities until 1978. See Daniel H. Ludlow, ed., *Encyclopedia of Mormonism* (New York: Macmillan, 1992), 3:1065–66.

8. Brigham Young, in *Journal of Discourses*, 2:33; James H. Anderson, "The Salt Lake Temple," *Contributor*, April 1893, 252–59.

9. Brigham Young, in *Journal of Discourses*, 1:133.

10. "Who Designed the Temple?" *Deseret News Weekly*, April 23, 1892, 578.

11. The demolition of the Endowment House also served as a visible signal that the Church was serious about ending plural marriages. In his 1890 "Manifesto," President Wilford Woodruff declared that because a plural marriage was alleged to have been performed there, "the Endowment House was, by my instructions, taken down without delay." Doctrine and Covenants, Official Declaration 1.

12. Richard Neitzel Hozapfel, *Every Stone a Sermon* (Salt Lake City: Bookcraft, 1992), 17; see also Marvin E. Smith, "The Builder," *Improvement Era*, October 1942, 630.

13. Manuscript History of Brigham Young, December 18, 1861, 49, in W. A. Raynor, *The Everlasting Spires: The Story of the Salt Lake Temple* (Salt Lake City: Deseret Book, 1965), 102.

14. Raynor, *Everlasting Spires*, 101–3; see also *Wilford Woodruff's Journal, 1833–1898, Typescript*, ed. Scott G. Kenney (Midvale, UT: Signature Books, 1984), 5:399.

15. Brigham Young, in *Journal of Discourses*, 10:254; see also *Wilford Woodruff's Journal*, 6:71.

16. Mark E. Petersen, *Priesthood Genealogical Research Seminar* (Provo, UT: Brigham Young University Press, 1974), 510, quoted in Richard O. Cowan, *Temples to Dot the Earth* (Springville, UT: Cedar Fort, 1997), 102–3.

17. Orson F. Whitney, *Life of Heber C. Kimball* (Salt Lake City: Bookcraft, 1967), 397.

18. James H. Anderson, "The Salt Lake Temple," *Contributor*, April 1893, 269–70. Concerning the seizure of Temple Square, see Joseph Fielding Smith, *Essentials in Church History* (Salt Lake City: Deseret Book, 1979), 489.

19. Brigham Young, in *Journal of Discourses*, 8:203.

20. Truman O. Angell Jr. to John Taylor, April 28, 1885, and Truman O. Angell Sr. to Taylor, March 11, 1885, in Hamilton, *Salt Lake Temple*, 54–57.

21. Paul C. Richards, "The Salt Lake Temple Infrastructure: Studying It Out in Their Minds," *BYU Studies* 36, no. 2 (1996–97): 212–18.

22. Hamilton, *Salt Lake Temple*, 147.

23. Truman O. Angell Sr., "A Descriptive Statement of the Temple Now Being Erected in Salt Lake City . . ." *Millennial Star*, May 5, 1874, 273–75.

24. Richard G. Oman, "Exterior Symbolism of the Salt Lake Temple: Reflecting the Faith that Called the Place into Being," *BYU Studies* 36, no. 4 (1996–97): 32–34.

25. Angell, "The Temple," *Deseret News*, August 17, 1854, 2.

26. Harold B. Lee, in Conference Report, October 1964, 86.

27. Hamilton, *Salt Lake Temple*, 143.

28. Recent scholarship has suggested other possible dates for the Savior's birth. See, for example, Jeffrey R. Chadwick, "Dating the Birth of Jesus Christ," *BYU Studies* 49, no. 4 (2010): 5–38.

29. Hamilton, *Salt Lake Temple*, 142–43.

30. Hamilton, *Salt Lake Temple*, 142.

31. Gordon B. Hinckley, "The Salt Lake Temple," *Ensign*, March 1993, 6.

32. Duncan M. McAllister, *Description of the Great Temple* (Salt Lake City: Bureau of Information, 1912), 7–10; Anderson, "Salt Lake Temple," 276.

33. *Deseret Weekly News*, April 9, 1892, 516.

34. Matthew B. Brown and Paul Thomas Smith, *Symbols in Stone: Symbolism on the Early Temples of the Restoration* (American Fork, UT: Covenant Communications, 1997), 127. Unfortunately, when the capstone was opened in 1993 many of the items it contained had been destroyed because of exposure to moisture.

35. *Wilford Woodruff's Journal*, 9:192–94 (April 6, 1892); compare James E. Talmage, *House of the Lord* (Salt Lake City: Bookcraft, 1962), 149–52.

36. Cyrus Dallin, in Levi Edgar Young, "The Angel Moroni and Cyrus Dallin," *Improvement Era*, April 1953, 234.

37. Matthias F. Cowley, *Wilford Woodruff: History of His Life and Labors* (Salt Lake City: Bookcraft, 1964), 562.

38. Anderson, "Salt Lake Temple," 274.

39. Anderson, "Salt Lake Temple," 283.

40. McAllister, "Temples of the Latter-day Saints: Purposes for Which They Are Erected," *Liahona*, February 22, 1927, 417; John R. Winder, "Temples and Temple Work," *Young Woman's Journal*, February 1903, 51.

41. For a description of these events, see Holzapfel, *Every Stone a Sermon*, especially chapter 9.

42. Anderson, "Salt Lake Temple," 279.

43. Gordon B. Hinckley, in Conference Report, April 1993, 92.

44. Hamilton, *Salt Lake Temple*, 182.

45. Arnold J. Irvine, "Temporary Annex Ready For Use," *Church News*, March 16, 1963, 8–9; George L. Scott, "New S. L. Temple Annex Opens," *Church News*, March 19, 1966, 7–11.

46. LeRoi C. Snow, "An Experience of My Father's," *Improvement Era*, September 1933, 677, 679.

47. Based on temple ordinance statistics in author's possession.

48. Spencer W. Kimball, ". . . To His Servants the Prophets," *Instructor*, August 1960, 257.

Temple Square, including the Salt Lake Tabernacle and Assembly Hall, as the Salt Lake Temple nears completion (ca. 1891). (© Intellectual Reserve, Inc.)

Chapter 5

The Salt Lake Tabernacle: A Witness to the Growth of God's Kingdom

Scott C. Esplin

"In great deeds something abides," reminisced Joshua Lawrence Chamberlain, a famed Civil War colonel. "On great fields something stays. Forms change and pass; bodies disappear, but spirits linger, to consecrate ground for the vision-place of souls. And reverent men and women from afar, and generations that know us not and that we know not of, heart-drawn to see where and by whom great things were suffered and done for them, shall come to this deathless field to ponder and dream; And lo! the shadow of a mighty presence shall wrap them in its bosom, and the power of the vision pass into their souls."[1] For Latter-day Saints, the historic Salt Lake Tabernacle has become one of those sacred sites—a consecrated hall where "something abides" and "spirits linger" and where modern visitors are wrapped in "the shadow of a mighty presence" while visions of the Restoration "pass into their souls." President Gordon B. Hinckley summarized the influence the

Scott C. Esplin is an assistant professor of Church history and doctrine at Brigham Young University.

Tabernacle has had on the Church: "The Spirit of the Lord has been in this structure. It is sacred unto us."[2]

With the construction of larger and more modern conference halls, the Salt Lake Tabernacle stands today as a silent witness to its pioneer past. Having undergone significant transformations throughout its life, the building serves not only as a monument to pioneer greatness but also as an example of changes in the Church's history. Its sacred heritage mimics the faith's own transformation into a recognizable worldwide church. Born of necessity, the Tabernacle began as a functional assembly hall for pre-railroad Utah in the 1860s. As the Church grew, the Tabernacle changed from a meeting place into a missionary messenger, a means for disseminating the faith. Improved technology, coupled with the increasing popularity of the building's famed choir, brought the structure into a new era. However, the recognition of the choir and of the Church eventually caused the faith to outgrow the building, leaving the structure as a memorial to pioneer ingenuity and resourcefulness. Throughout these transformations, the Salt Lake Tabernacle has hosted within its walls some of the most significant events associated with the growth of the Church and the establishment of Zion. It stands as a reminder of this past and as a witness that the Church's future remains connected to its prophetic founding.[3]

The Tabernacle as Functional Assembly Hall

The Salt Lake Tabernacle began as one of a series of options Church leadership explored to answer a problem that continually plagued early Mormonism: how to accommodate all who wanted to hear the prophet's voice. "It used to be in the days of the Prophet Joseph, a kind of common adage that Mormonism flourished best out of doors," noted Elder George A. Smith.[4] Indeed, throughout Joseph Smith's life, the Church struggled to provide adequate meeting space for its growing membership. Beginning with the Kirtland Temple, the first formally erected meetinghouse, the Church and its leaders failed to accommodate all who wanted to worship. "I felt to regret that any of my brethren and sisters should be deprived of the meeting," the Prophet Joseph Smith remarked, when more people than could fit crowded in to witness the Kirtland Temple dedication on March 27, 1836. Although those who did not fit in the temple were sent to a nearby schoolhouse and promised a second dedicatory service, many were still left out.[5] Later, in Nauvoo, the challenge to seat the Saints continued, with the Prophet and other leaders regularly addressing congregations outdoors because of the crowds. A canvas tabernacle requiring more than four thousand yards of cloth was planned for the lot directly west of the Nauvoo Temple, but the project was scrapped and the materials were used to outfit westbound wagons following the Prophet's death.[6]

In Salt Lake City, the problem of accommodating all who wished to gather for meetings persisted. As early as one week after entering the valley, leaders sought to protect Saints from the harsh elements by building an open-air bowery, a pavilion covered by evergreen branches. As many as five of these boweries stood for nearly two decades in and around Temple Square; the largest was built in the early 1860s and may have held more than eight thousand people.[7] While good for shade, these structures were useless against harsh winters. As early as 1852, a more permanent structure (known today as the "Old Tabernacle") was built along the southwest corner of Temple Square. Able to accommodate about 2,200 people, the hastily built structure served as a temporary measure until something larger and more lasting could be erected. Church leaders hoped the Salt Lake Tabernacle would solve this problem permanently when they announced plans for its construction at April conference in 1863.

Church leaders optimistically hoped the Tabernacle would be "enclosed [the first] fall, and when finished . . . seat nearly 9000 persons." The structure missed both estimates.[8] As construction stretched over more than four years, Church leaders began to realize that the building would never accomplish their goal of seating all the Saints. In the conference preceding its dedication, Elder George A. Smith predicted, "I expect that by the time our great Tabernacle is finished, we shall begin to complain that it is too small, for we have never had a building sufficiently large and convenient to accommodate our congregations at Conference times."[9] President Brigham Young similarly downplayed Saints' expectations:

> We calculate by next October, when the brethren and sisters come together, to have room for all. And if there is not room under the roof, the doors are placed in such a way that the people can stand in the openings and hear just as well as inside. I expect, however, that by the time our building is finished we shall find that we shall want a little more room. "Mormonism" is growing,

View of the interior of the Salt Lake Tabernacle, decorated with garlands and featuring a water fountain in the center. (© Intellectual Reserve, Inc.)

spreading abroad, swelling and increasing, and I expect it is likely that our building will not be quite large enough; but we have it so arranged, standing on piers, that we can open all the doors and preach to people outside.[10]

Elder Smith's and President Young's statements proved prophetic. When the building was first used the following October, the aisles and doorways were crowded, and many members were left standing outside.[11]

Resolved to increase the functionality of their new meeting hall, Church leaders took measures to enlarge the space. Just two years after the Tabernacle was completed, the Saints began adding a gallery that would significantly increase seating. Shortly before its completion in April 1870, the *Deseret News* remarked, "By the 5th of next month it is believed that the new gallery will be so far finished as to be ready for use by the public, and twelve thousand persons may then be comfortably seated within the walls of the spacious building. Under such circumstances it is presumed that Conference may be held in comfort, and that none who desire to attend will be under the necessity of staying away, for lack of comfortable accommodation, as has been the case on many occasions in the past."[12]

Indeed, with the Tabernacle's ability to accommodate large crowds, the pioneer builders next turned their attention to increasing the masses' comfort. From 1875 until the mid-1880s, a large water fountain flanked by four statues of lions rested twelve rows from the front podium in the center of the structure. Designed to cool the occupants, it also provided some comic relief when, on one occasion, a child made use of the fountain. "It seems that at one June conference, when the Tabernacle was very warm," LeRoi C. Snow recalled, "a family of good Saints from Hawaii was in attendance. They had entered the Tabernacle from a front side door and were attempting to make their way down the center aisle to find seats. To do so they had to detour around the fountain, for which purpose steps and a walkway were provided. One of the youngsters of the family, on coming abreast of the fountain fell a victim of temptation and eagerly dived in, and began a vigorous splashing. He was duly extricated, much to the amusement and probably the envy of the assembled Saints."[13] Though less exciting, additional amenities including gas lighting and heating were added to the structure in 1884.[14]

As they did their best to improve the comfort and use of the building, early leaders never forgot its primary purpose as an edifice where the Saints could gather to hear the word of God. President John Taylor's dedicatory prayer, finally offered in October 1875, eight years after the building was first used, highlighted the Tabernacle's original intent. "We, thy servants," Taylor prayed, "dedicate and consecrate this house unto thee, and unto thy cause, as a place of worship for thy Saints, wherein thy people may assemble from time to time, to obey thy commandment to meet often together to observe thy holy Sabbath, to partake of thy holy Sacrament of the Lord's Supper, and wherein they may associate for the purpose of prayer, praise and thanksgiving, for the transaction of business pertaining to thy Church and kingdom, and for whatsoever purpose thy people shall assemble in thy name." Further emphasizing the hall's primary focus, Taylor implored, "May thy holy angels and ministering spirits be in and round about this habitation, that when thy servants are called upon to stand in these sacred places, to minister unto thy people, the visions of eternity may be open to their view, and they may be filled with the spirit and inspiration of the Holy Ghost and the gift and power of God; and let all thy people who hearken to the words of thy servants drink freely at the fountain of the waters of life."[15]

Drinking "freely at the fountain of the waters of life" encapsulates the Tabernacle's purpose throughout much of its useful life. While it was regularly used for sacrament meetings until the 1890s and for weekly worship services into the 1920s, the building's best-known meeting function was always hosting the Church's general conferences. From the first conference held there in October 1867 to the last in October 1999, the Salt Lake Tabernacle served as the home of the semiannual gatherings. In fact, during that 132-year period, only five general conferences (held outside of Salt Lake due to the antipolygamy opposition of the 1880s) were ever convened outside the Tabernacle.[16]

As home to general conference for more than a century, the Tabernacle witnessed some of the Church's most significant events, including solemn assemblies for thirteen Church presidents, the canonizing of scripture, and announcements of official Church action (for example, the cessation of plural marriage in 1890 and the extension of priesthood access to all worthy males in 1978). It also hosted unique general conference sessions, including a special testimony meeting held as the last session of the October 1942 gathering. At the height of World War II, the sacrament was administered during this meeting, and those assembled "returned home better able to cope with the dark days ahead."[17] At the structure's rededication in 2007, Bishop H. David Burton recalled some of these historic Tabernacle occasions: "These old walls, if they could talk, would shout, 'We were here'" when Joseph F. Smith shared his vision of the redemption of the dead, when President Heber J. Grant inaugurated the Church welfare plan during the depth of the Depression, and when Harold B. Lee reiterated the First Presidency's 1915 call for family home evening.[18] President Boyd K. Packer likewise remembered:

> Here in 1880 the Pearl of Great Price was accepted as one of the standard works of the Church.
>
> Here also two revelations were added to the standard works, now known as Doctrine and Covenants sections 137 and 138. . . .
>
> Here in 1979, after years of preparation, the LDS version of the King James Bible was introduced to the Church.
>
> The new editions of the Book of Mormon, the Doctrine and Covenants, and the Pearl of Great Price were announced to the Church here.
>
> In 1908 in a general conference, President Joseph F. Smith read section 89 of the Doctrine and Covenants—the Word of

Wisdom. . . . Then a vote to accept it as binding upon the members of the Church was unanimously passed. . . .

Here the Book of Mormon was given the subtitle "Another Testament of Jesus Christ."[19]

In summary, as President Packer said, "Great events which shaped the destiny of the Church have occurred in this Tabernacle at Temple Square."[20]

In addition to many unique conference occasions, the Tabernacle's walls have also resounded with testimonies from every Church president from Brigham Young to Thomas S. Monson. During the building's eighty-fifth anniversary in 1952, Elder Stephen L Richards reflected upon the powerful doctrinal declarations that had been delivered in the building:

Ponder for a moment, my brethren and sisters, and all who listen, the glorious and vital truths which have been proclaimed in this building—the nature and composition of the Godhead, the organization of the universe, the history and placement of man in the earth, his purpose in living, and the divine destiny set for him, the laws governing his conduct and his eligibility for exaltation in the celestial presence, the true concept of family life in the eternal progression of the race, the truth about liberty and the place of governments in the earth, the correct concept of property, its acquisition and distribution, the sure foundations for peace, brotherhood, and universal justice. All these elemental things, and many others incident thereto, have been the burden of the message of truth which has come from this building through the generations.[21]

The impact of these truths caused Richards to conclude, "I stand today in a pulpit sanctified by its history. When I recall the noble servants of our Heavenly Father who have stood here and given inspired counsel to the people, and borne testimony with such power and conviction and spirit as to electrify every soul who heard; when I contemplate the operation of the still, small voice, which has come from simple and lowly words given here, which have touched the hearts and sympathies of the people; when I think of the vast volume of precious truth which has been proclaimed from this stand, I feel very small and weak within it."[22]

In addition to being home to the prophet's general conference addresses, the Tabernacle has also been the site for many of their final farewells. One of the earliest funerals in the Tabernacle was held for President Heber C. Kimball on June 24, 1868, just nine months after the building opened. The first funeral for a President of the Church in Salt Lake City occurred in 1877 when Saints bid farewell to Brigham Young in the historic structure. From then until the completion of the Conference Center in 2000, funeral services for every President of the Church (except President Joseph F. Smith, whose service was private because of the 1918 flu epidemic) and numerous other prominent men and women have been held in the Tabernacle. Elder Richards said, "Within these sacred walls have the great of our community found opportunity for the expression of their noblest thoughts and convictions, and from here they have been laid to rest in the closing of their lives."[23] Providing a place for the Saints to transact important Church business while greeting, learning from, and bidding farewell to Church leaders, the Tabernacle has served as the spiritual home of the Saints for more than a century.

The Tabernacle as Missionary Messenger

While originally built to host the Saints' spiritual events, the Salt Lake Tabernacle, easily the largest hall in the region, quickly took on other functions. During the late nineteenth century and throughout much of the twentieth century, the Tabernacle shifted from being a meeting hall to a missionary location. The Tabernacle "has stood as a great missionary," observed President Howard W. Hunter, "introducing the gospel of Jesus Christ to people all around the world—those who have entered its portals and those who have heard the message that has gone forth from here in music and the spoken word."[24] More so than the temples, which are reserved for members, the public Tabernacle became a place of intersection for Mormons and the outside world. "The Tabernacle was where early Mormonism revealed itself to contemporaries," historian Ronald W. Walker summarized.[25]

The Tabernacle's earliest missionary influence was its construction and size, both of which were unique in the West. Of the visitors who toured the structure, Walker observed, "Everyone agreed that the building was big, especially for its time. Travelers to Salt Lake City used such words as 'huge,' 'extraordinary,' 'immense,' and a 'monster in size' to voice their awe. . . . [However,] admiration for the building's engineering and size did not necessarily translate into praise for its design."[26] After lauding the orderliness of the city itself, one eastern visitor remarked, "The far-famed tabernacle strikes one as a huge monstrosity, a tumour of bricks and mortar rising on the face of the earth. It is a perfectly plain egg-shaped building, studded with heavy entrance doors all around; there is not the slightest attempt at ornamentation of any kind; it is a mass of ugliness; the inside is vast, dreary, and strikes one with a chill, as though entering a vault."[27] Another remarked that the building had "no more architectural character . . . than . . . a prairie dog's hole."[28]

Disdain for the building may have stemmed from contempt for the faith it represented, causing the Tabernacle to became "a frequent target for caricature."[29] Some called it "the Church of the Holy Turtle," others "half of an eggshell set upon pillars." Additional comparisons included a "culinary serving dish, . . . Noah's ark had it been capsized, . . . [and] balloons, bathtubs, bells, watermelons, a whale, and even mushrooms." In one instance of extreme exaggeration, one man remarked, "For my part, I decided that, so far as my experience goes, the oval tabernacle . . . is unsurpassed, even by its neighboring preaching shanty, for oppressive ugliness among all the buildings now standing in the world." Ronald Walker summarized, "In short, the building was a gigantic curio, something 'strange' and 'unique,' to be talked or written about because of its outlandishness. 'We have never seen anything like it,' said a British minister."[30]

Visitors could often overcome their disregard for the architecture, however, if they enjoyed the experience inside. In an effort to provide culture for its residents and welcome the world, the Church transformed the Tabernacle from merely a religious assembly hall into a community gathering place. In rededicating the structure, President Gordon B. Hinckley noted that the Tabernacle has not merely served the Church in religious functions. He observed:

> Through these many years, this has been a unique and wonderful place of assembly. Many men and women have spoken here, testifying of the Restoration of the gospel of Jesus Christ. From the time of Brigham Young to the present, every prophet has spoken from this pulpit. Other men and women of note have spoken, including various presidents of the United States. It has been a home for the arts and culture of this community. The Utah Symphony first used this as a place to perform. Great artistic productions have been presented here, such as the *Messiah* and the Tanner Gift of Music. Funeral services for men and women of prominence have been conducted here. It has truly been a centerpiece for this community through all of these many years.[31]

As a community centerpiece, the Salt Lake Tabernacle has witnessed some of the most significant civic events in Salt Lake's history. Prominent visitors to the state have sought out the Tabernacle. Ulysses S. Grant, the first United States president to come to Utah, toured the historic tabernacle shortly before its dedication in 1875.[32] Other United States presidents who visited or spoke in the historic structure include Rutherford B. Hayes, Theodore Roosevelt, William H. Taft, Woodrow

Wilson, Warren G. Harding, Herbert C. Hoover, Franklin D. Roosevelt, Harry S. Truman, John F. Kennedy, and Lyndon B. Johnson. President Hayes was amazed with the building's acoustics and the fact that he could carry on a conversation with General William T. Sherman from two hundred feet away.[33] Presidential candidates, some of whom later won election to the office, spoke from its podium, including Dwight D. Eisenhower, William Jennings Bryan, James G. Blaine, Richard M. Nixon, and Barry Goldwater. Other prominent visitors came from all over the world. They included General William Booth, Sir Arthur Sullivan, Susan B. Anthony, Emperor Dom Pedro II of Brazil, Queen Liliuokalani of Hawaii, actress Lillie Langtry, General Phillip Sheridan, actor Edwin Booth, Joseph Smith III, Ferdinand de Lesseps, Henry Ward Beecher, Dr. Norman Vincent Peale, and Harvard president Charles William Elliot.

In addition to prominent dignitaries, the Tabernacle has also regularly hosted the world's great performers. While Church leaders valued music, the idea of introducing sectarian singing into the Tabernacle was met with some protests. Although some members of the Twelve disapproved of sectarian uses for the building, the world-famous operatic soprano Adeline Patti gave one of the earliest concerts held in the historic structure in February 1884. By one account, Madame Patti won President John Taylor over to the idea of a concert by praising the magnificent Tabernacle and expressing "a strong desire that she might be allowed to try her voice there." Apparently, her appeal included "enthusiastic praise of the Mormon doctrines, and, in fact, . . . a strong wish to join the Mormon Church."[34] The event was significant not only because of the prestige of the performer but also because it marked the first event held on a winter night in the Tabernacle. Gas lamps and pot-bellied stoves were brought in to illuminate and warm the building. Patti had a special rail line built to take her car directly to the Tabernacle itself.[35] Though Patti's intent to convert is questionable, the concert was a success, with over fourteen thousand people reportedly present.

Since Patti's visit, musicians have made the Salt Lake Tabernacle a regular stop on their North American tours. The building has hosted some of the most famous musicians of the nineteenth and twentieth centuries, including Polish pianist Ignacy Jan Paderewski, Russian composer Sergei Rachmaninoff, Austrian violinist Fritz Kreisler, and, more recently, American vocalists Frederica von Stade and Gladys Knight.[36] *Deseret News* music editor Harold Lundstrom observed, "At least a dozen of the world's great artists . . . have told me that the principal reason for their accepting a concert date in Utah was so that they could include in their concert credits a 'performance in the Salt Lake Mormon Tabernacle.' At least four of them have said that a performance in the Tabernacle carried the prestige second only to Carnegie Hall."[37] Like soloists, famed performing groups have also sought out the hall as a venue. Over the years, the Tabernacle has hosted the New York Philharmonic, the Pittsburgh Symphony, the Chicago Symphony, the Berlin Philharmonic, and the Vienna Philharmonic.

Though visits by these performers and groups are significant, the Tabernacle's musical claim to fame remains its renowned namesake and chief occupant, the Mormon Tabernacle Choir.[38] In celebrating the building's renovation in 2007, President Packer remarked, "Worthy music of all kinds has its place. And there are endless numbers of places where it can be heard. But the Tabernacle on Temple Square is different from them all."[39] The difference may lie in the choir itself, which has become synonymous with the building. President Stephen L Richards best summarized the relationship: "I would not venture to say whether the Tabernacle has made the choir or the choir has made the Tabernacle famous."[40] In fact, though the adjacent Conference Center is much larger, President Hinckley carefully indicated that, upon completion of its renovation, the Tabernacle would remain the choir's home. "[This building] has become known across the world as the home of the Mormon Tabernacle Choir," he stated. "It will again be home to the Tabernacle Choir and the Orchestra on Temple Square."[41]

In addition to musical performances, numerous other civic events have been held in the building, including "nominating conventions for political offices, a mass protest meeting over the conduct of federal appointees in the territory, a benefit concert for the Johnstown flood victims, the Western Silver Conference, President Wilford Woodruff's 90th birthday celebration, [and] . . . a convention of Episcopalians."[42] Prominent among these civic events have been sacred memorials of national and international import. In 1923, for example, a memorial service was held in the Tabernacle mourning the death of United States president Warren G. Harding. Coincidentally, President Harding had spoken in the Tabernacle on his visit to Utah only six short weeks earlier. More recently, the hall served as a solemn gathering place for the Church following the terrorist attacks of September 11, 2001. As part of the National Day of Prayer and Remembrance, Church members and leaders gathered in the historic Tabernacle to sing, worship, and pray. Following the meeting, *Church News* editor Gerry Avant observed, "With seeming reluctance, people filed from the Tabernacle that, for the brief span of about an hour, had sheltered them as in a dome of peace and tranquility."[43]

Many of these civic events hosted in the Tabernacle include memorable Church productions aimed at distributing the Church's message both to its members and to the world. During the twentieth century, the Church frequently used the hall for various historical commemorations. In honor of the centennial of the Church in 1930, members participated in a pageant entitled "The Message of the Ages," held in the building throughout the month of April. Emphasizing the restoration of the gospel, it presented a chronological summary of the history of God's work on earth. One observer commented that this was "probably one of the most outstanding events ever held in the Tabernacle."[44] Seventeen years later, in 1947, a similar production was held to commemorate the arrival of the pioneers in Utah and the Church's reaching a milestone of one million members worldwide. More recently, the Tabernacle was used in Salt Lake's celebration of the 2002 Winter

Olympics and Paralympics, hosting concerts with the Tabernacle Choir and world-renowned artists throughout the games.

To accommodate its wide variety of uses and keep up with technological change, the Church has made frequent improvements to the Tabernacle. An article in the Church's *Improvement Era* during the building's centennial year summarized many of the changes: "The building has been remodeled and changed through the years as science and technology have opened new doors and avenues to improvement. The choir loft has been rebuilt half a dozen times; new electrical and heating systems have been installed; broadcast facilities have been added; the balcony stairs have been remodeled to allow for outside rather than inside access; and many other improvements have been made."[45]

Some of the earliest technological advancements brought to the building involved lighting and heat. Though the numerous doors and windows provided some natural light, artificial lighting soon became a necessity. A similar need to heat the hall was quickly recognized, as functionality was hampered during the cold winter months. In 1884, a heating and lighting system was installed. Three hundred gas-filled jets flooded the hall with light. Gradually, the gas was replaced with electricity, and the Tabernacle became one of the first structures in Utah to have electric lighting.[46] Later lighting changes have been driven by the needs of the various productions held in the structure.

While utility improvements have increased the functionality of the Tabernacle, safety improvements have increased its longevity. The *Improvement Era* remembered some famous near-disasters over the life of the building:

> The days of the Tabernacle have not been without excitement. During a Fourth of July celebration in 1887, fireworks ignited the roof, but, according to Church historical records, 'the flames were promptly put out by the fire brigade before doing much damage.' . . .

In 1933 water pipes froze and burst one bitterly cold night, causing extensive damage to some of the walls and carpets. Six inches of water accumulated in the basement under the organ, but the organ itself was not touched.

On a quiet January Sunday in 1938, four men were found spraying gasoline on the building. During the ensuing scuffle, one of them was severely burned.[47]

These and other potential disasters prompted safety improvements in the structure. A tin roof replaced the original four hundred thousand wooden shingles at the turn of the century, and an aluminum roof replaced the tin in 1947.[48] A sprinkler system was added to the interior in 1930. To protect the Tabernacle against earthquakes, the entire roof was reinforced with angle iron in 1942.[49]

In addition to improving safety, Church officials have sought to increase the comfort and serviceability of the Tabernacle. For example, in 1951 a quiet room was added for members with young families. Later, in 1968, a full basement was dug underneath the building to house mechanical equipment, radio and television facilities, offices, and storage. Especially important was the addition of dressing rooms and storage facilities for the Mormon Tabernacle Choir.

In many ways, the Salt Lake Tabernacle has become the public face of The Church of Jesus Christ of Latter-day Saints. The thousands who enter the hall to hear a politician, enjoy a concert, view a production, or listen to its choir experience a different side of Mormonism. As the Church's most visited historic site, Temple Square and its famed Tabernacle fulfill, in small measure, an earlier directive from the Lord regarding Nauvoo. "Let it be a delightful habitation for man, and a resting-place for the weary traveler, that he may contemplate the glory of Zion, and the glory of this, the corner-stone thereof; that he may receive also the counsel from those whom I have set to be as plants of renown, and as watchmen upon her walls" (D&C 124:60–61).

The Tabernacle as Pioneer Hallmark

The Salt Lake Tabernacle faced new challenges throughout the latter half of the twentieth century. It had to house general conference for a membership approaching thirteen million; balance cultural, civic, and choral demands; and serve as a state-of-the-art recording and broadcast studio. Though leaders did their best to keep the building up to date, technology and Church growth eventually brought significant changes to the edifice. The construction of the neighboring Conference Center, followed by the renovation of the Salt Lake Tabernacle itself, brought the building into a new phase of life. Today it stands as a pioneer hallmark, a visible connection to the Church's triumphant past.

Though technological and safety concerns certainly contributed to the choice to construct the Conference Center, a driving force behind the change was seating, the very issue that led to the Tabernacle's construction more than 140 years earlier. In announcing the construction of the Conference Center, President Hinckley remarked:

> I regret that many who wish to meet with us in the Tabernacle this morning are unable to get in. There are very many out on the grounds. This unique and remarkable hall, built by our pioneer forebears and dedicated to the worship of the Lord, comfortably seats about 6,000. Some of you seated on those hard benches for two hours may question the word *comfortably*.
>
> My heart reaches out to those who wish to get in and could not be accommodated. . . .
>
> We recognize, of course, that we can never build a hall large enough to accommodate all the membership of this growing Church. We've been richly blessed with other means of communication, and the availability of satellite transmission makes it possible to carry the proceedings of the conference to hundreds of thousands throughout the world.

But there are still those in large numbers who wish to be seated where they can see in person those who are speaking and participating in other ways.[50]

At the first general conference held in the completed Conference Center, President Hinckley further remarked, "The Tabernacle, which has served us so well for more than a century, simply became inadequate for our needs."[51]

While inadequate as a meeting hall, the building was preserved to serve a different function—as a monument to pioneer resourcefulness and a visual connection to both past struggles and future growth. President Packer commented on the building's symbolism, "The Tabernacle stands here next to the temple as an anchor and has become symbolic of the Restoration. It was built by very poor and very, very ordinary people. It is now known worldwide."[52] However, to continue to send this message, the Tabernacle needed to be preserved, necessitating the building's renovation from 2005 to 2007. Commenting on the renovation, President Hinckley observed, "We must do extensive work on the Salt Lake Tabernacle to make it seismically safe. . . . The time has come when we must do something to preserve it. It is one of the unique architectural masterpieces in the entire world and a building of immense historical interest. Its historical qualities will be carefully preserved, while its utility, comfort, and safety will be increased."[53]

As President Hinckley noted, making the building seismically safe was the primary focus of the Tabernacle's upgrade. A seismographic study may have, in fact, initiated the project. While building practices had changed dramatically since its construction, the Tabernacle's original design remained largely unchanged. However, an account of the renovation reported, "One day church leadership asked the very pertinent question, 'How would this building cope in an earthquake?' . . . The answer was not favorable." The Church commissioned the Salt Lake architectural firm FFKR to investigate. Using the 1994 Northridge California tremor as a model, they evaluated the effects

Preparing new steel and concrete foundations to reinforce external piers of the Tabernacle. (© Intellectual Reserve, Inc.)

a large quake would have on the historic structure. Architect Roger Jackson responded, "The study showed that the big stone piers, which are three ft. wide, nine ft. long and vary in heights from 12 to 21 ft., would start to tip over. And at about the same time, the big wood trusses would slide from the tops of them. So to the question, 'How would it cope?' the answer was, 'Not very well.'"[54] Structural engineer Jeff Miller summarized the problem: "The biggest deficiency in the whole structure was that nothing was really tied together, especially the roof." To protect against possible tragedy, engineers added steel trusses to each king truss, installed a steel-belt truss where the piers meet the roof, secured the balcony to the walls, and reinforced each pier with improved steel and concrete foundations. The work essentially tied together the structural elements of the Tabernacle "so that the edifice would move as a single mass in the event of a major earthquake."[55]

Utility, comfort, and safety were also improved significantly during the renovation. With the completion of the spacious Conference

Center in the spring of 2000, the need for maximum occupancy in the Tabernacle was reduced. Accordingly, seating was rearranged on both the main floor and the balcony, expanding spacing between rows and lowering the building's seating capacity by more than one thousand.[56] Replica pews made of oak replaced the original faux-painted white pine pews, though several were preserved near the rear of the facility for exhibition purposes.[57] While the new pews are more accommodating than the originals, President Hinckley still quipped at the building's rededication, "As you've already discovered, the new benches are just as hard as the old ones were!"[58] Additional comforts include air conditioning for the choir seats and podium and interior staircases for the balconies, which previously were accessible only from the exterior. Finally, although unseen by the average visitor, the basement facilities were significantly improved with renovated choir offices, dressing rooms, rehearsal areas, and a recording studio.[59] Work in the basement also included the addition of a large lift capable of moving "the organ console, parts of the lectern, a grand piano, and other elements between the basement and the main floor."[60] These changes allow the building to quickly transform into any one of its three major configurations: a full rostrum for large meetings, a limited rostrum for small meetings, and a stage for concerts with orchestra.[61]

Throughout the entire process, Church leaders charged construction crews to maintain the Tabernacle's historical integrity. Announcing the renovation, President Hinckley remarked, "Buildings, like men, get old. They don't last forever unless you look after them, and this building is old now."[62] The improvements made by the Church during renovation reflect an attempt to preserve and protect this jewel of Church architecture. President Hinckley continued, "I respect this building. I love this building. I honor this building. I want it preserved. I want the historicity of it preserved. I don't want anything done here which will destroy the historical aspect of this rare gem of architecture. Now in the process of working on it, they'll have to put in some steel work, yes, and so on. But I don't want a modern, 2004–2005 building. I want the old original Tabernacle, its weak joints bound together and preserved and strengthened and its natural and wonderful beauty preserved and strengthened."[63] He warned those involved in the project, "Now, [to] the engineers, the architects, I just want to say, be careful. Don't you do anything you shouldn't do, but whatever you do, do well and do right. . . . [Bishop H. David Burton is] going to take you through an exercise on exactly what they're going to do. But I am going to say this, when the drawings are all complete, I'm going to take another look at them to see that nothing is destroyed that shouldn't be destroyed."[64]

With the renovation complete, President Hinckley seems to have made good on his promise to ensure historical accuracy. Indeed, this goal appears to have guided the entire project. "President Hinckley's request to return the 'old original Tabernacle' became the standard for making difficult architectural and construction decisions. The phrase was used to express the essence and objective of the project,"[65] recalled Bishop Burton. Architect Roger Jackson summarized the difficulty: "The major challenge was to preserve the feel and character and the historic integrity of the building and to not let this work overshadow the building and its history."[66] At the building's dedication, Bishop Burton reported on their success: "A charge was extended to preserve, strengthen, and return the old original Salt Lake Tabernacle, revitalized and ready for another period of distinguished service. Today, dear President, we present this senior citizen of a building, all attired in a fresh new finish, fitly framed together in its historical elegance—although a bit more comfortable. The Presiding Bishopric, along with more than 2,000 craftsmen, proudly return the 'old original Tabernacle,' along with a 100-year warranty."[67]

Moving the Tabernacle through the renovation and into a new phase of utility has taught Latter-day Saints much about the building as well as their past. During the renovation, Church archivists acquired previously unknown early architectural renderings for portions of the building, adding to appreciation of pioneer craftsmanship. Scientists at Brigham Young University took advantage of access to early timbers during the project to date the lumber, and in the process learned about pioneer resourcefulness. They found that timbers from early structures, possibly the Temple Square boweries, were reused during the meager years when early settlers carved a living from a barren desert.[68] These are the kinds of lessons the renovation's champion, President Hinckley, encouraged. "It is good to look to the past to gain appreciation for the present and perspective for the future," he remarked. "It is good to look upon the virtues of those who have gone before, to gain strength for whatever lies ahead. It is good to reflect upon the work of those who labored so hard and gained so little in this world, but out of whose dreams and early plans, so well nurtured, has come a great harvest of which we are the beneficiaries. Their tremendous example can become a compelling motivation for us all, for each of us is a pioneer in his own life, often in his own family, and many of us pioneer daily in trying to establish a gospel foothold in distant parts of the world."[69] The preservation of the Tabernacle has moved the building into its third phase of utility, that of a historic landmark that teaches modern Saints about the past.

Conclusion

"A building develops a personality of its own," President Hinckley remarked of the historic Salt Lake Tabernacle.[70] In many ways, the personality of the Tabernacle reflects that of the Church. Born of pioneer necessity, the building's original purpose—to seat the Saints—has long been supplanted. However, in spiritual and historical significance, it cannot be replaced.

While witnessing the development of the kingdom, the Tabernacle has undergone changes in form and purpose to match those experienced by the Saints. As a meeting hall, the Tabernacle could never host all of the faithful. However, it has been transformed from a place of refuge and utility to one of outreach and now tribute to a triumphant past. President Taylor's plea at the building's dedication continues to be fulfilled: "Pour out thy Holy Spirit, we pray thee, upon every sincere soul now before thee."[71]

For nearly 150 years, the Tabernacle has stood as a silent witness to significant events in Church and world history. When it opened in 1867, it was the primary meeting place for a Church with a membership of approximately one hundred thousand located in only four stakes (Salt Lake, Weber, Utah, and Parowan) and ten missions.[72] A sixty-six-year-old Brigham Young presided over the first general conference in the building, an occasion at which the Church sustained twenty-eight-year-old Joseph F. Smith as the newest member of the Quorum of the Twelve. Now fourteen decades, fourteen Church Presidents, and thirteen million members later, the building still stands as a solid reminder of the faith, ingenuity, and vision of its pioneer builders.

The Tabernacle is the most significant functional assembly hall in the history of the Church. Originally designed to shield occupants from harsh frontier elements, it has since provided a place where listeners can be protected from a spiritual climate much more corrosive. Born of necessity and created with pioneer ingenuity, it has witnessed many of the faith's most prominent events and hosted its most influential people. The feelings of President Thomas S. Monson characterize its importance for General Authorities and lay members alike: "The Tabernacle is a part of my life—a part which I cherish."[73]

Notes

1. Joshua Lawrence Chamberlain, Dedication of the Monument to the 20th Maine, October 3, 1889, in Jim Lighthizer, "Reflecting on the 150th Anniversary of the Civil War," Civil War Preservation Trust, http://www.civilwar.org/150th -anniversary/message-from-jim-lighthizer.html.

2. Gordon B. Hinckley, "Good-bye to This Wonderful Old Tabernacle," *Ensign*, November 1999, 91.

3. For additional information on the history of the Salt Lake Tabernacle, see Scott C. Esplin, *The Tabernacle: An Old and Wonderful Friend* (Provo, UT: Religious Studies Center, Brigham Young University, 2007).

4. George A. Smith, in Journal History of The Church of Jesus Christ of Latter-day Saints, August 12, 1855, 1, Church History Library, Salt Lake City; hereafter cited as Journal History.

5. *History of the Church of Jesus Christ of Latter-day Saints*, ed. B. H. Roberts, 2nd ed. rev. (Salt Lake City: Deseret Book, 1957), 2:410–11.

6. Elden J. Watson, "The Nauvoo Tabernacle," *BYU Studies* 19, no. 3 (Spring 1979): 416–21.

7. Ronald W. Walker, "The Salt Lake Tabernacle in the Nineteenth Century: A Glimpse of Early Mormonism," *Journal of Mormon History* 32, no. 3 (Fall 2005): 200.

8. "The New Tabernacle," *Deseret News*, June 3, 1863, 387.

9. David W. Evans, "Discourse by Elder Geo. A. Smith, Delivered in the Tabernacle, Great Salt Lake City, April 7, 1867," *Deseret News*, May 15, 1867, 154.

10. David W. Evans, "Remarks by President Brigham Young, Delivered in the Tabernacle, Great Salt Lake City, April 7, 1867," *Deseret News*, July 10, 1867, 218.

11. "The Thirty-seventh Semi-annual Conference," *Salt Lake Telegraph*, in Journal History, October 6, 1867, 1.

12. "Fortieth Annual Conference," *Deseret Evening News*, in Journal History, April 5, 1870, 3.

13. Stewart L. Grow, "A Historical Study of the Construction of the Salt Lake Tabernacle," in Scott C. Esplin, *The Tabernacle: An Old and Wonderful Friend* (Provo, UT: Religious Studies Center, Brigham Young University, 2007), 251.

14. "All Ready," *Salt Lake Daily Herald*, April 1, 1884.

15. "The New Tabernacle Dedicatory Prayer," *Deseret News*, October 20, 1975, 594.

16. Kenneth W. Godfrey, "150 Years of General Conference," *Ensign*, February 1981, 70. The five conferences convened outside the Salt Lake Tabernacle include the April and October 1885 conferences held in Logan, the April 1886 conference held in Provo, the October 1886 conference held in Coalville, and the April 1887 conference held again in Provo.

17. Godfrey, "150 Years of General Conference," 70.

18. H. David Burton, "If These Old Walls Could Talk," *Ensign*, May 2007, 32–33.

19. Boyd K. Packer, "The Spirit of the Tabernacle," *Ensign*, May 2007, 27–28.

20. Packer, "Spirit of the Tabernacle," 27.

21. Stephen L Richards, in Conference Report, April 1952, 46.

22. Richards, in Conference Report, 45.

23. Richards, in Conference Report, 46.

24. Howard W. Hunter, "The Tabernacle," *Ensign*, November 1975, 96.

25. Walker, "Salt Lake Tabernacle," 199.

26. Walker, "Salt Lake Tabernacle," 208–9.

27. Lady Hardy, "The Tabernacle, Salt Lake City," in *Historic Buildings of America as Seen by Famous Writers*, ed. Esther Singleton (New York: Dodd, Mead and Company, 1906), 217–18.

28. In Walker, "Salt Lake Tabernacle," 210.

29. In Walker, "Salt Lake Tabernacle," 210.

30. In Walker, "Salt Lake Tabernacle," 210–12.

31. Gordon B. Hinckley, "A Tabernacle in the Wilderness," *Ensign*, May 2007, 43.

32. Hunter, "Tabernacle," 95–96.

33. Arnold J. Irvine, "8 Prophets Spoke from Its Podium," *Church News*, September 30, 1967, 5.

34. Kate B. Carter, *The Great Mormon Tabernacle* (Salt Lake City: Daughters of Utah Pioneers, 1967), 62.

35. Harold Lundstrom, "Voices of the Musical Great Echoed in Historic Salt Lake Tabernacle," *Church News*, September 30, 1967, 6.

36. Eleanor Knowles, "Focal Point for Important Events," *Improvement Era*, April 1967, 24.

37. Lundstrom, "Voices of the Musical Great," 7.

38. For additional information on the choir, see Lloyd D. Newell's work herein.

39. Packer, "Spirit of the Tabernacle," 26–27.

40. Richards, in Conference Report, April 1952, 44.

41. Hinckley, "Tabernacle in the Wilderness," 43.

42. Irvine, "8 Prophets Spoke from Its Podium," 5.

43. Gerry Avant, "'Balm for Wounded Hearts' at Memorial," *Church News*, September 22, 2001, 3.

44. In Carter, *Great Mormon Tabernacle*, 64.

45. Knowles, "Focal Point for Important Events," 23.

46. Carter, *Great Mormon Tabernacle*, 62.

47. Knowles, "Focal Point for Important Events," 25.

48. Carter, *Great Mormon Tabernacle*, 61–62.

49. Carter, *Great Mormon Tabernacle*, 61.

50. Gordon B. Hinckley, "This Glorious Eastern Morn," *Ensign*, May 1996, 65.

51. Gordon B. Hinckley, "This Great Millennial Year," *Ensign*, November 2000, 68.

52. Packer, "Spirit of the Tabernacle," 28.

53. Gordon B. Hinckley, "Condition of the Church," *Ensign*, November 2004, 5–6.

54. Lynne Lavelle, "A Singing Endorsement," *Traditional Building* 22, no. 6 (December 2009); www.traditional-building.com/Previous-Issues-09/ Decembert-Project09FFKR.html.

55. Brett Hansen, "Gathering Strength," *Civil Engineering* 8, no. 77 (August 2007): 49.

56. Hansen, "Gathering Strength," 52–53. Architect Roger Jackson said that the number of balcony rows was reduced from nine to seven and the spacing on the floor was expanded from nine to fourteen inches. Roger Jackson, "If These Walls Could Talk: Preserving the Historic Salt Lake Tabernacle" (lecture, Brigham Young University, Provo, UT, January 18, 2008).

57. "Tabernacle Project Fact Sheet," Newsroom; http://lds.org/ldsnewsroom/v/ index.jsp?vgnextoid=437858f5e99a1110VgnVCM100000176f620aRCRD&vg nextchannel=9ae411154963d010VgnVCM1000004e94610aRCRD.

58. Hinckley, "Tabernacle in the Wilderness," 43.

59. Jennifer Dobner, "Mormon Tabernacle Reopens after Renovations, Seismic Upgrade," *Deseret News*, April 1, 2007.

60. Hansen, "Gathering Strength," 53. Unfortunately, the addition of this lift also led to what may be the renovation's "largest casualty from the standpoint of preservation"—the "timber framing system that was used to support the original podium" had to be removed to accommodate the lift. "It was hopelessly in the way," remarked architect Roger Jackson. "That was a piece of old fabric that would have been really nice to keep" (53).

61. Hansen, "Gathering Strength," 53.

62. Gordon B. Hinckley, "Tabernacle Renovation Press Briefing," October 1, 2004; see newsroom.lds.org.

63. Hinckley, "Tabernacle Renovation Press Briefing."

64. Hinckley, "Tabernacle Renovation Press Briefing."

65. Burton, "If These Old Walls Could Talk," *Ensign*, May 2007, 32.

66. Hansen, "Gathering Strength," 49.

67. Burton, "If These Old Walls Could Talk," 32.

68. Matthew F. Bekker and David M. Heath, "Dendroarchaeology of the Salt Lake Tabernacle, Utah," *Tree-Ring Research* 63, no. 2 (2007): 95.

69. Gordon B. Hinckley, "The Faith of the Pioneers," *Ensign*, July 1984, 3.

70. Hinckley, "Good-bye to This Wonderful Old Tabernacle," 91.

71. "The New Tabernacle Dedicatory Prayer," *Deseret News*, October 20, 1875, 594.

72. Henry A. Smith, "137th Conference Will Note Tabernacle's 100th Birthday," *Church News*, September 30, 1967, 3.

73. Thomas S. Monson, "Tabernacle Memories," *Ensign*, May 2007, 42.

An exterior view of the Salt Lake Theatre. (Courtesy of L. Tom Perry Special Collections, Brigham Young University.)

Chapter 6

The Salt Lake Theatre: Brigham's Playhouse

Kenneth L. Alford and Robert C. Freeman

A s we imagine a world without the Internet, videos, televisions, recorded music, or radios, we can better understand the important role that theatres[1] once played in our society. Throughout history, an enduring commitment to music, art, and other forms of culture has been at the very heart of great societies. This pattern seems to transcend any particular political, religious, or societal context. Humanity yearns for refinement. For members of The Church of Jesus Christ of Latter-day Saints, the roots of cultural identity—including music, drama, and dance—date back to the beginning years of the Restoration.

A Rich Dramatic Tradition

Drama and the arts were well established among Latter-day Saints before their arrival in the western desert. In Nauvoo during the 1840s,

Kenneth L. Alford is an associate professor of Church history and doctrine at Brigham Young University. Robert C. Freeman is a professor of Church history and doctrine at Brigham Young University.

the Saints embraced the notion that a reprieve from the daily struggle of living was indispensable to their mental and spiritual health. The Prophet Joseph Smith led the effort to encourage such interests by organizing a dramatic company in Nauvoo.[2] The multistory Cultural Hall (also known as the Masonic Hall) was built on Main Street in the early 1840s, and numerous plays were performed there. In April 1844, just two months before the martyrdom of Joseph and Hyrum Smith, Brigham Young appeared in two scenes of the play *Pizarro, or the Death of Rolla* as "the High Priest, costumed in robes of scarlet and gold, with white muslin . . . in a nonspeaking part."[3] In that same Nauvoo production of *Pizarro*, a young man named Hiram Clawson accepted a small part as a stage hand;[4] he later played a major role in creating and establishing the Salt Lake Theatre.[5]

After their forced exodus from the City Beautiful, the Saints sought rest from their travels and travails through song and dance. Lifting the spirits of weary travelers helped them tremendously and served as a kind of healing balm. The Lord himself encouraged such activity when he instructed the Saints at Winter Quarters, "If thou art merry, praise the Lord with singing, with music, with dancing, and with a prayer of praise and thanksgiving" (D&C 136:28). During the journey west, performances were sometimes conducted on the open ground or on makeshift stages that were as mobile as wagons. As one historian noted, "even in these, the darkest days of 'Mormon' history, the innate love of the people for clean and wholesome social enjoyment lightened their cares and eased their burdens."[6]

Salt Lake before the Theatre

The first pioneers arrived in the Salt Lake Valley in July 1847, and plays were being produced under the boughs of the original bowery on Temple Square as early as 1850.[7] Hiram Clawson had a prominent role in many of those performances.[8]

Shortly after the first plays were presented in the bowery, "the dramatic instinct existed and soon found voice in the organization of the Deseret Dramatic Association," according to Phil Margetts, one of Utah's nineteenth-century theatrical stars.[9] President Young was invited to be an honorary member of the board. Soon after, President Young called on the Saints to construct an edifice where they might enjoy social interactions on a regular basis and be sheltered from the elements. The historic Social Hall was dedicated on New Year's Day, 1853.[10] Hiram Clawson was again among the stalwart performers.[11]

The Social Hall, a very modest forty feet by sixty feet, could seat only about three hundred patrons, though up to four hundred people were sometimes squeezed into the building.[12] Appropriately, a bust of Shakespeare was placed on stage, confirming that this was, first and foremost, a playhouse. Participant changing rooms were located underneath the performance floor. The Social Hall served as a center of pioneer social activity from 1852 until 1857, when the threatened invasion of the United States Army interrupted its use during the so-called Utah War.[13]

By the following summer, the threat of military action had faded, and calls for a new and larger building soon emerged. The need for a theatre in Salt Lake City was briefly filled by the organization of the Mechanics' Dramatic Association in 1859 and the generosity of Harry Bowring, who was building a new home on First South between Third and Fourth East.[14] The exterior walls of his home were built, but the interior walls had not yet been added. Mr. Bowring offered the entire ground floor of his home for use as a small theatre. "A stage was built in one end, and rising tiers of lumber seats were built in the auditorium. . . . The first scenery consisted of rugs and sheets hung up, but a little later calico curtains were used. The increasing popularity of the Mechanics' Dramatic Association, and consequent increasing box office receipts made it possible for them to replace the calico curtains with painted scenery."[15] Utah historian Edward W. Tullidge wrote: "It is worthy of note that this was the first place in Utah that bore the name of theatre. . . . It was a theatre now, no longer a bowery; no longer a Social Hall; secular, not sacred. . . . It was the beginning of our proper dramatic era."[16] It was apparently in Bowring's Theatre that President Young decided that Salt Lake needed a large and proper theatre. One account records:

> Phil Margetts had organized the Mechanics' Dramatic Association without the sanction of the Church president, though there is no record of any opposition to it. At any rate Phil was anxious to get the favor of the "Mormon" leader for his company. So he called on him one day and extended an invitation to him and his family to witness a performance, fixing a time for the visit. President Young asked:
>
> "Why can't Heber [meaning Heber C. Kimball, his counselor] and I come tonight? What are you playing?"
>
> "Luke the Laborer," answered Phil.
>
> "I'll come tonight," President Young promised, and in witnessing the performance he was so well pleased that he accepted an invitation for himself and Heber C. Kimball and their families for the following evening.
>
> The next night the two families, including Hiram B. Clawson arrived,—*ninety* in all; and although they crowded the little theatre beyond its capacity they managed to squeeze in. . . .
>
> At the close of the play Phil made a curtain speech to which Brigham Young responded in a complimentary way. That very night President Young was impressed that the time was ripe for the building of a big theatre and immediately thereafter instructed Hiram B. Clawson to negotiate at once for a suitable site upon which to construct a great playhouse.[17]

As President Young famously said, "The people must have amusement as well as religion."[18] He recognized, as one Salt Lake Theatre actress noted, that the Saints "demanded amusement. We were far away from everywhere, cut off from the world, with nothing but the faults and foibles of our neighbors to amuse us."[19]

Not everyone was enamored, though, with the idea of a theatre in the city. There was even disagreement among Church leaders. The idea of erecting a playhouse when the temple of the Lord was incomplete seemed to be of questionable merit. Some authorities argued that if they built a theatre before a temple, it would invite condemnation both locally and nationally.[20] Brigham Young was resolute, however, and the theatre became a priority. He is reported to have said at this time that "there is nothing lovely in this world but the Lord created it for the good of his children. It is the abuse and not the use of anything that constitutes evil."[21]

Almost half the funds used to build the Salt Lake Theatre were obtained "in a very unusual manner, thanks to Uncle Sam. Johnson's [*sic*] army, doing detail duty in Utah, had very large supplies when they were suddenly ordered East"[22] to fight in the Civil War. Before the army's redeployment, the government auctioned off large quantities of supplies, building materials, and foodstuffs. Brigham Young sent Clawson to the auction as his agent with four thousand dollars in gold to "buy the things we most needed."[23] As Clawson recounted in a 1907 address to the Daughters of Utah Pioneers:

I found building material, glass, nails, tents, sugar and other groceries, and many necessities. I was cordially received and favored by the officers. . . . I made my purchases as instructed. Tents with cook stoves that sold in New York City for $12 or $15, I bought for $1, nails worth $40 a box for $6, and other things in proportion. From the sale of a part of the things that I purchased, which realized $40,000.00, and with nails, glass and other building material, so conveniently provided, the building of the Salt Lake Theatre was made possible.[24]

Few were surprised when President Young selected Clawson as the first manager of the Salt Lake Theatre.[25] Clawson quickly secured a site for the new theatre on the northeast corner of First South and State Street.[26] In addition to the funds obtained through the sale of military surplus, it is reported that President Young also used funds that had previously been set aside to build a Seventies Hall in Salt Lake City. "We have a large fund on hand," President Young is reported to have said, "for the erection of a Seventy's hall, but not enough to build such a hall as I want for the Seventies; so we will use that fund to help build the theatre, and when we get the theatre running we can pay back the Seventy's hall fund with good interest, and in that way the Seventy's will get their hall sooner than if they started to build it now."[27]

Building the Salt Lake Theatre

The theatre's foundation was laid in July 1861, and the walls had been raised by October. The building was enclosed by Christmas and completed in March 1862. The theatre was built entirely of timber, stone, and adobe,[28] and the finished cost was over one hundred thousand dollars.[29] George W. James, a travelogue author, called it "one of the noted buildings in America."[30] The Salt Lake Theatre was described in an 1888 illustrated guide to Salt Lake City:

> This imposing and massive edifice . . . was erected at the instance and under the personal direction of the late President Brigham Young. It has undergone many improvements since his demise, and no pains are spared by its present proprietors to make it one of the best appointed in the West. It is a capacious building, 175 feet in length and 80 feet in width, and 60 feet from floor to ceiling inside, having a stage 65 feet deep and 32 feet at the proscenium,[31] and it is fully supplied with traps, properties and scenery. It has a parquette, dress and three upper circles, and two private boxes each side of the proscenium. It will seat

comfortably 1,500 persons. The outside presents an imposing appearance, granite finish on adobe walls, fluted columns, massive cornices in the simple Doric style of architecture. The interior is decorated with taste, and when lighted up is very fine. The scenery is the production of the best artists, and looks so real that it commands the admiration of all spectators. In all its appointments the theatre is first class.[32]

M. B. Leavitt, a famous theatrical promoter, declared in 1912, "At the time of its erection, it was not surpassed in magnitude, completeness and equipment by any other existing house. Its stage, 130 feet deep, remains the most capacious of any in this country."[33] One non-LDS author, in 1914, went so far as to declare that the Salt Lake Theatre was "one of the Seven Wonders of the theatrical world."[34]

The theatre was dedicated on Thursday, March 6. President Young sent invitations which announced the upcoming event:

> Mr. _____ and family are respectfully invited to be present at the dedication of the New Theatre, on Thursday evening, March 6, 1862, at 6 o'clock.
>
> Brigham Young
>
> P.S. Children under four years not admitted. As the house is not finished, care should be taken to come warmly clothed.
>
> This ticket must be presented at the door of the Theatre.
>
> Great Salt Lake City,
> Feb. 28, 1862[35]

Over 1,200 people attended the dedication—reportedly nearly all of them were Church officials and their families. In the dedicatory prayer, Daniel H. Wells, a member of the First Presidency, invoked the blessings of the Lord that the building would be a place "for pastime, amusement, and recreation; for plays, theatrical performances, for lectures or celebrations."[36] One account of the dedicatory prayer reflected some disappointment at the proceedings:

> "Squire" Wells as he was popularly called . . . no doubt made a good city mayor and an efficient general of the Nauvoo Legion, but the worthy "Squire" was not an orator, moreover, he had his piece written for this occasion and read it; his peculiar mode of delivery was tiresome even when at his best, when he had his choice of subject and all the latitude he could desire; but it was especially so on this occasion, when he was circumscribed to a most monotonous enumeration of everything that entered into the construction of the huge building. Beginning with the ground on which it stood and going in systematic order up through it foundation, walls, floors, doors, windows, to the roof, particularizing even the timbers, nails and bolts, the laths and plaster, the glass and putty, no detail he could think of was omitted. Each and all were especially dedicated to their particular purpose and use, and the blessing of the Almighty invoked to be and continue with each of these materials, and with the structure as a whole. Even to those who believed in dedications, who were the great majority of those present, the dedicatory prayer was just a little wearisome and the audience experienced a feeling of relief when it was over.[37]

The dedicatory service also included a speech by President Young entitled "The Capacity of the Human Body and Mind for Development." During his talk, he stated, "If I had my way, I would never have a tragedy played on these boards. There is enough of tragedy in everyday life, and we ought to have amusement when we come here."[38] The theatre, Young continued, is "one of the privileges and blessings which an All-Wise Creator had placed within the reach of creatures to enjoy."[39] Heber C. Kimball and John Taylor also spoke. A choir and orchestra performed "The Star Spangled Banner," "La Marseillaise," a special anthem written for the dedication by Eliza R. Snow, and other hymns. There was dancing after the formal program ended.[40]

After a brief initial opening run of a few weeks, the theatre was closed after the April 1862 general conference so that work on the interior could be completed. The theatre reopened on Christmas Eve 1862.[41]

For the first decade of its existence, the theatre was lit by 385 oil lamps dispersed throughout the building. Later, in 1872, gas lighting, which was much preferred, was installed.[42] Shortly thereafter, other enhancements were added. These included the replacement of the old benches with chairs and new stage boxes and the modification of the floor to provide a better slant toward the stage. Despite these improvements, there were still many challenges. In 1873, George Reynolds wrote President Young that the theatre was struggling. He cited poor attendance due to inclement weather and illness among the Saints as well as their animals. Another concern was a new music hall that had recently opened in Salt Lake City that featured women dancing in provocative ways. Reynolds reported that the new hall seemed to attract both those who were curious and those who were more inclined toward amusements other than those that President Young and others had worked so hard to establish.[43]

The Salt Lake Theatre in Operation

The first play performed in the new theatre was entitled *The Pride of the Market*.[44] Unlike other theatres, no performances were ever given on Sunday,[45] and every performance opened with prayer regardless of what type of event was being held. Smoking and drinking were prohibited. Customers were required to check their firearms at the box office, and, instead of popcorn, attendees often ate parched corn and dried fruit during a performance.[46] When the theatre first opened, its ticket prices ranged from fifty cents for the upper galleries to seventy-five cents for the better seats.[47] The theatre reflected the community in

The interior of the Salt Lake Theatre was designed by E. L. T. Harrison, a London-trained architect who patterned the house after the famous Drury Lane and Boston theaters. (Used by permission, Utah State Historical Society. All rights reserved.)

which it flourished; "almost anything was taken in exchange for admittance—eggs, butter, cheese, flour, vegetables and other merchantable produce. Large melons bought a ticket and a small melon in change; a peck of potatoes might buy a ticket with a bit of flour as change."[48]

In the early years of the theatre, actors usually worked without pay and were expected to learn "three, four, sometimes five, new plays a week; frequently two plays the same night." Sometimes actors were expected to memorize their parts "on a day's notice."[49]

President Young took an active role in the operation of the Salt Lake Theatre. After it opened, he attended as many rehearsals and performances as possible. He reportedly even used his private carriage to take actresses to and from the theatre to help them avoid opportunities for embarrassment and annoyance.[50] Ever the matter-of-fact and practical leader, "he was a splendid fireman about the theatre, and took every possible precaution against fire. Once, when George Francis Train was delivering a lecture in the theatre, two or three of the coal-oil footlights began to smoke and flare. [President Young] stepped quietly out of the stage box, strolled over to the lamp, and, with his broad-brimmed hat, wafted out the light and returned to his box without any remark."[51]

Several stories about Brigham Young and the theatre were passed around Salt Lake City. In one story, a young actor fell in love with Sara Alexander, a ward of President Young's. When the actor asked for permission to court the young woman, Brigham Young reportedly told him, "Young man, I've seen you attempt Richard III and Julius Caesar with fair success, but I advise you not to aspire to Alexander."[52] In a second story, a leading lady needed a dark-haired wig to complete her costume but could not find one in the wardrobe department. When President Young heard of the problem, he approached John McDonald, an actor with long black hair, and asked him to cut his hair so that a wig could be made. McDonald reportedly said, "If the success of the play depends upon my hair, Brother Brigham, you shall have it!," and he cut his hair as requested.[53] A third story involved the subject of censorship:

> The first time Brigham Young imposed any censorship on the theatre was during the first professional ballet to appear in it. Young instructed the manager that all ballet skirts must be ankle length. The manager protested that it would be impossible for the troupe to dance, but Young was insistent.
>
> During the first performance, many of the dancers tripped and fell on the long skirts. Before the second performance, the manager cut one inch off the skirts.
>
> When this went unnoticed by Young, the manager cut off another inch at the next performance and continued doing this until, by the final night of the ballet, the skirts had been

shortened to their original length. Brigham Young had attended every performance and either hadn't noticed or pretended he hadn't![54]

To ensure that the Salt Lake Theatre presented proper entertainment, rules and regulations were introduced sometime in the 1864–65 performance season and hung on the theatre wall.[55] The following were some of the house rules:

1. Gentlemen are not to wear their hats in the Green Room, except in costume, or talk vociferously. . . . For any breach of this article, Fifty Cents will be forfeited. . . .

2. All rehearsals must be punctually attended, according to the call. For absence from each scene, a fine of Fifty Cents; whole rehearsal, Five Dollars. . . .

5. Any person appearing intoxicated on the stage shall forfeit a week's salary, and be liable to be discharged. . . .

8. A performer introducing his own language or improper jests, not in the author, or swearing in his part, shall forfeit One Dollar.

9. A performer restoring what is cut out by the managers or omitting advertised songs, will forfeit One Dollar. . . .

12. No person permitted, on any account to address the audience, but with the consent of the managers. Any violation of this article will subject the party to forfeiture of a week's salary, or discharge, at the option of the managers. . . .

16. Every gentleman engaged in the Theatre is to provide himself with such silk or cotton tights, stockings, wigs, hats, feathers, swords, shoes and boots, as may be appropriate and necessary to the costume he is wearing. If the costume be of present period, the whole of it must be provided by the performer. . . .

19. The use of profane or ungentlemanly language is strictly prohibited in the Theatre.

20. Smoking is strictly prohibited on the stage of the Theatre, in the entrances, Green Room,[56] auditorium, or in the ante-rooms.[57]

During the first eight years of operation, the theatre reportedly produced "more than 500 plays, farces, and operas, . . . a record unequaled by any American theatre of that time."[58] Many of those performances included the talents of national and international dramatic stars, including "P.T. Barnum; Drew, Ethel, John, and Lionel Barrymore; Sarah Bernhardt; Edwin Booth; Billie Burke; 'Buffalo Bill' Cody; Fanny Davenport; John Drew; Eddie Foy; Charles and Daniel Froham; Al Jolson; Lillian Russell; Dewitt Talmage; and scores besides."[59]

One famous American actress, Julia Dean Hayne, enjoyed and appreciated the Salt Lake Theatre so much that she extended a planned brief stop in Salt Lake into a performance run over one year long. At her last performance in July 1866, she stepped out of character and was called in front of the curtain. In her farewell speech, she said, "To President Young, for the many courtesies to a stranger, alone and unprotected, I return these thanks which are hallowed by their earnestness; and I trust he will permit me, in the name of my art, to speak my high appreciation of the order and beauty that reigns throughout this house. I would the same purity prevailed in every temple for the drama's teaching. Then, indeed, the grand object would be achieved, and it would become a school."[60]

President Young owned the theatre until his death. For a brief time following President Young's passing in 1877, the property was maintained in the name of the Salt Lake Theatre Corporation, but the keys were held by the US marshal when the theatre became involved in estate litigation. In 1879, the theatre keys were conveyed to President John Taylor, who assumed responsibilities and reorganized it into the Salt Lake Dramatic Association.[61] During the theatre's existence, three

Presidents of the Church (Brigham Young, John Taylor, and Joseph F. Smith) as well as one future Church President (Heber J. Grant) held a majority ownership and control of the theatre.[62]

Numerous prominent Salt Lake families were closely associated with the Salt Lake Theatre. The children or grandchildren of Hyrum Smith, Edward Partridge, Heber C. Kimball, Orson Pratt, Lorenzo Snow, Newel K. Whitney, Parley P. Pratt, Jedediah M. Grant, Joseph Fielding, Willard Richards, John Taylor, William E. McLellin, George A. Smith, Newel Knight, Amasa M. Lyman, Reynolds Cahoon, and many others were involved in productions.[63] Elder Orson F. Whitney, who was called in 1906 to serve as an Apostle, also took part in theatrical performances at the Salt Lake Theatre.[64]

Annie and Maude Adams, a mother-and-daughter team, were famous local actresses who performed regularly at the theatre. Annie started acting there as a child, and her daughter, Maude, first appeared on stage as a baby in the early 1870s. A farce entitled *Lost Child* was to be performed with Phil Margetts as the lead comedian. The play called for a baby to be displayed on stage, but a problem arose:

Actress Maude Adams.

Instead of providing a real baby, as the property man had been instructed to do, he had a grotesque-looking rag baby, not at all to the comedian's taste in the matter. Millard, the property man, declared he had been unable to procure a live baby, nobody was willing to lend a baby for the part— older children he could get, but he could not get a baby, and the rag baby was the best that he could do under the circumstances, and on such short notice. Margetts was in distress. "What, in Utah!" he exclaimed. "The idea!" Where babies are our best crop, to be unable to procure one for his favorite farce. It was simply preposterous, absurd, incredible; he objected to play with nothing but a miserable makeshift of a rag baby. . . . Sudden as a bolt from a clouded sky, while the altercation was still at its height, Mrs. Kiskadden [Annie Adams] appeared in the centre of the stage with her baby in her arms, and in a good-natured tone that ended all the trouble, exclaimed, "Here's Maude, use her!" Maude was indeed a good substitute for the inartistic-looking "prop" the property man had provided. Phil was happy and played the distracted parent with a realism and a pathos he never could have summoned for the rag baby.[65]

In later years, Maude Adams would become one of America's most famous and beloved actresses.

In addition to providing a suitable place for plays and musical performances, the Salt Lake Theatre hosted numerous other events such as magicians, musclemen, lectures on numerous topics (including phrenology), dances, charity events, and even political caucuses and conventions.[66]

Conclusion

President Young was sometimes criticized for the active role he had taken in the creation and development of the Salt Lake Theatre. Addressing that criticism, he said:

I built the theatre to attract the young of the community and provide amusement for the boys and girls rather than have them run all over creation for recreation.

Upon the stage of a theatre can be represented evil and its consequences, good and its happy returns and rewards, the weakness and the follies of man, the magnanimity of virtue and the greatness of truth.

The stage can be made to aid the pulpit in impressing upon the minds of the community an enlightened sense of a virtuous life, also a proper horror of the enormity of sin and dread of its consequences.[67]

A history of the Salt Lake Theatre written in 1915 suggested: "Every thoughtful visitor to the place confesses to feeling an influence, an undefinable impression unlike that imparted by any other building of its kind. Who shall say? Perhaps something of the spirit of good, invoked upon the edifice in the prayers of the old pioneers may still linger within its walls to hallow them, and keep alive the aims and hopes of its founders."[68]

The Salt Lake Theatre was in business for sixty-six years and was "a castle, indeed, which . . . stood as an historic monument to Drama, Music, and Art in Utah and the Rockies, and which . . . sent forth geniuses and influences affecting even their development throughout America."[69] By the 1920s, the building was in need of costly repairs, and audiences diminished with each passing year. In 1928, President Grant, who had owned a controlling interest in the Salt Lake Theatre in earlier times, made the difficult decision to sell the building for two hundred thousand dollars.[70] The last performance in the Salt Lake Theatre on October 20, 1928, was a mixed program that included several plays and speeches, intended primarily as a stroll down memory lane for the audience. And, of course, the final evening ended with prayer.[71]

The actual destruction of the building was more difficult than the engineers assigned to the task had envisioned. "Its large, red-pine structural timbers were sound and the building remained unusually tightly fitted. Such pioneer workmanship, combined with the structure's bastion-like walls, meant that several more months of demolition than planned was required."[72] Mountain States Telegraph and Telephone, who had purchased the theatre, built a telephone exchange on the site.[73] Several furnishings from the Salt Lake Theatre, including the original stage curtains and Brigham Young's box seats, have been preserved and are on display at the Pioneer Memorial Museum in Salt Lake City.

After the theatre was demolished, there remained individual memories and the realization that culture was an indispensable part of the Latter-day Saint heritage. One tribute and lament summarized community feelings regarding the destruction of the grand old theatre:

> And now, this art heritage of a passing pioneer people, with its four glittering horseshoes, and many gilded pillars, is to be swept away for the progress of business and a paltry sum of $200,000. The building which stood as a giant in the sixties seems small in the shadow of the twentieth century skyscraper. . . . the last performances have been given. A wrecking crew will lay low the "homey" theatre. . . .
>
> As if to link the glory of the past with the power of the present, Ethel Barrymore stood before the curtain recently, too sad to talk, as she recalled that on this stage had played her grandmother, her mother and father, her uncle, and her two brothers.
>
> And what a record of plays the old call board registers! From the dust of the hills the adobe building came, to dust in the hills it will soon be blown, but the memory of the Salt Lake Theatre will be as imperishable as the granite cliffs in the Wasatch crags, and as tenderly sweet as the scent of a desert rose.[74]

Inspired by such traditions, Latter-day Saints continue to have a deep and abiding love for beautiful, inspiring, and enduring values. President Young once said that if he were stranded on a cannibal island and challenged to bring civilization, he would build a theatre.[75] His comment is indicative of the Mormon way. Industry, hard work, and perspiration mark the Mormon ethic. But clearly one secret to Latter-day Saint success both in pioneer times and today has been the inclination to unstring the bow, relax, and be entertained with healthy cultural amusements. The Salt Lake Theatre filled that role well.[76]

Notes

1. While the preferred US spelling today is usually "theater," this chapter will retain the preferred nineteenth-century British-influenced spelling—"theatre."

2. Horace G. Whitney, *The Drama in Utah: The Story of the Salt Lake Theatre* (Salt Lake City: Deseret News, 1915), 3.

3. Stanley B. Kimball, "Also Starring Brigham Young," *Ensign*, October 1975, 52.

4. George D. Pyper, *The Romance of an Old Playhouse* (Salt Lake City: Seagull, 1928), 26.

5. Hiram Bradley Clawson was born in 1826 at Utica, New York, and arrived in Utah in 1848. He was a "member 17th quorum seventies. Diplomatic missionary to Salt Lake City and elsewhere 1855–77. First treasurer Salt Lake City. Adjutant-general Nauvoo Legion. First superintendent Zion's Co-operative Mercantile Institution. Died March 29, 1912, Salt Lake City." See *Pioneers and Prominent Men of Utah* (Salt Lake City: Utah Pioneers, 1913), 810. He was a son-in-law to Brigham Young. See Charles L. Metten, "Salt Lake Theatre," in *Encyclopedia of Mormonism*, ed. Daniel H. Ludlow (New York: Macmillan, 1992), 1255.

6. Pyper, *Romance of an Old Playhouse*, 23.

7. George Wharton James, *Utah: The Land of Blossoming Valleys* (Boston: Page, 1922), 137.

8. Whitney, *Drama in Utah*, 5.

9. There appears to be some debate regarding the exact date of the creation of the Deseret Dramatic Association. Some sources claim 1850, others 1852. See Pyper, *Romance of an Old Playhouse*, 38, 44.

10. Pyper, *Romance of an Old Playhouse*, 45.

11. Whitney, *Drama in Utah*, 5.

12. Pyper, *Romance of an Old Playhouse*, 45.

13. For additional information regarding the relationship between Salt Lake City and the United States Army, please see the chapter entitled "Camp Douglas—Keeping a Watchful Eye on the Saints," in this volume.

14. Pyper, *Romance of an Old Playhouse*, 68.

15. Myrtle E. Henderson, *A History of the Theatre in Salt Lake City from 1850 to 1870* (Evanston, IL: n. p., 1934), 43–44.

16. Quoted in Pyper, *Romance of an Old Playhouse*, 69–70.

17. Pyper, *Romance of an Old Playhouse*, 71–72.

18. Andrew Jenson, *Encyclopedic History of The Church of Jesus Christ of Latter-day Saints* (Salt Lake City: Deseret News, 1941), 762.

19. Annie Adams Kiskadden and Verne Hardin Porter, "The Life Story of Maude," *Green Book Magazine*, June 1914, 892.

20. John D. Fitzgerald, "Theatre in the Wilderness," *Family Weekly*, October 12, 1958, 22.

21. Fitzgerald, "Theatre in the Wilderness," 22.

22. T. Earl Pardoe, "The Showplace of the Pioneers," *Drama Magazine*, January 1929, 106.

23. Pyper, *Romance of an Old Playhouse*, 75.

24. Pyper, *Romance of an Old Playhouse*, 75–76.

25. Whitney, *Drama in Utah*, 9. Clawson served as manager of the Salt Lake Theatre from its opening in 1862 until May 1889. See Pyper, *Romance of an Old Playhouse*, 333.

26. Henderson, *History of the Theatre*, 47.

27. John S. Lindsay, *The Mormons and the Theatre* (Salt Lake City: n.p., 1905), 23. The Salt Lake Seventies Hall was never built.

28. Whitney, *Drama in Utah*, 11. Up to a quarter million adobe bricks were used during the construction.

29. Arthur Hornblow, *A History of the Theatre in America* (Philadelphia: J. B. Lippincott, 1919), 347. For additional information see Roberta Reese Asahina, "Brigham Young and the Salt Lake Theater, 1862–1877" (PhD diss., Tufts University, 1980).

30. James, *Utah*, 135.

31. A proscenium is "the part of a modern stage in front of the curtain." See *Merriam-Webster's Collegiate Dictionary*, 10th ed., "proscenium."

32. *The "Mormon" Metropolis: An Illustrated Guide to Salt Lake City and Its Environs* (Salt Lake City: J. H. Parry, 1888), 33–34.

33. M. B. Leavitt, *Fifty Years in Theatrical Management* (New York: Broadway Publishing, 1912), 406.

34. Kiskadden and Porter, "Life Story of Maude," 885.

35. Pardoe, "Showplace of the Pioneers," *Drama Magazine*, January 1929, 106.

36. Henderson, *History of the Theatre*, 7.

37. Lindsay, *Mormons and the Theatre*, 24–25.

38. James, *Utah*, 137.

39. Leavitt, *Fifty Years in Theatrical Management*, 406.

40. Whitney, *Drama in Utah*, 8. See also Lindsay, *Mormons and the Theatre*, 25.

41. Whitney, *Drama in Utah*, 9.

42. Henderson, *History of the Theatre*, 55.

43. George Reynolds to Brigham Young, February 5, 1873, correspondence, Vault MSS 95, L. Tom Perry Special Collections, Harold B. Lee Library, Brigham Young University, Provo, UT.

44. Whitney, *Drama in Utah*, 8.

45. Kiskadden and Porter, "Life Story of Maude," 894.

46. Fitzgerald, "Theatre in the Wilderness," 22.

47. Whitney, *Drama in Utah*, 8.

48. Kiskadden and Porter, "Life Story of Maude," 894.

49. Kiskadden and Porter, "Life Story of Maude," 890.

50. James, *Utah*, 137–38.

51. Leavitt, *Fifty Years in Theatrical Management*, 408.

52. Fitzgerald, "Theatre in the Wilderness," 22.

53. Fitzgerald, "Theatre in the Wilderness," 22.

54. Fitzgerald, "Theatre in the Wilderness," 23.

55. Henderson, *History of the Theatre*, 64.

56. A "green room" in a theatre or other public building is a room that is designed to accommodate performers or speakers when they are not on stage.

57. Henderson, *History of the Theatre*, 64–66.

58. Fitzgerald, "Theatre in the Wilderness," 22.

59. Ronald W. Walker, "Salt Lake Theatre," in *Utah History Encyclopedia*, ed. Allan Kent Powell (Salt Lake City: University of Utah Press, 1994), 484.

60. Whitney, *Drama in Utah*, 18.

61. Management in the Association was maintained by three individuals—John T. Caine, president; Hiram B. Clawson, secretary; and David McKenzie, treasurer. See Pyper, *Romance of an Old Playhouse*, 332–33.

62. Whitney, *Drama in Utah*, 46.

63. See Pyper, *Romance of an Old Playhouse*, 21–22.

64. Whitney, *Drama in Utah*, 37.

65. Lindsay, *Mormons and the Theatre*, 60.

66. Walker, "Salt Lake Theatre," 484–85.

67. Fitzgerald, "Theatre in the Wilderness," 23.

68. Whitney, *Drama in Utah*, 48.

69. Pyper, *Romance of an Old Playhouse*, 11. On pages 12 and 13, Pyper relates the following story regarding how he became manager of the Salt Lake Theatre:

> One day, more than thirty years ago, Heber J. Grant, then owning a controlling interest in the Salt Lake Theater, now President of the Church of Jesus Christ of Latter-day Saints ("Mormon" Church) said to me, "George, which would you rather be—manager of the Heber J. Grant Insurance Company, or manager of the Salt Lake Theater?"
>
> "I would rather be manager of the Salt Lake Theater than anything else on earth!" I answered.
>
> A few days later he said:
>
> "Go down and put your name on the boards."
>
> And so, for thirty years I have been managing the destinies of the very playhouse.

70. Pardoe, "Showplace of the Pioneers," 106.

71. Henderson, *History of the Theatre*, 107.

72. Walker, "Salt Lake Theatre," 485. See also Ronald W. Walker and Alexander M. Starr, "Shattering the Vase: The Razing of the Old Salt Lake Theatre," *Utah Historical Quarterly* 57 (Winter 1989): 64–88

73. Ann W. Engar, "Theater in Utah," *Utah History to Go*, http://historytogo.utah .gov/utah_chapters/utah_today/theaterinutah.html.

74. Pardoe, "Showplace of the Pioneers," 106.

75. Clarissa Young Spencer, *Brigham Young at Home* (Salt Lake City: Deseret Book, 1961), 147.

76. Visitors to Salt Lake City can still see what the Salt Lake Theatre looked like. Both the Daughters of Utah Pioneers Museum (located at 300 North Main Street) and Kingsbury Hall on the University of Utah campus (located at 1395 Presidents Circle) in Salt Lake City are patterned after the original Salt Lake Theatre.

Beehives on the doorknobs of the Salt Lake Temple. (© Intellectual Reserve, Inc.)

Chapter 7

The Beehive and Deseret: Mormon Symbols in Salt Lake City

Susan Easton Black

W hen looking for symbols of the Book of Mormon in Salt Lake City, there is nothing so evident as the beehive and an obscure word buried in the book of Ether: "And they did also carry with them deseret, which, by interpretation, is a honey bee; and thus they did carry with them swarms of bees" (Ether 2:3). The honeybee, depicted on heroic-sized beehives, is seen atop such prominent buildings as the Beehive House and Joseph Smith Memorial Building in downtown Salt Lake City. Smaller replicas of the beehive have been stamped on license plates, park benches, and other objects. Monuments and souvenirs galore tout the beehive as the symbol of Salt Lake City much as Atlanta claims the peach as its symbol. To Latter-day Saint residents of Salt Lake City, the beehive is more than a symbol of the city as a home of hard workers or of industry. The beehive symbol was Brigham Young's way to remind residents of the Jaredite civilization in America.

Susan Easton Black is a professor of Church history and doctrine at Brigham Young University.

This paper will show that in the 1840s the symbol of the beehive and the word *deseret* were not yet wedded as one. In fact, the two words were not linked together until after the Latter-day Saints had a foothold in the Great Salt Lake Valley. It was then that *Deseret* was chosen as the name of the Mormon territory in the West and the beehive symbol adopted as the state symbol. This paper will trace the beehive's rise to prominence in Salt Lake City and the reasons that the word *deseret* took center stage in the valley. It will also show that as the federal government intervened to prevent the creation of a state called *Deseret*, the beehive symbol gained widespread acceptance but the term *deseret* lost favor, retaining importance only as a trademark of Church-owned entities.

The Beehive Symbol Is Introduced into Mormon Society

Some Latter-day Saint scholars link the word *beehive* to the ancient Jaredite word *deseret*, meaning honeybee (see Isaiah 7:18; 2 Nephi 17:18). The words therefore share an obvious organic connection but not the same precise definition. Adding to the potential confusion, some have suggested that the beehive and *deseret* are symbols of industry. Kevin L. Barney states that Brigham Young chose the beehive symbol and the word *deseret* because he "liked the imagery of cooperative labor and industry brought to mind by honeybees and their hives."[1] S. S. Ivins agrees with Barney, claiming that Brigham chose "the honey bee as their symbol of industry."[2] W. Jeffrey Marsh adds that *deseret* is "a Book of Mormon term for honeybee, signifying unity, industry, and cooperation."[3]

Hugh Nibley says there is more to the beehive symbol than the simplistic view of industry and cooperation. He points out that there is great significance in the fact that the Jaredites brought swarms of honeybees to the new land. According to Nibley, the transporting of bee swarms was a common practice among ancient Egyptians, who held the "bee sign" to be sacred. Nibley sees a strong correlation between the

Jaredites, the honeybee, and early practices in Lower Egypt.[4] He writes, "The bee, like the red crown, was identical with the majesty of Lower Egypt. . . . The bee symbol spread in other directions from its original home, enjoying a prominent place in the mysteries of the Hittites, the Finnish, and surviving in some nations in certain Easter rites." Nibley also points out, "In certain editions of the Book of Mormon, though not the first, the word *deseret* is capitalized, for the editors have recognized that it is really a title. . . . One might be justified, though we will not insist on it, in seeing in *Deseret* the national symbol or as it were the totem of Jared's people."[5] Paul Y. Hoskisson cautions that uncovering the meaning of the word *deseret* and the purpose for the Jaredites bringing honeybees to the new land should be left to the future, for "unless and until it can be determined from which cultural background the Jaredites departed, it will be impossible to do anything but guess about etymologies for Jaredite names," including the name *deseret*.[6]

A few Latter-day Saint historians suggest that because the beehive is prominent in the Third Degree of Freemasonry, Freemasonry introduced Brigham to the symbol.[7] According to Masonic scholar Allen E. Roberts, "The bee . . . works hard and tirelessly, not for himself, but for the swarm. He has a strength and knowledge of materials that cannot be duplicated. He works in complete cooperation, and without dissension, with his fellow bees. He protects the Queen, refuses admittance to enemies, builds, makes honey, and lives in a society ruled by law."[8] In his attempt to link bees to the activities of Freemasonry, Roberts writes of the ancient Masonic lodge as a "Hive of Free-Masons." He calls dissensions that threaten the hive and attempts to separate and form new lodges "swarming," a reference to the pattern of bees and ancient masonry.[9] What historians fail to recognize is that the beehive symbol was introduced and placed in circulation in Nauvoo over a year before Freemasonry officially entered town.[10]

On February 27, 1841, Governor Thomas Carlin signed into law "an Act to Incorporate the Nauvoo Agricultural and Manufacturing Association."[11] The purpose of the association was to promote agriculture and husbandry and to manufacture flour, lumber, and other necessary articles. According to the act, capital stock in the association (a maximum of $100,000) was to be subdivided into $50 shares. Shares or stock certificates were to be numbered and dated before being issued. On the face of each certificate the symbol of the beehive was to appear.[12]

The Nauvoo Agricultural and Manufacturing Association made no attempt to mention or link the beehive to *deseret* on the certificates. Likewise, published accounts of meetings and suggestions given for improving agricultural and manufacturing output in Nauvoo did not reference the word *deseret*.[13]

It was Peter Haws, one of seven principals of the association,[14] who kept the beehive symbol in circulation among Latter-day Saints long after the Nauvoo Agricultural and Manufacturing Association had become defunct. While camped at Garden Grove in Iowa Territory, Peter embossed on the front side of a brass token dated 1846 an ornate beehive with the slogan "Do Your Duty." On the obverse side, he embossed clasped hands with the motto "Union Is Strength."[15] His token was circulated in Garden Grove and throughout Pottawattamie County and used as a barter or exchange among Latter-day Saints. As the Nauvoo Agriculture and Manufacturing Association certificates, there was no attempt by Peter Haws to link the beehive symbol to *deseret*.[16]

The Jaredite Word *Deseret* Becomes a Household Word in Mormon Society

In 1849, Brigham Young and a committee consisting of Heber C. Kimball, Willard Richards, John Taylor, and John M. Bernhisel introduced the word *deseret* into the everyday vocabulary of Salt Lake City residents. The committee, with Brigham acting as lead, met to create and approve a memorial requesting that the US Congress charter "a Territorial Government of the most liberal construction authorized by our excellent Federal constitution, with the least possible delay, to be

obverse   reverse

Haws's 1846 brass token with beehive (variety 1). (© Intellectual Reserve, Inc.)

known by the name of Deseret."[17] The memorial argued that Deseret should be included within the United States because "all political power is inherent in the people; inhabitants of a region are best qualified to judge the type of government suited to their needs."[18] The memorial proposed the boundaries of the new territory be "Oregon on the north, the Green River on the east, Mexico on the south, and the Sierra Nevada on the west, including a portion of the Southern California seacoast."[19] The committee approved a twenty-two-foot-long memorial containing 2,270 signatures signed in support of the proposed territorial status of Deseret.[20] On May 3, 1849, Dr. John M. Bernhisel left Salt Lake City bound for Washington DC with the memorial in hand.[21] In the nation's capitol, his efforts and that of other leading Latter-day Saints to advance the cause of Deseret were thwarted at every turn.

In the meantime, the State of Deseret functioned without federal approval for nearly two years under a formal constitution based upon the US Constitution and the Iowa Constitution of 1846. The preamble to the Deseret Constitution says, "We the People, Grateful to the Supreme Being for the blessings hitherto enjoyed, and feeling our dependence on Him for a continuation of these blessings, do ordain, and establish a free and Independent Government, by the name of the State of Deseret."[22] No mention was made in the constitution of the beehive symbol, nor was it mentioned at rhetorical occasions such as speechmaking. The same could be said about other planned activities of the State of Deseret.

For example, there was no mention of the beehive in the elections held in the bowery to determine which officials would govern the State of Deseret. The General Assembly of the State of Deseret passed ordinances regulating elections and the militia, creating a judiciary system, establishing roads and waterways, and incorporating the Perpetual Emigrating Company and The Church of Jesus Christ of Latter-day Saints. In addition, the general assembly incorporated cities and established the University of Deseret.[23] The board of regents of the university approved the Deseret Alphabet.[24] Then came the first newspaper in Salt Lake City, the *Deseret News.*[25] It is noteworthy that Eliza R. Snow celebrated the proposed State of Deseret in a children's song:

> In our lovely Deseret,
> Where the Saints of God have met,
> There's a multitude of children all around.
> They are generous and brave;
> They have precious souls to save;
> They must listen and obey the gospel's sound.[26]

On September 9, 1850, US President Millard Fillmore signed an act creating the Territory of Utah. When word was received in Salt Lake City of the president's executive decision, Brigham Young ordered the General Assembly of Deseret to dissolve the State of Deseret on April 5, 1851, in favor of the territorial status of Utah.

Deseret and the Beehive Symbol as One

Although the initial proposal was rejected, Brigham did not discard his plans for a State of Deseret within the United States. As governor of the Territory of Utah, Brigham ordered the building of the Beehive House as his official residence and office in 1854 (note that he did not order the building of a Utah House). More than any other residence in Salt Lake City, construction of the Beehive House sent a signal of Brigham's continued hopes and plans for a State of Deseret. In reference to these hopes, he said, "[We will] sustain in time to come our free and glorious institutions to the latest generation."[27] Atop his newly constructed house was placed a gilded beehive. Beehives also adorned the interior of the home, with multiple beehives etched into stair railings. Latter-day Saint residents of the city, believing there was a message in the Beehive House, embraced the beehive as the symbol of Deseret and followed Brigham's example. Soon the beehive symbol, now a reference to the hoped-for State of Deseret, appeared in business and residential districts throughout the city. To many, it was a symbol of defiance—a way to visibly show irritation with federal government interference. To others, it conveyed a willingness to persist in establishing Deseret as a state within the United States. In spite of the replicated beehive symbols throughout the city, the drafting of new constitutions, and the boundary changes made to fit within the prescribed limits of Utah Territory, efforts to create the State of Deseret within the Union failed in 1856, 1862, and 1872.[28]

Frustrated, if not angered, by repeated rejections, Brigham redoubled his efforts to link *deseret* with the beehive symbol. Take, for instance, the Deseret Agricultural and Manufacturing Society, a society similar in composition to the Nauvoo Agricultural and Manufacturing Association of 1841. Brigham Young was president of the new society and, as such, selected the beehive as the society's symbol. Next came the Deseret Currency Association, the first banking establishment in the city. Brigham Young was president of that association also. One purpose of the association was to provide a medium of exchange because US coins were rare in the city. On the notes and certificates issued by the society was the familiar beehive.[29] The difference between these notes and certificates and those issued in Nauvoo was the direct link between *deseret* and the beehive.

The beehive symbol was also prominently displayed on notes issued by the Deseret Typographical Association. The Deseret Dramatic Association, Deseret Livestock Company, Deseret Museum, and

Deseret Music and Dramatic Association are but a few of the organizations that boasted the name *deseret* and the beehive symbol. Others were the Deseret University Bank, Deseret Meat Market, Deseret Mercantile Association, and Deseret Telegraph.

A three-dollar Deseret Currency Association note. (Courtesy of Church History Library.)

Deseret and the Beehive Are Separated

Linking *deseret* with the symbol of the beehive was short lived in a temporal sense. The 1872 federal rejection of the State of Deseret greatly weakened the connection between *deseret* and the beehive. It was further weakened when government officials of the State of Utah, several of which were Latter-day Saints, embraced the beehive symbol and rejected the term *Deseret*.[30] For example, on April 3, 1896, the Great Seal of the State of Utah was adopted. The seal incorporates the word *industry* and an ornate beehive. Prominently displayed on the state flag is also the word *industry*. In the center of the flag's shield is a beehive. On March 4, 1959, the beehive became the official state emblem. On that same date, the state motto "Industry" was adopted. Today the beehive symbol has become so ubiquitous in Salt Lake City that native-born residents scarcely take notice. Does any resident notice that an ordinary sidewalk in downtown Salt Lake City has a honeycomb pattern permanently etched in the cement squares? Does anyone pause to consider the Book of Mormon symbolism when seeing the beehive emblem on the state flag? Ask an outsider, a long-time resident, or any elementary school child. Utah is not Deseret; Utah is the "Beehive State."

The Church has not severed the word *deseret* from the beehive symbol. The Church-owned Deseret Industries, a leader in humanitarian outreach efforts, uses the beehive as its logo. Deseret Mutual Benefit Association, a Latter-day Saint insurance and investment company, currently uses the beehive symbol. The Church-backed Deseret Book, a publisher and chain of Latter-day Saint bookstores, also once used a beehive logo.

Conclusion

Book of Mormon names are again surfacing in Salt Lake City, both for smiles and for profits. In King Benjamin's Court, a subdivision located near the Jordan River Temple, streets are named for Book of Mormon leaders. The Olympus Cove development touts streets named Zarahemla, Abinadi, Hagoth, and Helaman. Resident Michelle Romero gestures to the upscale homes on the street before saying with a laugh, "Only this neighborhood could get away with it."[31] It was not Brigham Young's intention to flood Salt Lake City with symbols of the Book of Mormon for amusement or financial gain. He wanted a symbol that would endure throughout time. He did not select the angel Moroni, although he might have been tempted to do so. He selected the beehive symbol and linked the symbol to *deseret*, a word used only once in the Book of Mormon.

To the casual observer the link no longer depicts the passion evoked in yesteryear. Historian Dale L. Morgan writes, "'Deseret' is almost a lost word in Utah. It survives colorlessly, in the name of a few business firms and religious organizations. Latter-day Saint children sing hymns to 'our lovely Deseret' with little understanding of the passionate devotion the name once commanded or the aspiration which

Beehive atop the Beehive House. (Courtesy of Kenneth L. Alford.)

it encompassed."[32] The beehive stands alone as the symbol of Utah. It symbolizes industry and unity in strength, but little more. To the thoughtful observer, the link between the beehive and *deseret* still holds meaning. It is a visual reminder that an ancient people originating from the Tower of Babel roamed this land. It is a reminder that the Book of Mormon influence reaches from the sidewalks, with their honeycomb patterns, to the heavens, with beehives atop the Joseph Smith Memorial Building and the Beehive House. From top to bottom, the city of the Great Salt Lake is an expression of Book of Mormon influence. It brings to mind sacred scriptural passages: "There shall be none greater than the nation which I will raise up unto me of thy seed, upon all the face of the earth" and "whatsoever nation shall possess [the land] shall serve God, or they shall be swept off when the fulness of his wrath shall come upon them" (Ether 1:43; 2:9). For those who look for truth, the symbol of the beehive is a reminder that the influence of the Book of Mormon still holds sway in the city.

Notes

1. Kevin L. Barney, "On the Etymology of *Deseret*," *BCC Papers* 1/2 (November 3, 2006), http://bycommonconsent.com/2006/11/03/bcc-papers-1-2-barney.

2. S. S. Ivins, "The Deseret Alphabet," *Utah Humanities Review* 1, no. 3 (July 1947): 223.

3. W. Jeffrey Marsh, "Brigham Young and the Book of Mormon," *Journal of Book of Mormon Studies* 10, no. 2 (2001): 13.

4. See Hugh Nibley, *Lehi in the Desert; The World of the Jaredites; There Were Jaredites*, vol. 5, *The Collected Works of Hugh Nibley: The Book of Mormon* (Salt Lake City: Deseret Book; Provo, UT: FARMS, 1988), 189–90; Hugh Nibley, "There Were Jaredites," *Improvement Era*, April 1956, 244; Hugh Nibley, *Abraham in Egypt* (Salt Lake City: Deseret Book; Provo, UT: FARMS, 1981), 233; Jeffrey Ogden Johnson, "Deseret, State of," in *Encyclopedia of Mormonism*, ed. Daniel H. Ludlow (New York: Macmillan, 1992), 1:371–73.

5. Hugh Nibley, "The World of the Jaredites," *Improvement Era*, January 1952, 22–23.

6. Paul Hoskisson, "An Introduction to the Relevance of and a Methodology for a Study of the Proper Names of the Book of Mormon," in *By Study and Also by Faith: Essays in Honor of Hugh W. Nibley*, ed. John M. Lundquist and Stephen D. Ricks (Salt Lake City: Deseret Book; Provo, UT: FARMS, 1990), 2:132.

7. See H. L. Haywood, *Symbolical Masonry* (New York: George H. Doran, 1923); Henry W. Coil, *A Comprehensive View of Freemasonry* (Richmond, VA: Macoy Publishing, 1973).

8. Allen E. Roberts, *The Craft and Its Symbols: Opening the Door to Masonic Symbolism* (Richmond, VA: Macoy Publishing, 1974), 74.

9. Roberts, *Craft and Its Symbols*, 73.

10. Freemasonry entered the town unofficially with Latter-day Saint converts who had been or still were masons.

11. *History of the Church of Jesus Christ of Latter-day Saints*, ed. B. H. Roberts, 2nd ed. rev. (Salt Lake City: Deseret Book, 1957), 4:303. It should be noted that when the Nauvoo Agricultural and Manufacturing Association was organized, Brigham was in England. On February 27, 1841, the same date the act was signed, "President Brigham Young went to Manchester, and preached in Lombard Street." *History of the Church*, 4:305.

12. It should be noted that the beehive was a prominent symbol used in American communities before being introduced in Nauvoo. The beehive is found on antique clocks made in Connecticut, cast-iron string holders, ovens built with ash-chutes, and even seventeenth-century coiffures.

13. See E. Robinson, "Special Notice," *Nauvoo Neighbor*, January 10, 1844, 3; "Trades Meeting," *Nauvoo Neighbor*, February 5, 1845, 3–4.

14. Lyndon W. Cook, *The Revelations of Prophet Joseph Smith: A Historical and Biographical Commentary of the Doctrine and Covenants* (Provo, UT: Seventy's Mission Bookstore, 1981), 260.

15. There are two varieties of the token. Variety 1 does not have initials on the obverse side. Variety 2 has the initials P. H. on the obverse side below the clasped hands. The P. H. stands for Peter Haws, a private coiner indicted for counterfeiting United States coins in Nauvoo. There is no clear evidence that the motto "Union Is Strength" adopted by the second, third, fourth, and fifth wards in Salt Lake City in 1890 traces its origin to the Peter Haws brass token. See Alvin E. Rust, *Mormon and Utah Coin and Currency* (Salt Lake City: Rust Rare Coin, 1984), 33–35.

16. The coining of Peter Haws in Garden Grove was unacceptable to Brigham Young. When Brigham learned that Peter Haws had a coining press in his wagon on May 12, 1846, he reproved him: "While I was standing with Prest. Kimball at his tent, an outcry was heard from Peter Haws' Camp; . . . Haws had let Williams have some bogus money on shares. . . . I reproved them for dealing in base coin and told Haws he could not govern himself, his family, or a company; and unless

he repented and forsook such dishonesty, the hand of the Lord would be against him and all those who partook of such corruption." *Manuscript History of Brigham Young, 1846–1847*, ed. Elden J. Watson (Salt Lake City: J. Watson, 1971), 158.

17. Memorial to US Congress, April 30, 1849, in *Manuscript History of Brigham Young, 1847–1850*, ed. William S. Harwell (Salt Lake City: Collier's, 1997), 198. There is conjecture as to which member of the committee suggested the name *Deseret*. The suggestion that the name was put forward by Joseph Smith years earlier cannot be substantiated. Known sources of Joseph Smith's words do not evidence that he spoke the word *deseret*.

18. Dale L. Morgan, *The State of Deseret* (Logan: Utah State University Press with the Utah Historical Society, 1987), 37. The entire memorial is found in "The Constitution of the New State of Deseret," *Millennial Star*, January 15, 1850, 23–25.

19. Johnson, "Deseret, State of," 371.

20. See Journal History of The Church of Jesus Christ of Latter-day Saints, December 10–11, 13, 1848; March 27, 1849; and April 30, 1849, Church History Library, Salt Lake City.

21. William S. Harwell, *Manuscript History of Brigham Young, 1847–1850*, 200. Five states "made a spontaneous effort at self-creation"—Texas, Franklin ("the embryo state of Tennessee"), Oregon, Deseret, and California. California was the only entity successful in achieving statehood. Morgan, *State of Deseret*, 7, 7n1.

22. Morgan, *State of Deseret*, 121.

23. The University of Deseret had a Deseret University Bank. For information on the bank, see Rust, *Mormon and Utah Coin*, 108–11.

24. During the decade 1859–69, publications in this unique alphabet were *Deseret First Book*; *Deseret Second Book*; the Book of Mormon to the end of the Words of Mormon, designed to be the Deseret Third Book; and the complete Book of Mormon. Historian Andrew Jenson reported that even some of the Church records were inscribed in the Deseret Alphabet. Andrew Jenson, *Encyclopedic History of the Church of Jesus Christ of Latter-day Saints* (Salt Lake City: Deseret News, 1941), 184; Leah R. Frisby and Hector Lee, "The Deseret Readers," *Utah Humanities Review* 1, no. 3 (July 1947): 240–44.

25. The *Deseret News* was founded in 1850. Its columns were filled with Church-related items, Mormon theology, and values.

26. Eliza R. Snow, "In Our Lovely Deseret," *Hymns* (Salt Lake City: The Church of Jesus Christ of Latter-day Saints, 1985), no. 307.

27. B. H. Roberts, *A Comprehensive History of the Church of Jesus Christ of Latter-day Saints* (Provo, UT: Brigham Young University Press, 1965), 3:492.

28. Eugene England, *Brother Brigham* (Salt Lake City: Bookcraft, 1980), 159.

29. See Rust, *Mormon and Utah Coin*, 74–86.

30. Edward Leo Lyman, "Statehood for Utah," in *Utah History Encyclopedia*, ed. Allan Kent Powell (Salt Lake City: University of Utah Press, 1994), 529–31.

31. Rosemary Winters, "Funky Utah Street Names Can Hit You Where You Live," *Salt Lake Tribune*, March 29, 2009.

32. Morgan, *State of Deseret*, 7.

Chapter 8

Thomas Bullock: "The Lord's Clerk"

Arnold K. Garr

Salt Lake City's early history was shaped by prominent pioneers like Brigham Young and Heber C. Kimball but also by lesser-known settlers who left a lasting mark on both the city and the Church. One of these individuals was Thomas Bullock, who served in numerous civic and ecclesiastical posts during the first twenty years of Salt Lake's history. The contributions Bullock made not only helped shape his own community but continue to influence people interested in Latter-day Saint Church history today.

A defining moment in the life of Thomas Bullock took place on the morning of September 18, 1846, in Nauvoo, Illinois. By this time, the main body of Latter-day Saints had fled Nauvoo for their new homes in the West, and only about six hundred remained in the city.[1] Brigham Young had asked his trusted clerk, Bullock, to remain in Nauvoo and record its final days as a Latter-day Saint community,

Arnold K. Garr is a professor emeritus of Church history and doctrine at Brigham Young University.

and it was a heart-wrenching story. On September 13, a renegade anti-Mormon army commenced an attack on the small Nauvoo militia. Several Latter-day Saints were killed, and the survivors were forced to surrender. Within days, the last remnant of destitute Mormons would flee across the Mississippi River.[2] During the retreat, a band of about thirty mobocrats confronted a sickly Thomas Bullock. The captain of the band pointed his sword at Bullock's throat. Four others directed their bayonets at his chest. The leader then threatened, "If you are not off from here in twenty minutes, my orders are to shoot you." Bullock snapped back, "Shoot away, for you will only send me to heaven a few hours quicker." The captain then countered, "If you will renounce Mormonism you may stay here, and we will protect you." To this, the courageous Bullock declared, "I am a Mormon, and if I live, I shall follow the Twelve." The captain then ended the confrontation with one final warning, "If you are not gone when I return in half an hour, my orders are to kill you and every Mormon in the place."[3] Soon thereafter, Thomas and his impoverished family complied with the merciless order, making their way across the Mississippi River to safety in Iowa.

This traumatic incident reveals Thomas Bullock's character. First, he was a man of incredible courage; second, he had unwavering faith in the restored gospel; and third, he possessed exceptional loyalty to the leaders of the Church. This episode demonstrated that Thomas would rather die than denounce his allegiance to Brigham Young and the Twelve Apostles. He manifested this remarkable loyalty many times over throughout the rest of his life.

A chief way Thomas exhibited his faithfulness to Church leadership was to magnify his talent as a professional clerk. Throughout his life, he served as clerk, secretary, scribe, recorder, or proofreader for Joseph Smith, Brigham Young, Willard Richards, the Quorum of the Twelve Apostles, the Church Historian's Office, the Nauvoo City Council, the Nauvoo Masonic Lodge, Church general conferences, the Nauvoo poor camp, the vanguard pioneer company, the Utah Territorial House of Representatives, Salt Lake County, Brigham Young's exploration parties, the Council of Fifty, the *Deseret News*, the Perpetual Emigrating Fund Company, the Nauvoo Legion of Utah, and the First Presidency.

On November 27, 1832, Joseph Smith received a revelation that described the responsibilities of the Lord's clerk: "It is the duty of the Lord's clerk, whom he has appointed, to keep a history, and a general church record of all things that transpire in Zion" (D&C 85:1). Joseph Smith called several men to serve as clerks. Some were more faithful than others, but none was more valiant than Thomas Bullock. His life may be divided into two main periods: first, in his early years in England, in Illinois, and on the pioneer trail, when he developed and refined the skills that he would use for the rest of his career; and second, during his Salt Lake City years, when he made a major contribution as a clerk and historian.

Early Years

Thomas Bullock was born on December 23, 1816, in Leek, Staffordshire, England.[4] He was the youngest of nine children born to Thomas and Mary Hall Bullock.[5] His career as a clerk began in March 1830, when he was only thirteen. At that time, he took a position in the law office of John Cruso, where he worked for the next eight years. In nineteenth-century England, many boys were apprenticed out to learn a skill or trade. In 1838, Thomas began working in the government's excise department.[6] On one occasion, he referred to himself in this position as "one of Her Majesty, Queen Victoria's Officers of Excise."[7] In 1838, Thomas married Henrietta Rushton, whom he had courted for about five years.[8]

On November 20, 1841, Thomas and Henrietta participated in an event that would change their lives forever. They were baptized members of The Church of Jesus Christ of Latter-day Saints "on a cold . . . night, when ice was on the canal, and the keen frosty air was blowing in all its severity."[9] Bullock's loyalty to the Church was tested shortly after his conversion. He "was pelted with stones" and threatened to be run over by a carriage. On one occasion, somebody actually tried to throw him "down an old coal pit." Yet, through it all, he believed that the Lord had delivered him out of "each trial and difficulty."[10] Thomas and Henrietta soon began making plans to move to America and unite with the Saints in Nauvoo.

On March 8, 1843, Thomas, his wife, and their three children boarded the ship *Yorkshire* and embarked on their journey to the United States. Bullock and his father-in-law, Richard Rushton, were selected to supervise a company of eighty-three Mormons on the vessel. Thomas even paid the passage for several Latter-day Saint families.[11] After a hazardous trip across the ocean during which their ship almost capsized, the *Yorkshire* arrived in New Orleans.[12] There they boarded the steamboat *Dove*, which carried them to St. Louis.[13] While they were in St. Louis, they switched to the steamer *Amaranth*, which transported them to Nauvoo. Their date of arrival at the great Mormon gathering place was May 31, 1843.[14]

Much to his delight, on the day Thomas arrived in Nauvoo, he met the Prophet Joseph Smith. It did not take long for the Prophet to recognize Bullock's skills, and within five months he called Thomas to be his personal clerk, a position he would hold until Joseph was martyred in June the following year.[15] As a result of this appointment, Thomas was at the center of many activities during the last eight months of the Prophet's life.

One of the first major responsibilities Joseph Smith assigned to Bullock was to be clerk for the April 1844 general conference.[16] This occasion provided the setting for the Prophet's King Follett Discourse, which some have called his greatest sermon. Thomas was one of four men who recorded that discourse—the other three were Wilford Woodruff, Willard Richards, and William Clayton. However, Bullock's account was more thorough and extensive than the others.[17] This conference is also when the Twelve called for volunteers to serve as "electioneer" missionaries to campaign for Joseph Smith in his run for president of the United States. At that time, 244 men stepped forward and received their assignments.[18]

During the two months following general conference, Thomas began clerking for several other institutions. On April 18, he joined the Masons and within ten weeks was appointed clerk of the Nauvoo Masonic Lodge.[19] On May 9, a court-martial was held in Joseph Smith's office for Major-General Wilson Law of the Nauvoo Legion on charges of "unofficer-like conduct," and Bullock was assigned to be secretary for the proceedings.[20] Then on May 13, Joseph asked Thomas to keep the records of the steamboat *Maid of Iowa*, a vessel owned jointly by the Prophet and Dan Jones.[21]

Unfortunately, Bullock's close association with Joseph Smith came to a tragic end when the Prophet and his brother Hyrum were brutally martyred in the Carthage Jail on June 27, 1844. A few years after the fact, Thomas wrote a touching tribute to the martyrs: "I do know they were the anointed of the Lord, the Prophet and Patriarch of God, and they were two good men when living, and they died good men; they died martyrs for the truth, and they sealed their testimony with their blood; and their testimony is true, and all the powers of earth and hell can not render it null and void."[22]

After the death of Joseph Smith, a new era began in the life of Thomas Bullock. Soon thereafter, Willard Richards of the Quorum of the Twelve Apostles became an important person in Thomas's life. In addition to being an Apostle, Elder Richards had been appointed Church historian in December 1842, general Church recorder in July 1843, and Nauvoo city recorder in August 1843.[23] On December 8, 1844, Elder Richards opened an office in his newly completed home and appointed Thomas Bullock as deputy city recorder. Thomas began putting the Nauvoo city records into order inasmuch as they had been neglected for several months due to Elder Richards's extended illness.[24]

In February 1845, Bullock began his greatest endeavor as a historian, writing the manuscript for the "History of Joseph Smith." Up to that time, Elder Richards and others had written 394 pages of the manuscript.[25] However, between February 1845 and February 1846, Bullock, under the direction of Elder Richards, wrote an incredible 674 pages of the history.[26] Then, on February 4, 1846, Bullock and Richards packed the manuscript for the pioneer trek to the Rocky Mountains. Because of the western migration and subsequent Mormon colonization, Bullock's further work on the "History of Joseph Smith" would be suspended until 1854.

Thomas Bullock recorded many of the most important events pertaining to the Latter-day Saint exodus from Nauvoo and the pioneer journey to the Salt Lake Valley——certainly one of the most arduous yet faith-promoting eras in the history of the Church. As assigned, he recorded the sorrowful demise of Nauvoo as the Mormon capital. "For a whole week the war of cannon and the sharp cracking of rifles kept us in an awful state of suspense and anxiety," wrote Bullock. "Our devoted city was defended by about 150 poor, sickly, persecuted Saints, while it was cannonaded by about 1500 to 2000 demoniacs, in the shape of men, who had sworn to raze our temple to the ground, to burn the city, ravish our wives and daughters, and drive the remainder into the river."[27]

The Mormons who survived this brutal attack fled for their lives across the Mississippi River to Iowa. There the "Poor Camp," as they were called, were safe but impoverished and without food. This became the setting for the "miracle of the quail," which took place on October 9. On this occasion, according to the faithful, the Lord miraculously provided food from heaven, in the form of quail, for his starving Saints. Once again we are indebted to Thomas for writing a descriptive account of a significant event in Church history:

> But hark! what noise is that? See! the quails descend; they alight close by our little camp of twelve wagons, run past each wagon tongue, when they arise, fly round the camp three times, descend, and again run the gauntlet past each wagon. See the sick knock them down with sticks, and the little children catch them

alive with their hands! . . . They rise again, the flocks increase in number, . . . continually flying round the camp, sometimes under the wagons, sometimes over, and even into the wagons, where the poor sick Saints are lying in bed; thus having a direct manifestation from the Most High, that although we are driven, He has not forsaken us.[28]

After this episode, it took Bullock about two months to get to Winter Quarters at the Missouri River. He arrived on November 27, 1846, "finding a city of about 700 houses, and upwards of 4,000 Saints, built in less than three months."[29] There he was reunited with his good friend and fellow historian, Willard Richards. In December, Elder Richards told Bullock that he must be at his side writing "from this time henceforth and forever."[30] At about that same time, President Young told Bullock that he would take him to the Rocky Mountains "even if he had to put [him] in his pocket."[31] On April 11, 1847, President Young called Thomas to be the chief clerk for the vanguard company of pioneers going to the Salt Lake Valley.

Accordingly, two days later Bullock left his family behind, departing from Winter Quarters to the Rocky Mountains with eight Apostles and a total of 143 pioneers.[32] Thomas's journal is the official record of the vanguard pioneer company and one of the most important documents in Church history. During the trek west, Bullock also served as clerk for meetings of the Twelve Apostles, which at that time constituted the presiding quorum of the Church. One example was "the council in the grove," a meeting held on June 28, 1847, at the Little Sandy River. On that occasion, Jim Bridger gave a rambling, sometimes incoherent description of the country in and around the Great Basin.[33]

About four weeks after this rendezvous with Bridger, the pioneers finally arrived at the Great Salt Lake Valley. Bullock's first impression of the historic location was obviously favorable. On July 22, he recorded, "A very extensive valley burst upon our view, dotted in 3 or 4 places with Timber. I should expect the valley to be about 30 miles long & 20 miles wide." He continued, "I could not help shouting 'hurra, hurra, hurra, there's my home at last'—the Sky is very clear, the air delightful and all together looks glorious."[34] On July 24, President Young saw the valley for the first time and, according to Wilford Woodruff, declared, "This is the right place, drive on."[35] During the next three months, ten additional pioneer companies entered the valley.[36]

Salt Lake City Years

Thomas Bullock, early Salt Lake civic and ecclesiastical leader. (© Intellectual Reserve, Inc.)

The pioneers went to work as soon as they entered the Salt Lake Valley. On July 24, Bullock recorded that they "removed to the spot where the city would be built . . . and dedicated the place to the Lord."[37] On July 28, he recorded another significant event. On that historic day, he accompanied President Young and the Apostles to a location "between the two creeks." There, President Young chose the site for construction of the Salt Lake Temple. Elder Orson Pratt made a motion "that the Temple be built upon this Spot of ground," and it carried.[38] During the first month in the valley, "we ploughed and planted about eighty-four acres with corn, potatoes, beans, buck wheat, turnips and a variety of garden sauce," Bullock recorded. "We irrigated all the land; surveyed and laid out a city, with streets running east and west, north and south." Bullock's lot was located "on the second block, south of the temple."[39]

On August 22, the pioneers had a conference. On September 1, Bullock accompanied 107 men on a return trip to Winter Quarters.[40] President Young and seven Apostles led these "returning pioneers." Bullock again was the official clerk for the expedition. They arrived back at Winter Quarters two months later on October 31, 1847.[41] There, Thomas was finally reunited with his family after being apart for over six months.

The Winter Quarters area in December 1847 provided the location for one of the most important decisions ever made pertaining to Church government. The question to be resolved was whether or not to reorganize the First Presidency of the Church. Bullock served as the clerk for the entire development. During the three and a half years since Joseph Smith's martyrdom, Brigham Young had been leading the Church as President of the Quorum of the Twelve Apostles, but he had not reorganized the First Presidency. The other members of the Twelve sustained President Young as their leader, but they had differences of opinion as to whether the Presidency should ever be reconstituted. President Young had not pressed the issue until the Twelve returned to Winter Quarters, but now he strongly believed he should reorganize the First Presidency. However, he wanted to have the sustaining vote of the Quorum of the Twelve.[42] Therefore, the Apostles met on December 5, 1847, at Elder Orson Hyde's home on the east side of the Missouri River at Kanesville, Iowa. After much discussion, the Apostles in attendance voted unanimously to sustain Brigham Young as President of the Church with authority to choose two counselors. Accordingly, President Young chose Heber C. Kimball and Willard Richards to serve with him in the First Presidency.[43] The Twelve then held a special conference in the Kanesville Tabernacle across the Missouri River. On December 27, Bullock recorded that the membership of the Church unanimously sustained the new First Presidency.[44] One historian called this episode "the single, most important development" during the Winter Quarters era of Church history.[45]

As the spring of 1848 approached, Bullock with his family began making preparations to return to the Salt Lake Valley with the leaders of the Church. Again President Young assigned Bullock to keep the official journal for the trip. In addition, Bullock was given the responsibility of caring for the Church records during the journey. These records filled an entire wagon, called the "big wagon," and contained the manuscript for the "History of Joseph Smith," which Thomas Bullock and Elder Richards had worked on so diligently back in Nauvoo. Bullock faithfully carried out his duties as church scribe in addition to looking out for the safety of his own family during the westward trek. They departed on May 24 and arrived in the Salt Lake Valley on September 22.[46]

There was much to be done when President Young and his company returned to the valley in 1848. One of the first responsibilities President Young gave to Thomas, as his clerk, was to issue land inheritances. The pioneers had surveyed the area and laid out Salt Lake City the year before, but the plots had never been officially distributed. In 1848, the city was subdivided into five-, ten-, fifteen-, twenty-, forty-, and eighty-acre lots. The three men who had the responsibility of issuing the plots were Brigham Young, Heber C. Kimball, and Thomas Bullock. The job turned out to be extremely demanding and time-intensive. Sometimes, as many as "fifty persons were in the office at a time." Altogether, 776 people made applications for a grand total of "9,630 acres, or 15 square miles" of land.[47]

By the fall of 1848, there were approximately 4,200 people living in the valley, but there was no official currency for the community. Therefore, on December 28, 1848, the municipal council authorized President Young, President Heber C. Kimball, and Bishop Newel K. Whitney to issue paper money. The pioneers did not have a printing press, so President Young assigned Thomas Bullock and Robert L. Campbell, clerks for the First Presidency, to write all the bills by hand. For the next few days the two clerks carried out this tedious task of creating handwritten denominations of fifty cents, one, two, three, and five dollars, which were all dated January 2, 1849. Each bill required the signatures of four people——Brigham Young, Heber C. Kimball, Newel K. Whitney, and Thomas Bullock. Finally, each bill was stamped with the private seal of the Twelve Apostles. This unique seal contained sixteen letters—P.S.T.A.P.C.J.C.L.D.S.L.D.A.O.W. These letters were an acronym for "Private Seal of the Twelve Apostles, Priests of the Church of Jesus Christ of Latter-day Saints, in the Last Dispensation All Over the World." Thomas spent all of New Year's Day stamping and signing the bills. On the same day, President Young and President Kimball affixed their signatures to the notes which Bishop Whitney had signed previously. Unfortunately, the supply of money did not meet the demands of the people, so the committee decided to authorize the use of bills printed by the defunct Kirtland Safety Society, a Mormon financial institution in Ohio that had failed back in 1837. The use of this money, according to Bullock, fulfilled "a prophecy of Joseph that one day [the Kirtland Safety Society notes] would be as good as gold."[48]

In the meantime, somebody had discovered a case of type, and with it Truman O. Angell constructed a makeshift press that produced the first printed currency. This greatly expedited the printing of money, but Young, Kimball, Whitney, and Bullock still had to personally sign the bills, and Thomas was required to stamp the notes with the seal of the Twelve Apostles. The production of these bills was the first printing of any kind done in the Salt Lake Valley.[49] The pioneers used paper money exclusively for about eight months. Then, on September 12, 1849, Thomas Bullock and John Kay[50] started melting gold for the purpose of making hard currency. On the following day, they minted the valley's first gold coins.[51]

In addition to his moneymaking activities, Bullock became clerk for several other entities in 1848 and 1849. In September 1848, he was elected to the office of Salt Lake County recorder.[52] Three months later, he also began taking minutes for the Council of Fifty.[53] This body was a behind-the-scenes political organization headed by the President of the Church; it included all the members of the Quorum of the Twelve Apostles and many other leaders.[54] On February 13, 1849, Bullock was appointed to serve on a committee to divide Salt Lake City into wards. The chairman of the committee was Bishop Whitney, and the other members were President Young, President Kimball, Elder Parley P. Pratt, Elder John Taylor, and Elder Amasa M. Lyman.[55] In September 1849, Bullock was the clerk for President Young's exploration party to Brownsville (later Ogden). Thomas would serve as clerk for several other exploration parties over the next seven years.[56] Bullock also served as official clerk for the general conference held in October 1849. He would act as clerk for all general conferences thereafter until 1856 when he departed on a mission to England.[57]

One would think that with all of his heavy assignments, Bullock would become overwhelmed with his workload. Nevertheless, during the year 1850, he took on several more demanding responsibilities. Early in the year, President Young called on four capable men to establish the first newspaper in the community—to be called *Deseret News*. Elder Richards became the first editor; Horace K. Whitney, the printer; Brigham H. Young, the pressman; and Thomas Bullock, the proofreader. On June 15, the first edition of the *Deseret News* rolled off the press, and it has been in continuous publication ever since.[58] It is still "one of the most influential newspapers in the Intermountain West."[59]

By the middle of the nineteenth century, thousands of Latter-day Saints in the eastern United States and Europe desired to gather with the Saints in the Rocky Mountains but did not have the money to do so. In the fall of 1849, Church leaders established the Perpetual Emigrating Fund (PEF) to help finance the migration of these low-income individuals. In return, the immigrants were expected to reimburse the PEF for their loans. By 1850, the organization was incorporated, and its name was expanded to Perpetual Emigrating Fund Company. On September 15, Brigham Young asked Thomas Bullock to be the official recorder for the organization. The PEF remained in business until 1887 and did much good. It has been estimated that it "assisted more than 30,000 individuals to travel to Utah."[60]

In 1849, before Utah had become an official territory of the United States, the Mormon pioneers organized a provisional government they called the State of Deseret. Brigham Young was chosen governor, and territorial leaders recommended the establishment of a bicameral legislature patterned after the federal government.[61] On December 2, 1850, the general assembly of the State of Deseret met in the newly constructed Council House. On that occasion, Thomas Bullock was chosen as the official clerk for the House of Representatives.[62] Soon thereafter, the State of Deseret was dissolved, but Bullock continued as clerk for the House of Representatives for several years after Utah officially became a United States territory.

After Utah became a territory, Governor Young assigned Bullock the responsibility of taking a census for the entire territory. This proved to be one of the most unique and demanding assignments Bullock would undertake during all of his years in governmental service. The governor gave the assignment to Bullock in a formal letter, on March 28, 1851. Thomas efficiently completed the arduous assignment three months later. His count reported 11,354 residents in the territory.[63]

After finishing the census, it did not take Bullock long to get involved in other important projects. By 1852, the Mormons had been living in the Salt Lake Valley for nearly five years, but there was still no library in the city. Therefore, Bullock took action, and on January 9, 1852, he helped organize the community's first official library. "He assisted in making a catalogue of the books and stamped them with 'Utah Library.'"[64]

Soon after the pioneers entered the valley, they organized a militia and called it the Nauvoo Legion, with General Daniel H. Wells as commander. On April 12, 1852, Wells appointed none other than Thomas Bullock to be the military secretary. Within the next three years, the dedicated clerk had achieved the rank of lieutenant colonel.[65]

Bullock's responsibilities in the Church, government, and community were so wide-ranging and significant that it causes a person to wonder, which of all his assignments did he consider the most important? Perhaps the answer might be found in a letter that he wrote to his cousin on September 21, 1850. After quickly enumerating many of his responsibilities, Bullock humbly wrote this insightful sentence: "I am honored with the office of Secretary to the first Presidency, and have the privilege of receiving instructions which tens of thousands of people would be glad to have."[66]

One of Bullock's primary assignments was to continue his work with Church historical records. From the time the Mormons entered the Salt Lake Valley in 1847 until June of 1853, Elder Willard Richards and Thomas Bullock were so busy helping to establish their pioneer community that they did not have the time to even unpack the historical records they brought with them from Nauvoo. Finally, on June 7, 1853, the two dedicated historians unloaded a whole wagon full of manuscripts, letters, periodicals, and other documents. On December 1, 1853, Elder Richards resumed work on the "History of Joseph Smith." He wrote one line and then became so ill that he was unable to contribute anything else. He died on March 11, 1854.[67]

During the April 1854 general conference, President Young called Elder George A. Smith to take Elder Richards's place as Church historian.[68] Elder Smith and Thomas Bullock, chief clerk in the Church Historian's Office, resumed work on the "History of Joseph Smith" on April 10, 1854. They were assisted in the project by at least three other clerks—Robert Campbell, Leo Hawkins, and Jonathan Grimshaw. These men worked diligently for the next two years and completed the history in August 1856. During this time, they produced over eight hundred pages of manuscript.[69]

Several scholars have tried to calculate Bullock's contribution to the "History of Joseph Smith," but perhaps Elder Smith's assessment is the best. In 1856, Smith wrote to Wilford Woodruff: "Thomas Bullock acted with me as chief clerk in the history office previous to, and at the time of Prest. Smith's death, and he continued in it ever since. His pen wrote the principal part of the rough manuscript from my dictation, and his acquaintance with all the papers was of great assistance to me."[70]

In addition to Elder Smith's tribute, a contemporary historian gave the following appraisal of Bullock's contribution:

> Thomas Bullock in some ways contributed as much as Willard Richards or George A. Smith to the "History of Joseph Smith." Though he was not the immediate author of the manuscript, his journals and memory were extensively drawn on. He wrote the final or rough draft of the manuscript for each year from 1839 to 1844. His participation in the history spanned from nearly the beginning of the renewed emphasis on the work in 1843 until it was completed in 1856, something neither Richards [nor] Smith could claim.[71]

The "History of Joseph Smith" was first published as a series of articles in the *Times and Seasons* in Nauvoo and the *Deseret News* in Salt Lake City from 1842 to 1858. It was also published in the *Millennial Star* in England from 1842 to 1863.[72] The "History of Joseph Smith" eventually became the basis for the *History of the Church*, which B. H. Roberts was assigned to edit in May 1901. The first six volumes of that work contained the "History of Joseph Smith" and were published from 1902 to 1912.[73] It continues to this day to be the most frequently cited primary source of the teachings and events in the life of the Prophet Joseph Smith.

As soon as Thomas completed his work on the "History of Joseph Smith," the Church called him on a mission to his beloved homeland, England. There he served faithfully from 1856 to 1858. Upon his return to Utah, he continued in some of the assignments he had before his mission, specifically chief clerk in the Church Historian's Office and clerk to the House of Representatives. In 1863, the Territorial

Legislative Assembly voted to make Bullock one of the regents of the University of Deseret (later University of Utah). This assignment was his highest academic honor.

The previous year he had moved to the little town of Wanship, Summit County, east of Salt Lake City. Thereafter his assignments in the Salt Lake Valley began to decrease as he accepted increasing responsibilities in Summit County such as county clerk and recorder. In 1868, Thomas moved to Coalville, Utah, where he lived the rest of his days. He died on February 10, 1885, at age sixty-eight.[74]

Conclusion

Thomas Bullock was a man of tremendous capacity and talent. People sometimes use the term *Renaissance man* to describe a person who is "knowledgeable or proficient in more than one field."[75] Bullock was clearly deserving of the designation *Renaissance man*. He was heavily involved in the affairs of church, government, education, politics, publishing, the military, pioneering, moneymaking, and census taking. Historian Thomas Carlyle once summarized the effect of studying heroes: "Great Men, taken up in any way, are profitable company. We cannot look, however imperfectly, upon a great man, without gaining something [from] him."[76] Does Thomas Bullock deserve to be called great? The world tends to apply this term to people who are rich, famous, powerful, and beautiful. However, the New Testament gives a much different definition for the word. The Savior proclaimed, "He that is greatest among you shall be your servant" (Matthew 23:11). If this is the criteria for greatness, Bullock clearly qualifies. His service as secretary to the First Presidency, clerk for the Territorial House of Representatives, journalist for the vanguard pioneer company, chief clerk in the Church Historian's Office, and major scribe for the "History of Joseph Smith" surely qualify him for greatness. Thomas Bullock was a man of courage, a man of loyalty, a man of ability, a man of achievement, a man of honor, and a man of God. He certainly magnified the distinctive title of "the Lord's clerk," leaving a lasting legacy in Salt Lake City as well as the entire Church.

Notes

1. Many authors say there were between 600 and 650 Mormons in Nauvoo in September 1846. See B. H. Roberts, *A Comprehensive History of the Church of Jesus Christ of Latter-day Saints* (Provo, UT: Brigham Young University Press, 1965), 3:135; James B. Allen and Glen M. Leonard, *The Story of the Latter-day Saints*, 2nd ed. rev. (Salt Lake City: Deseret Book, 1992), 234; Kenneth W. Godfrey, "Nauvoo, Battle of," in *Encyclopedia of Latter-day Saint History*, ed. Arnold K. Garr, Donald Q. Cannon, and Richard O. Cowan (Salt Lake City: Deseret Book, 2000), 818. However, Thomas Bullock estimated that there were only about 150 Mormons in the city at the time. See Thomas Bullock "Letter from the Camp to Elder Franklin D. Richards," *Millennial Star*, January 15, 1848, 28.

2. See Godfrey, "Nauvoo, Battle of," 818–19.

3. Bullock, "Letter from the Camp," 28.

4. Andrew Jenson, *Latter-day Saint Biographical Encyclopedia* (Salt Lake City: Andrew Jenson History Company, 1914), 2:599.

5. C. Ward Despain, "Thomas Bullock: Early Mormon Pioneer" (master's thesis, Brigham Young University, 1956), 6.

6. "Thomas Bullock—Pioneer," in *Our Pioneer Heritage*, comp. Kate B. Carter (Salt Lake City: Daughters of Utah Pioneers, 1965), 8:265.

7. "Letter from Elder Thomas Bullock to Elder John O. Angus," *Millennial Star*, July 3, 1852, 299.

8. Jerald F. Simon, "Thomas Bullock as an Early Mormon Historian," *BYU Studies* 30, no. 1 (Winter 1990): 71.

9. "Letter from Elder Thomas Bullock," 299.

10. "Letter from Elder Thomas Bullock," 299.

11. "Thomas Bullock—Pioneer," 230.

12. "Letter from Elder Thomas Bullock," 299.

13. Gregory R. Knight, "Introduction to the 1845–1846 Journal of Thomas Bullock," *BYU Studies* 31, no. 1 (Winter 1991): 6.

14. *History of the Church of Jesus Christ of Latter-day Saints*, ed. B. H. Roberts, 2nd ed. rev. (Salt Lake City: Deseret Book, 1964), 5:415.

15. "Thomas Bullock—Pioneer," 232.

16. Smith, *History of the Church*, 6:302.

17. Donald Q. Cannon, "The King Follett Discourse: Joseph Smith's Greatest Sermon in Historical Perspective," *BYU Studies* 18, no. 2 (Winter 1978): 179, 185.

18. *History of the Church*, 6:325. For more on Joseph Smith's campaign for president, see Arnold K. Garr, *Joseph Smith: Presidential Candidate* (Orem, UT: Millennial Press, 2007).

19. Despain, "Thomas Bullock: Early Mormon Pioneer," 15.

20. *History of the Church*, 6:362.

21. *History of the Church*, 6:377.

22. "Letter from Thomas Bullock to Elder John O. Angus," 299.

23. Dean C. Jessee, "The Writing of Joseph Smith's History," *BYU Studies* 11, no. 4 (Summer 1971): 454; H. Dean Garrett, "Richards, Willard," in *Encyclopedia of Latter-day Saint History*, 1025.

24. B. H. Roberts, ed., *History of the Church of Jesus Christ of Latter-day Saints, Period 2: Apostolic Interregrum*, 2nd ed. rev. (Salt Lake City: Deseret Book, 1932), 7:324.

25. Simon, "Thomas Bullock as an Early Mormon Historian," 76.

26. Jessee, "Writing of Joseph Smith's History," 469.

27. Thomas Bullock, "Letter from the Camp," 28.

28. Bullock, "Letter from the Camp," 29.

29. Bullock, "Letter from the Camp," 30.

30. "Thomas Bullock—Pioneer," 8:238.

31. "Thomas Bullock—Pioneer," 8:238.

32. "Thomas Bullock—Pioneer," 8:239.

33. Will Bagley, ed., *The Pioneer Camp of the Saints: The 1846 and 1847 Mormon Trail Journals of Thomas Bullock* (Spokane: Arthur H. Clark, 1997), 209–13.

34. Bagley, *Pioneer Camp of the Saints*, 232.

35. Allen and Leonard, *Story of the Latter-day Saints*, 257.

36. *Deseret News 1997–1998 Church Almanac* (Salt Lake City: Deseret News, 1998), 167–68.

37. "Letter from Thomas Bullock," *Millennial Star*, April 15, 1848, 117.

38. Bagley, *Pioneer Camp of the Saints*, 241–42.

39. "Letter from Thomas Bullock," 117–18.

40. Bagley, *Pioneer Camp of the Saints*, 276–77.

41. Bagley, *Pioneer Camp of the Saints*, 318n96.

42. For an in-depth discussion on the issue of reorganizing the First Presidency, see Richard E. Bennett, *Mormons at the Missouri: Winter Quarters, 1846–1852* (Norman: University of Oklahoma Press, 1987), 199–214. See also Gary James Bergera, *Conflict in the Quorum: Orson Pratt, Brigham Young, Joseph Smith* (Salt Lake City: Signature Books, 2002), 53–83.

43. *History of the Church*, 7:621.

44. *History of the Church*, 7:623.

45. Bennett, *Mormons at the Missouri*, 214.

46. Despain, "Thomas Bullock: Early Mormon Pioneer," 47, 52.

47. Despain, "Thomas Bullock: Early Mormon Pioneer," 55.

48. Despain, "Thomas Bullock: Early Mormon Pioneer," 57–58.

49. Despain, "Thomas Bullock: Early Mormon Pioneer," 58.

50. John Moburn Kay was born on October 6, 1817, in Bury, Lancashire, England. As a boy he worked in his uncle's iron and brass foundry. He joined the Church in 1841 and immigrated to the Salt Lake Valley in 1848. After he arrived in the valley his "trade of moulding and pattern-making in iron and brass came at once into play." For further information on John Kay, see Andrew Jenson, *LDS Biographical Encyclopedia,* vol. 3 (Salt Lake City: Andrew Jenson History Company, 1920), 661–63.

51. Despain, "Thomas Bullock: Early Mormon Pioneer," 59.

52. Despain, "Thomas Bullock: Early Mormon Pioneer," 67.

53. D. Michael Quinn, "The Council of Fifty and Its Members, 1844 to 1945," *BYU Studies* 20, no. 2 (Winter 1980): 185, 193.

54. For more on the Council of Fifty, see Kenneth W. Godfrey, "Council of Fifty" in *Encyclopedia of Latter-day Saint History*, ed. Arnold K. Garr, Donald Q. Cannon, and Richard O. Cannon (Salt Lake City: Deseret Book, 2000), 256–57; James R. Clark, "The Kingdom of God, the Council of Fifty, and the Star of Deseret." *Utah Historical Quarterly* 26 (April 1958): 130–48; and Andrew F. Ehat, "It Seems Like Heaven Began on Earth': Joseph Smith and the Constitution of the Kingdom of God," *BYU Studies* 20, no. 3 (Spring 1980): 253–79.

55. Despain, "Thomas Bullock: Early Mormon Pioneer," 60.

56. "Thomas Bullock—Pioneer," 8:261.

57. Despain, "Thomas Bullock: Early Mormon Pioneer," 60.

58. "Thomas Bullock—Pioneer," 8:262.

59. J. Michael Hunter, "*Deseret News*," in *Encyclopedia of Latter-day Saint History*, 291.

60. David F. Boone, "Perpetual Emigrating Fund (PEF)," in *Encyclopedia of Mormonism*, ed. Daniel H. Ludlow (New York: Macmillan, 1992), 3:1075; see also Despain, "Thomas Bullock: Early Mormon Pioneer," 63; "Thomas Bullock—Pioneer," 260; Allen and Leonard, *Story of the Latter-day Saints*, 291; and *2010 Deseret News Church Almanac* (Salt Lake City: Deseret News, 2010), 278.

61. Richard D. Poll, "Deseret," in *Utah History Encyclopedia*, ed. Alan Kent Powell (Salt Lake City: University of Utah Press, 1994), 138–39.

62. "Thomas Bullock—Pioneer," 8:261.

63. Following are the results of his census, as of April 1, 1851:

	Males	Females	Total
1st Great Salt Lake County	3,119	3,036	6,155
2nd Davis County	596	532	1,128
3rd Weber County	691	452	1,143
4th Utah County	1,125	880	2,005
5th San Pete County	197	168	365
6th Iron County	191	169	360
7th Tooele County	85	67	152
8th Green River Precinct	22	24	46
Total	6,026	5,328	11,354

(See Despain, "Thomas Bullock: Early Mormon Pioneer," 64–66).

64. Despain, "Thomas Bullock: Early Mormon Pioneer," 69.

65. Despain, "Thomas Bullock: Early Mormon Pioneer," 69–70.

66. "Thomas Bullock—Pioneer," 8:266.

67. Jessee, "Writing of Joseph Smith's History," 470.

68. Howard C. Searle, "Authorship of the History of Joseph Smith: A Review Essay," *BYU Studies* 21, no. 1 (Winter 1981): 117.

69. Jessee, "Writing of Joseph Smith's History," 460, 470, 472; Simon, "Thomas Bullock as an Early Mormon Historian," 77.

70. Simon, "Thomas Bullock as an Early Mormon Historian," 77.

71. Simon, "Thomas Bullock as an Early Mormon Historian," 79.

72. Searle, "Authorship of the History of Joseph Smith," 113, 119.

73. Searle, "Authorship of the History of Joseph Smith," 120.

74. Despain, "Thomas Bullock: Early Mormon Pioneer," 73, 94, 96–98, 101.

75. *Random House Webster's College Dictionary*, "Renaissance man."

76. Thomas Carlyle, *On Heroes and Hero Worship, and the Heroic in History* (Boston: Ginn & Company, 1902), 2.

Entrance to the Salt Lake City Cemetery, which was established just one year after the first pioneers arrived in the valley. (Courtesy of David F. Boone.)

Chapter 9

"And Should We Die": Pioneer Burial Grounds in Salt Lake City

David F. Boone

Four decades ago, avid researcher, historian, teacher, and preservationist T. Edgar Lyon wrote a significant article in the *Improvement Era* about the uniqueness of nineteenth-century Latter-day Saint pioneers.[1] He noted that, despite our admiration of the pioneers, many aspects that we often associate with the Church's migration and colonization are not unique to the Church. Latter-day Saints were not, for example, the first group to go west, and they did not pioneer any of the major routes they followed, nor did their members comprise the majority of individuals who traversed the continent. Lyon's thesis was to identify the truly unique aspects of the Church's efforts to pioneer the great American West. One of the unique elements of Latter-day Saint migration noted by Lyon was their concern for the very old and the very young and their unusual respect for life and death. In other words, they took time to properly care for the sick, afflicted, or less

David F. Boone is an associate professor of Church history and doctrine at Brigham Young University.

fortunate, and when an individual died along the trail, those who survived took the time, as conditions permitted, to respectfully and even reverently care for and inter the departed.

Latter-day Saint leaders have long taught about the sanctity of life, which includes the passing from mortality. The Prophet Joseph Smith taught:

> I would esteem it one of the greatest blessings, if I am to be afflicted in this world, to have my lot cast where I can find brothers and friends all around me [and] . . . to have the privilege of having our dead buried on the land where God has appointed us to gather His Saints together. . . . The place where a man is buried is sacred to me. . . . Even to the aborigines of this land, the burying places of their fathers are more sacred than anything else. . . .
>
> It has always been a great calamity not to obtain an honorable burial: and one of the greatest curses the ancient prophets could put on any man, was that he should go without a burial.[2]

Because the pioneers were so concerned and took time to bury their loved ones who died along the pioneer trail even when conditions were so difficult for them to make the necessary burial arrangements, it stands to reason that their respect for the deceased would not change when they reached their destination. This chapter will trace the burial practices of early Latter-day Saints in the Salt Lake Valley and highlight the establishment of prominent pioneer burial grounds, including the Salt Lake City Cemetery.[3]

Earliest Pioneer Deaths in the Salt Lake Valley

Within days of the entry of Brigham Young's company into the Salt Lake Valley on July 24, 1847, plowing, planting, and building had begun. Soon other groups began arriving.

Milton Howard Therlkill. On July 29, a group of Latter-day Saint pioneers from the South, known as the "Mississippi Saints," were the second company to arrive. The Mississippi Saints departed from Monroe County, Mississippi, on April 8, 1846, and wintered in Pueblo, Colorado, where they learned that they were ahead of Brigham Young's party. They were joined in Pueblo by members of the Mormon Battalion's sick detachment, and in spring they followed President Young's company westward.

Less than two weeks after the Mississippi Saints arrived in Salt Lake on August 11, 1847, one of their number, three-year-old Milton Howard Therlkill, the son of George and Matilda Jane Crow Therlkill, drowned when he fell into City Creek. Milton was buried a short distance from where the pioneers were camped on property later designated as the Crow lot.[4] As the city continued to grow, the area of the burial was designated as Block 49 in downtown Salt Lake City. The death of Milton Therlkill indicated the need to prepare for others who would follow. As others died, they too were buried in the same plot or block. This became the first Latter-day Saint burying ground in what became the state of Utah.

Carolina Van Dyke Grant. An example of the unusual respect paid to those who died is found in the Jedediah M. Grant family. Jedediah Grant was the captain of the "third hundred families" in a company that departed Winter Quarters, Nebraska, on June 19, 1847, and arrived in the Salt Lake Valley on October 4. Jedediah's family consisted of his wife, Carolina (called Caroline) Van Dyke Grant, and two daughters: two-year-old Caroline, called Caddie, and an infant named Margaret, born at Winter Quarters just a month before their departure. Caroline was recovering from a difficult delivery. "Caroline had been so weak that she could barely begin the journey a month later."[5] Her desire was to be with her husband and the Saints, so she stoically embarked on the journey.

Caroline rallied significantly along the trail, and her improvement seemed to indicate she was winning the battle for her life. Unfortunately, when the company arrived at Devil's Gate along the Sweetwater River, "an epidemic of cholera had broken out, spreading first among the animals and then attacking the people, especially the children."[6] Due to their weakened condition, both Caroline and her daughter Margaret contracted cholera. Despite their sickness, the train moved on, but the disease was more than their weakened bodies could sustain.

On Thursday, September 1, 1847, Jacob Gates, a member of the pioneer company, recorded, "Word came that Capt Grants wife was dying which hindered us a while." The following day, Gates further recorded, "This morning bro Grants babe dead and she [Caroline] failing," and on Saturday, September 3, "Buried the dead babe."[7]

Margaret, like many other pioneer dead, was buried beside the trail. Jedediah buried his daughter in a beautiful white dress that had been prepared earlier by her mother. The pioneers interred the child without a coffin or other means to protect the small body. Soon after, the pioneer company moved on.

With the anguish added by the death of her infant, coupled with the effects of cholera, Caroline continued to decline. "Most in the company expected her own death at any time,"[8] but she fought courageously for her life, and the train continued onward. "In a moment," remembered Sarah Snow, who had cared for Grant's older daughter while her mother was sick, "we were both by the bed, while Caddie kissed her mama and tried to huddle into the covers. Sister Grant looked at us knowingly, then as she contentedly closed her eyes again and seemed to be sinking. I heard her whisper to Jedediah, 'All is well! All is well! Please take me to the valley—Jeddy. Get Margaret—bring her—to me!' Brother Grant answered tenderly . . . as he sobbed with sorrow, 'Yes, yes, Caroline. I'll do my best. I'll do my best.'"[9]

To fulfill his wife's dying request, Jedediah had to move quickly. "While the women of the third hundred prepared the body of their leader's young wife, the men built a box from a dismantled wagon bed." Captain Grant strapped the improvised coffin to the side of his wagon and drove the seventy-five remaining miles to the valley that his wife had so badly wanted to see. "Driving day and night, he made the infant settlement near the Great Salt Lake on the evening of September 29." They buried her near the site where Milton Therlkill was interred only weeks before. Grant's biographer, Gene A. Sessions, credits Carolina Van Dyke Grant as being the first adult buried in Salt Lake City.[10]

With her interment in the Salt Lake Valley, Jedediah's promise to his dying wife was only partially fulfilled. The day after the burial, he left the valley for a return trip to the mountains with help for his company." After seeing to the immediate needs of those under his charge, he continued eastward with a close friend, Joseph Bates Nobel, in an effort to recover the body of little Margaret. Upon arrival at the place where she was interred, they found that the wolves had uncovered the grave, carried away the body, and scattered any evidence of the child's remains. Brokenhearted, he returned to his new mountain home.

The Salt Lake City Cemetery

In late September 1847, the Abraham O. Smoot and George B. Wallace company arrived in the valley.[11] Mary Melissa Wallace, the young daughter of George B. and Melissa Melvina King Wallace, was born January 8, 1847, at Winter Quarters and died September 27, 1848, at just twenty-one months of age. No cause of death was listed.

Instead of burying their daughter outside of the pioneer fort in Salt Lake City, as had been done with earlier deaths, George took her tiny body, climbed the city's east bench, and buried his daughter in a secluded spot in the foothills. George made this unusual move perhaps because as the new settlement grew, the pioneer fort was being surrounded and crowded, so he looked for a place where the grave would not be disturbed. Several other families followed Wallace's example, and soon the foothill overlooking the Salt Lake Valley became an unofficial burying ground for the Saints in addition to Block 49 east of the fort.

In February 1849, a committee consisting of George B. Wallace, Daniel H. Wells, and Joseph Heywood selected a site in the foothills to recommend as a permanent city cemetery. Wallace was interested in recommending this site for several reasons. First, he had "acted as undertaker during some of the most trying days experienced by the Saints [in Nauvoo]."[12] Second, he had already buried his daughter Mary and another child in the foothills of the Salt Lake Valley. Third, others had buried children there.

Daniel H. Wells reported, "They thought the most suitable place was northeast of the city. Twenty acres was [initially] included in the survey."[13] The committee's recommendation was accepted, and today it is the site of the Salt Lake City Cemetery. Mary Wallace is recognized as the first burial in the cemetery. In January 1851, the General Assembly of the State of Deseret incorporated Salt Lake City. "A City Council was organized, which administered the affairs of the graveyard."[14] George Wallace was appointed the first sextant and was responsible for planning, improving the cemetery grounds, recording information about each burial, and overseeing other cemetery operations.

The cemetery was twenty acres when the city was incorporated,[15] and since then it has grown in acreage and number of graves. "From 20 acres and two graves, the Salt Lake City Cemetery grew to 350 acres . . . [and] 110,000 graves." Today "it's the largest municipally-owned cemetery in the nation." There are now two Chinese and two Japanese sections, a section for paupers and prisoners, three Jewish cemeteries, and a Catholic cemetery "now cared for by those congregations."[16] There is also a mausoleum and areas for Congregation Montefiore (Orthodox Jews), children, soldiers, war veterans, and dignitaries.

In February 1856, a city ordinance was passed that required that all bodies be buried in the city cemetery, not on public land. All exceptions to burials outside of the cemetery had to be cleared "by the Mayor and the Committee on Municipal Laws."[17] But as the city continued to develop and land was apportioned to individuals, it was not unusual that some residents desired to bury their loved ones on their own land. This practice was in part for convenience, but it was also to provide a final resting place that could be watched over and protected from desecration.

The concern was justified because of local grave robbers. One such character was John Baptiste, who had worked in Salt Lake about three years before he was suspected of grave robbing. When it was discovered that personal property buried with the deceased was missing, corpses were exhumed, John was suspected, and surveillance was established. In time, he was caught with stolen goods and admitted a portion of his guilt.[18] "His home was searched and found to be full of clothing," and it was determined that "after a burial he would open up the grave, take all the clothing, jewelry, etc., and replace the body paying little attention as to how it was done." He then would soak and dry the clothes and sell them along with items of value taken from the graves. "When the investigation was concluded and the news of this outrage was learned, the cemetery was alive with people digging up their dead. The clothing at his home was all taken to the City Hall where people went and identified their own."[19] Apparently, no family was exempt; John had exhumed the graves of men, women, and children alike. Elder Wilford Woodruff wrote in his journal, "It was afterwords reported that John Baptist was branded in the forehead as A Robber of the dead . . . & placed upon Millers Island."[20] Elder Woodruff wrote that it was "one of the most Damniable, Diabolical, Satanical, Helish Sacraleges . . . Committed upon the bodies of the Dead Saints."[21]

Private Family Cemeteries

Early in the history of Salt Lake City, several families, including those of Church leaders, created and maintained burial grounds on their personal property or in close proximity to their homes. These private cemeteries remained even after the ordinance barring these memorials was passed. In fact, Temple Square was surrounded on all four sides by private family cemeteries. The best known of these are the Kimball-Whitney graveyard on the north, the Brigham Young Family Cemetery on the east, the Willard Richards burial ground on the south, and the Smith family plot on the west side.

Nathaniel V. Jones, bishop of Salt Lake City's Fifteenth Ward, addressed the city council with a concern about private cemeteries: "In the western part of the 15th Ward, where waters can be obtained by digging at a depth of three feet, the inhabitants inter their dead in many instances on their Lots, and the waters continually filtering through the corpse must be unwholesome and liable to engender disease." Bishop Jones's proposal, therefore, was to pass "an Ordinance forbidding any persons to inter their dead on their Lots," and if they had already done so, "to remove them to the burying ground in the Grave Yard, unless by petition they are otherwise permitted to bury on their Lots." In April 1856, the Salt Lake City Council met to discuss "the subject of permitting certain deceased person interred upon their City Lots [to] remain undisturbed."[22] The buried remains of the Heber C. Kimball family, George A. Smith family, and others were allowed to stay where they were. The city council also decided "that the remains of the friends of J. M. Grant, V. Shirtleff, General Rich and others buried on the mound in the lot belonging to V. Shirtleff (Section 7, Block 49) be permitted to remain."[23] All the approved interments were from the private burial grounds and from the burials in the block east of the old fort. In spite of these ordinances, private family cemeteries persisted in the downtown area. Some survive to this day. The Young and Kimball-Whitney cemeteries remain downtown, while other family cemeteries have been displaced to make way for the growing city.

Kimball-Whitney Cemetery. The Kimball-Whitney Cemetery is on property set aside in 1848 for one of the first formally dedicated burial grounds within the valley. Elder Heber C. Kimball and Bishop Newel K. Whitney dedicated the land to the Lord as a private cemetery for their two families. Ann Houston Whitney was the first to be buried there in November 1848. Bishop Whitney died two years later and was laid to rest beside his wife.[24]

The cemetery can be reached from North Main Street via Kimball Lane, approximately one hundred yards directly west from Main Street. The grounds contain a large monument commemorating the burial sites of more than sixty Kimball and Whitney family members, along with their employees, friends, and others. In total, "there are about thirty-five Kimballs, fifteen Whitneys and eleven hired help and friends buried there."[25]

In 1886, when Solomon Kimball, the son of Heber and Vilate Kimball, returned to Utah from his colonization efforts in Arizona, "he found the cemetery in a bad condition. There was no fence around it. Nine-tenths of the graves could not be identified, and worse yet, the title to the property was in the hands of four different individuals, each of whom was determined to make merchandise [commercialize it]." Later, he learned that the little cemetery had been sold by the city to recoup unpaid taxes on the property. Upon investigation, Solomon discovered that a territorial law exempted burial places from taxation, and he reacquired the property in the name of the Kimball family. He purchased a right-of-way from Main Street, had an iron fence installed, and increased the size of the cemetery. Furthermore, he received perpetual right from the city council "to allow the honored dead to remain there on condition that the family improve, beautify, and take care of this piece of property and allow no more internments to be made there."[26]

Custodianship of the burial ground remained within the Kimball family through J. Golden Kimball. Afterward, the Church assumed perpetual care of the Kimball-Whitney Cemetery.[27] Several other private cemeteries would follow suit.

Brigham Young Cemetery (Mormon Pioneer Memorial Monument). The Brigham Young Family Cemetery is located on East First Avenue on Brigham Young's farm property. Today it is referred to as the Young Family Cemetery and also known as the Mormon Pioneer Memorial Park.[28] The Memorial Park is the burial site of Brigham Young, several of his wives (including Eliza R. Snow), many of his children, and others.

The first burial in the Brigham Young Family Cemetery is believed to be Alva Young, son of Brigham and Louisa Beeman Young, who was buried October 1, 1848. Extant markers suggest there are at least twelve individuals interred on this site, but the identity of others also believed to be buried there would raise that number significantly. Kate B. Carter noted, "The earliest burial date [on a tombstone] in the cemetery is 1874 and the last, 1892, but there must have been burials before [the earliest date] for ten of Brigham Young's children died in infancy to childhood. . . . It is presumed that at least some of these individuals were interred in their family burial ground."[29] Later, city laws and ordinances discontinued the practice of private burial grounds, and later still, on March 18, 1927, Richard W. Young, president of the Brigham Young Cemetery Association, "conveyed title by warranty deed" of the cemetery property "to the Corporation of the President of the Church of Jesus Christ of Latter-day Saints." It further covenanted "that the burials now situated in and upon the aforesaid land shall in no manner or way be disturbed or removed except upon the legal mandate of the municipal or the proper governmental authority."[30] It is not known how, why, or when the Brigham Young private burial plot escaped the municipal city government's ban on private cemeteries.

Willard Richards Family Cemetery. The Willard Richards family home was located on the south side of South Temple Street and on "the east half of the block on the west side of Main Street between South Temple and First South Streets." When Willard Richards died on March, 11, 1854, "he was buried in the plot that had been set apart for that purpose near the middle of this property." In addition to President Richards, "three of his wives and several children also had been buried there" well after the city ordinance prohibiting private burying grounds. This suggests that Willard Richards, like Heber C. Kimball, petitioned for and was granted permission to have a private burial ground for this family. In 1890, Richards's sons Joseph and Willard were interested in developing the Richards Street property. Heber John Richards, custodian of the Richards property south of Temple Square, in concert with his brother's interests, "decided to move the graves to the [family] lot in the City Cemetery."[31] The Journal History of the Church confirms that "the remains of the late Willard Richards and others were removed from the family burial ground, east of the Deseret Museum, in [downtown] Salt Lake City and placed in the [city] cemetery."[32] Alice Ann Richards, daughter of Willard Richards, recorded, "We had a family cemetery in our lot in an oak grove, and Aunt Sarah [Sarah Longstroth Richards] was buried there with father [Willard Richards] and other members of our family. Uncle George [Longstroth] and Uncle Moses [Whitaker] were buried in a corner of grandma's lot. The graves were all well taken care of and the ground beautiful with walks, grass and flowers."[33]

Smith Family Cemetery. Two lots facing West Temple Street belonged to pioneer leaders John Smith and his son, George A. Smith. This area was the home of George's son John Henry Smith, who later became an Apostle, and the birthplace of George Albert Smith. Today the site is home to the Church History Museum, an original pioneer log home, and the Family History Library. In 1856, Elder George A. Smith petitioned the city council to allow his father and mother to remain where they were buried. On April 19, 1856, the petition was granted.[34]

Other Cemeteries

Fort Douglas Military Cemetery. Camp Douglas, which was later named Fort Douglas, was a military encampment established by General Patrick Edward Connor and the California Volunteers on the east bench of Salt Lake City in October 1862.[35] The southeast corner of the property claimed by the military was reserved for a cemetery, and the first grave was prepared in January 1863. Many of the burials were soldiers who died in skirmishes with Native Americans. At least sixteen soldiers and officers of the California Volunteers who died in armed conflict are interred there.[36] The cemetery's most famous inhabitant is General Connor himself.[37]

Mount Olivet Cemetery. General Connor also established another Salt Lake City cemetery, although not specifically for the military. "Under the leadership of Connor and Episcopalian Bishop Daniel S.

Tuttle, non-LDS residents of Salt Lake City pushed for the establishment of a separate cemetery to serve the needs of those not associated with the LDS Church."[38] Although the Salt Lake Cemetery was a municipal burial site, Connor felt it was important to provide an alternate choice for burying the dead. The Mount Olivet Cemetery was established in 1874 and remains the "only public cemetery in the United States established by an act of Congress."[39]

A forty-acre plot of what was originally the military reserve was "to be maintained forever and in perpetuity." The first burial on site of the new facility came before the government finalized the transaction, and "Emily Pearsall, an Episcopalian missionary who had worked in Utah for two years was buried there in 1872."[40] The next burial did not occur until 1877.

Through the intervening decades, significant improvements have been made at this site, and today it is an attractive, gardenlike setting. Ironically, there are quite a few Latter-day Saints buried in the Mount Olivet facility, as evidenced by etchings on tombstones and information regarding Latter-day Saint temple ordinances. Rather than an attempt at religious segregation, as originally planned, today the cemetery is more representative of a financial segregation and caters to the needs of wealthier families.

Recent Discoveries

In 1986, 139 years after Milton Therlkill, Caroline Grant, and others were buried, a construction company was digging up the ground near the old pioneer fort in preparation for building an apartment complex. It was known that there were graves in the vicinity, but the knowledge of their exact location had been lost for more than one hundred years. During the construction process, the remains of several individuals were unearthed.[41] Construction was halted while a more careful examination could proceed. Ultimately, thirty-three graves[42] were found in the area, including what was believed to be the remains of early settlers, both male and female, young and old, Caucasian and Native American. "A total of thirty-four human burials were recovered from Block 49. All but one of these burials dated to the historic use of the early burial ground between 1847–56."[43] The single exception was judged to be the remains of Native Americans, which were returned to the Paiute Tribal Council for a ceremonial reburial.

Multiple studies were made by the Brigham Young University Anthropology Department on many of the remains. The site was painstakingly studied before the remains were exhumed. Grave sites were mapped and charted, and countless measurements were taken. The work of exhuming the remains was conducted with the help of numerous volunteers, including college students, descendants of some of those believed to be buried in the area, and individuals who heard of the dig and wanted to be involved.

The remains of the deceased were individually encased and sent to the University of Wyoming, where George Gill, a forensic archaeologist, tried to identify them. Gill applauded the BYU archaeologists "for doing an outstanding job removing and preserving the bones."[44] Gill and his staff studied to estimate age, gender, stature, cause of death, and background. These facts were recorded and compared with historical information from early Salt Lake City burials. Gill was able to determine that "most of the bodies were those of children . . . [including] eight adults, one adolescent and 24 children." At least five "were related, to at least a cousin relationship."[45] Many of the remains were identified with a high degree of accuracy, while the identity of others is less clear. Among those identified were Milton Howard Therlkill and Carolina Van Dyke Grant.

It was debated whether the bodies should be reburied in the Salt Lake City Cemetery or kept together somewhere else. The latter option was chosen, and they were buried in Pioneer Trails State Park (now This Is the Place Heritage Park) in a re-creation of a pioneer village overlooking Salt Lake City known as Old Deseret. The park is located on the east side of Salt Lake City near the "This Is the Place" monument. The remains were buried in coffins built by the carpenter at Old

Deseret, and those coffins were enclosed in six large, donated burial vaults.[46]

The Old Deseret Cemetery recreates the original configuration of the downtown burial ground (see fig. 1).[47] None of the headstones marking the graves have epitaphs or other writing, presumably because not all of the remains have been identified. A memorial stone nearby reads, "As the identity of most of these graves remains unknown, this memorial has been dedicated to the memory of all pioneer children who died and who, like those whose bodies lie here, should not go unremembered."[48] The headstones for the adults are larger, and those marking the grave of children are smaller.

The site was dedicated by President Thomas S. Monson in a ceremony on Memorial Day in 1987 at This Is the Place Heritage Park to rebury the individuals and dedicate the site. There were musical numbers, representatives from most of the families whose ancestors were being reburied, and dozens of guests, many of whom helped to exhume, identify, and study the remains. As with the Tomb of the Unknown Soldier, President Monson said that part of him "hoped not all the remains would be identified with certainty, allowing every Utahn to believe that one of the bodies may be that of his or her own ancestor."[49]

As Dr. Lyon noted, "The Mormon people placed great value on human life."[50] The pioneers spent significant time welcoming the newborn, as well as reverencing the departure of the dying, and, when possible, taking great pains to prepare the grave site against molestation from man or beast. This, in addition to the heroics of transcontinental migration, is a significant part of the Latter-day Saint legacy in the colonization of the West.

Gravesites of Church Presidents

On a lighter note, for years I have taken Church history students on field trips in conjunction with our classes, believing that seeing the

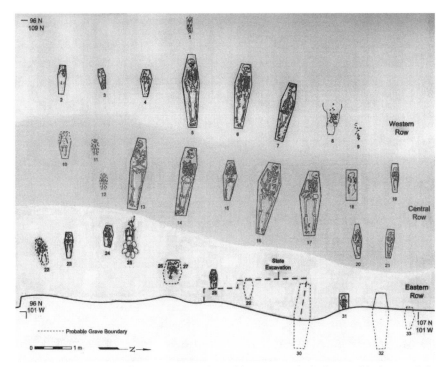

Fig. 1. Organization of pioneer graves, burial layout on Block 49, one block east of the orignial pioneer fort. Adapted from Richard K. Talbot, Lane D. Richins, and Shane A. Baker, The Right Place: Fremont and Early Pioneer Archaeology in Salt Lake City *(Provo, UT: Office of Public Archaeology, Brigham Young University, 2004), 105.*

sites we discussed in class can help imprint the history lessons into their lives. It takes a full day, from before dawn until nearly dark, and we visit many different sites. We cannot visit all there is to see, but one consistent attraction is the Salt Lake City Cemetery.

We visit the graves of many notables who have passed to their reward. Favorites include Orrin Porter Rockwell, Mary Fielding Smith, Karl G. Maeser, and many others. There always seems to be particular interest in the grave sites of the Presidents of the Church. The Salt Lake City Cemetery contains a wealth of history waiting to be shared. Every tombstone has its own story, and some have many stories. Even the sites of less prominent individuals hold a fascination for inquiring students.

Before arriving at the cemetery or going to the grave sites, I begin with a little discussion and a few questions. I ask, for example, how many Church Presidents there have been in this dispensation. This they know, but then I will ask a loaded question, "How many of the prophets are buried in the Salt Lake City Cemetery?"

Many will know that the Prophet Joseph Smith was buried in Nauvoo, Illinois, along with other family members. Quite a few students will realize that President Young was buried in his own cemetery in downtown Salt Lake City. Most do not know where his private cemetery is until we visit it as a class. Fewer still know that President Lorenzo Snow was buried in Brigham City, Utah, because he lived there many years. Some of the students know that President Ezra Taft Benson is buried in Whitney, Idaho. Some of the older students remember the funeral procession to the family burial plot.

The place where I am able to catch most students, however, is when they are able to account for all but one of the prophets. With rare exception, they are stumped until they are reminded that the current prophet was included in our count, and he is not yet buried!

After we have accounted for all the prophets of this dispensation, we then know whose graves we might find. The students delight in seeing the graves. Some seem to pay their quiet respects to the Presidents and what they accomplished. Others enjoy learning more about their lives. But invariably there seems to be a connection made, a reverence for the Presidents in the wake of their service.

The students typically want to take pictures, write in notebooks, or pause in thought. I try not to hurry them unduly, but neither do we linger too long because of many other things to see. But the students always seem to be a little more subdued, both at the grave sites and immediately after our departure. As the Prophet Joseph Smith taught, there seems to be a serenity, a realization that the final resting place is sacred—a place of peace, a place set apart from the world where time hesitates for a few moments. Below is a chart showing the final resting places of each latter-day prophet buried, along with coordinates to locate their grave sites.

The grave site of President Brigham Young is located just east of Temple Square in Salt Lake City. (Courtesy of Scott C. Esplin.)

Fig. 2. *Grave sites of Church Presidents*

Church President	Date of Birth	Place of Birth	Date of Death
1. Joseph Smith	23 Dec 1805	Sharon, VT	27 Jun 1844
2. Brigham Young	1 Jun 1801	Whitingham, VT	29 Aug 1877
3. John Taylor	1 Nov 1808	Milnthorpe, England	25 Jul 1887
4. Wilford Woodruff	1 Mar 1807	Farmington, CT	2 Sep 1898
5. Lorenzo Snow	3 Apr 1814	Mantua, OH	10 Oct 1901
6. Joseph Fielding Smith	13 Nov 1838	Far West, MO	19 Nov 1918
7. Heber Jeddy Grant	22 Nov 1856	Salt Lake City	14 May 1945
8. George Albert Smith	4 Apr 1870	Salt Lake City	4 Apr 1951
9. David Oman McKay	8 Sep 1873	Huntsville, UT	18 Jan 1970
10. Joseph Fielding Smith	19 Jul 1876	Salt Lake City	2 Jul 1972
11. Harold Bingham Lee	28 Mar 1899	Clifton, ID	26 Dec 1973
12. Spencer Woolley Kimball	28 Mar 1895	Salt Lake City	5 Nov 1985
13. Ezra Taft Benson	4 Aug 1899	Whitney, ID	30 May 1994
14. Howard William Hunter	14 Nov 1906	Boise, ID	3 Mar 1995
15. Gordon Bitner Hinckley	23 Jun 1910	Salt Lake City	27 Jan 2008

Fig. 2. cont.

Place of Death	Burial date	Place	Burial reference (plat/block/lot grave)
Carthage, IL	29 Jun 1844	Smith Fam. Cem., Nauvoo, IL (SW of Smith Homestead)	
Salt Lake City	2 Sep 1877	B. Young Memorial Cem., SLC SE corner)	
Kaysville, UT	29 July 1887	SLC Cemetery	F-11-9-2E
San Francisco	8 Sep 1898	SLC Cemetery	C-6-10-1E
Salt Lake City	13 Oct 1901	Brigham City Cem.	B-16-58-5
Salt Lake City	22 Nov 1918	SLC Cemetery	Park-14-12-2E
Salt Lake City	18 May 1945	SLC Cemetery	N-2-1-2E
Salt Lake City	7 Apr 1951	SLC Cemetery	I-5-15-1-E
Salt Lake City	22 Jan 1970	SLC Cemetery	West-3-79-1W
Salt Lake City	6 Jul 1972	SLC Cemetery	Park-14-14-1E
Salt Lake City	29 Dec 1973	SLC Cemetery	West-6-76-1E
Salt Lake City	9 Nov 1985	SLC Cemetery	West-13-44-3W
Salt Lake City	4 Jun 1994	Whitney, ID	4-4-31
Salt Lake City	3 Mar 1995	SLC Cemetery	West-12-36-3E
Salt Lake City	3 Feb 2008	SLC Cemetery	West-3-178-2W

Notes

1. Special recognition and appreciation are extended to Randall Dixon of the Church History Department for his work in collecting information on early Latter-day Saint burials and for his gracious willingness to share parts of his research. T. Edgar Lyon, "Some Uncommon Aspects of the Mormon Migration," *Improvement Era*, September 1969, 33–40.

2. *Teachings of the Prophet Joseph Smith*, comp. Joseph Fielding Smith (Salt Lake City: Deseret Book, 1976), 294–95.

3. Many early burial grounds were created "in an *ad hoc* manner primarily in response to the immediate needs of the very first pioneers after their arrival in the summer of 1847." Burial grounds are typically not "formally designated or consecrated as a cemetery." Richard K. Talbot, Lane D. Richins, and Shane A. Baker, *The Right Place: Fremont and Early Pioneer Archaeology in Salt Lake City* (Provo, UT: Office of Public Archaeology, Brigham Young University, 2004), 83–84.

4. Robert Crow, grandfather of Milton Therlkill, owned the plot of ground. Journal of Horace K. Whitney, August 12, 1847, Church History Library, The Church of Jesus Christ of Latter-day Saints, Salt Lake City. Apparently, the Crows were allowed to bury their grandson in this area because of the accident, the family's grief, the neighbors' desire to assist in a time of need, and availability of the vacant lot.

5. Gene A. Sessions, *Mormon Thunder: A Documentary History of Jedediah Morgan Grant* (Urbana: University of Illinois Press, 1982), 59.

6. Sessions, *Mormon Thunder*, 62.

7. Jacob Gates Journal, in the Mormon Pioneer Overland Travel database, 1847–68, The Church of Jesus Christ of Latter-day Saints.

8. Sessions, *Mormon Thunder*, 64.

9. Sessions, *Mormon Thunder*, 68.

10. Sessions, *Mormon Thunder*, 68.

11. The Mormon Pioneer Overland Travel database identifies that they arrived on September 25, 26, and 29, which suggests that they, like other companies, were strung out by the time they reached the Salt Lake Valley; http://lds.org/churchhistory/library/pioneercompanysearch/1,15773,3966-1,00.html.

12. Andrew Jenson, *Latter-day Saint Biographical Encyclopedia* (Salt Lake City: Andrew Jenson, 1901), 1:291.

13. Kate B. Carter, comp., *Heart Throbs of the West: A Unique Volume Treating Definite Subjects of Western History* (Salt Lake City: Daughters of Utah Pioneers, 1943), 6:326.

14. Carter, *Heart Throbs*, 6:326.

15. "Salt Lake City Cemetery History," a fact sheet provided by sexton Mark E. Smith and distributed from his office at the cemetery.

16. Susan Lyman, "A Walk Through Time: Salt Lake Cemetery Is Filled with History, Drama," *Deseret News*, May 29, 1988, S1.

17. "Salt Lake City Cemetery History."

18. On January 28, 1862, Baptiste was taken "to the graveyard to day to point out the graves which He had opened. . . . He did not point out more than a doz[en] Graves . . . for fear he would be killed." Elder Woodruff continued, "I would probably range [estimate] from One to three Hundred." *Wilford Woodruff Journal, 1833–1898, Typescript*, ed. Scott G. Kenney (Midvale, UT: Signature Books, 1983), 6:14.

19. Carter, *Heart Throbs*, 6:328–29.

20. *Wilford Woodruff's Journal*, 6:14–15 (July 28, 1862). Baptiste was banished to Miller Island (later Fremont Island), which was being grazed by livestock owned by a Miller family. David E. Miller, "Footnote to History: The Man Who Was Banished," *Home Magazine*, April 15, 1956, H3; see also "Affairs in Utah," *New York Times*, February 28, 1862, 3.

21. *Wilford Woodruff's Journal*, 6:13 (January 27, 1862).

22. Carter, *Heart Throbs*, 6:326.

23. "First Cemetery in the Salt Lake Valley, 1847–48 (Also the Kimball-Whitney and Brigham Young Private Cemeteries)," *Heritage Gateways*, http://heritage.uen.org/resources/Wcd7132cdf9bbb.htm.

24. When Heber C. Kimball died in June 1868, he was buried near his family in the same plot as were his wives Vilate Murray, Laura Pitkin, Sarah Noon, Sarah Ann Whitney, Anna Gheen, Ellen Sanders, and Theresa Morley. See Orson F. Whitney, "The Kimball Cemetery," *Deseret Evening News*, June 14, 1890. His wife Ellen Sanders was one of the first three women to enter the Salt Lake Valley. At the turn of the century, a newspaper column noted, "A beautiful pine tree today grows over [Kimball's] exact sleeping place, while around him are the bodies of several of his

wives and friends." See "The Kimball-Whitney Cemetery," *Deseret Evening News*, June 15, 1901.

25. Carter, *Heart Throbs*, 6:334.

26. Carter, *Heart Throbs*, 6:334–35. The proceeds from the sale of Elder Orson F. Whitney's *Life of Heber C. Kimball*, "which have been extensive," were used to make significant improvements to the cemetery. Orson F. Whitney, "The Kimball Cemetery."

27. "First Cemetery in the Salt Lake Valley, 1847–48."

28. "Some Not-So-Common Sites to See around Temple Square," *Mormon Times*, Saturday, May 15, 2010, 11.

29. Carter, *Heart Throbs*, 6:334.

30. Carter, *Heart Throbs*, 6:333.

31. Carter, *Heart Throbs*, 6:335.

32. Journal History of The Church of Jesus Christ of Latter-day Saints, Church History Library, March 29, 1890, 3.

33. Alice Richards Smith, *The Living Words of Alice Ann Richards Smith* (n.p.), 5, Leonard J. Arrington Historical Archives, Utah State University, Logan, Utah.

34. Great Salt Lake City Council Minutes, April 19, 1856, Church History Library, MS 8623 reel 35.

35. For additional information about the establishment of Camp Douglas, see Kenneth L. Alford's chapter in this volume.

36. Talbot, Richins, and Baker, *Right Place*, 89.

37. After completing his military service, General Connor returned to Salt Lake to become a prospector and a self-appointed reformer, whose goal was to dilute the authority of the Latter-day Saints and create interest for non-Mormons to reside in Utah.

38. Talbot, Richins, and Baker, *Right Place*, 89.

39. Talbot, Richins, and Baker, *Right Place*, 89.

40. Talbot, Richins, and Baker, *Right Place*, 89–90.

41. The discovery was by chance, because only the year before a company from Colorado was hired to find the burial ground established by the earliest pioneers to the Salt Lake Valley. Thousands of dollars and many days were spent searching for the burial sites without success. It was a year later, and after construction on the site had resumed, that an antique bottle collector looking for pioneer artifacts found some

bones. Chuck Gates, "Discovery of Graves Culminates a Search for 'Roots,'" *Deseret News*, March 8, 1987, B2.

42. Talbot, Richins, and Baker, *Right Place*, 103. "The 33 historic burials . . . were distributed across an area approximately ten meters east to west and eleven meters north to south (110 sq. meters)." In total, "32 graves containing human remains, and two other possible graves which contained no skeletal material. The discrepancy between the 33 burials and 32 graves is due to the fact that 2 infants were buried in a single grave." These two were believed to be conjoined twins, connected at the head, seemingly in a state of embrace in death.

43. Talbot, Richins, and Baker, *Right Place*, 103.

44. Gates, "Discovery of Graves Culminates a Search for 'Roots,'" B2.

45. Conrad Walters, "Pioneers' Bones Are Back for Reburial," *Salt Lake Tribune*, April 17, 1987.

46. Chuck Gates, "State Park Preparing to Rebury 32 Pioneers," *Deseret News*, April 17, 1987, B1–B2. The vaults were used in case additional studies need to be performed on the skeletal remains. There is always a chance that new tests, procedures, or science could be developed that would help to prove the identify of yet-unidentified individuals or to further study the remains.

47. This is why the original layout of the original cemetery on Block 49 where the skeletal remains were exhumed became so important.

48. Personal observation during a visit to This Is the Place Heritage Park, June 2010.

49. Phoenix Roberts, "Utah's Tomb of the Unknowns: Discovering a Lost Cemetery," *Salt Lake Magazine*, June 2004, 50. Only nine out of the thirty-three were positively identified, and several others were identified with some question of absolute certainty. Most of those individuals without an exact identity were infants, but for some of the twenty-four a surname was known. In addition, with the identities fixed, another monument was erected in downtown Salt Lake City. The monument is located at the intersection of 200 West and 300 South in Salt Lake City on the southwest corner of the intersection and the northeast corner of Block 49. This is the closest point to the burials on public property that the monument could be affixed.

50. Lyon, *Uncommon Aspects*, 40.

A drawing of Camp Douglas in 1862. (Used by permission, Utah State Historical Society.
All rights reserved.)

Chapter 10

Camp Douglas:
Keeping a Watchful Eye
on the Saints

Kenneth L. Alford

Camp Douglas is the only military installation in the United States on a site purposely chosen so that its guns could fire, if necessary, upon American citizens nearby. The establishment of Camp Douglas on the bench above Salt Lake City is an interesting but little known story of the American Civil War. Utah is generally viewed as a quiet bystander to the Civil War, but events in Utah played an important supporting role. While Camp Douglas (later renamed Fort Douglas) experienced a long and colorful history, this paper focuses on the period between the camp's founding in 1862 and the end of the Civil War.

Background

President Brigham Young and the first Latter-day Saint pioneers arrived in the Salt Lake Valley in July 1847. At that time, President

Kenneth L. Alford is an associate professor of Church history and doctrine at Brigham Young University.

Young reportedly said, "If the United States will now let this people alone for ten years to come, we will ask no odds of them or any one else but God."[1] In 1857, exactly ten years later, President James Buchanan declared Utah to be in open rebellion and ordered several thousand soldiers to march on Utah and install a new territorial governor. After harassment of the army, the evacuation of northern Utah, negotiation sessions, and the issuance of a blanket presidential pardon, the conflict was settled peacefully. Colonel Albert Sidney Johnston's forces marched quietly through Salt Lake City in June 1858.[2]

The soldiers established Camp Floyd (named after John B. Floyd, President Buchanan's secretary of war) forty miles southwest of Salt Lake City. The camp's distance from Salt Lake City was probably viewed favorably by most Salt Lake inhabitants. Relations with Camp Floyd were sometimes strained but resulted in economic benefits for many Utah residents. Camp Floyd was renamed Fort Crittenden after Secretary Floyd resigned in December 1860 to join the Confederacy.

In 1861, when the first shots of the Civil War were fired, Utah found itself at a strategic crossroads—mail, telegraph lines, gold from California, and emigrants all needed to pass freely through the Utah Territory, but Union soldiers were needed in the East far more than they were required at Fort Crittenden. In May 1861, the War Department "issued orders for the immediate withdrawal of all the regular troops from New-Mexico and Utah."[3] Fort Crittenden was evacuated and closed. The soldiers garrisoned there were moved east during July. An auction held in August disposed of materials and buildings at the fort.[4] One citizen's August 1861 letter summed up the feelings of many Utah residents: "The troops are gone. Camp Floyd, which for three years past has resounded with the orgies of the ungodly and become a nest for every unclean thing, has reverted to its wonted quietude and simplicity. Sometimes I regret that I never visited it; yet at other times I feel grateful that I have kept myself entirely aloof from Gentile influences and associations."[5]

While some residents celebrated the fort's closing, others questioned the wisdom of the decision. A *New York Times* writer predicted that "the removal of the small force from Utah will prove a fatal blunder, as it will leave the great overland routes to California and Oregon unprotected, and invite aggression both from lawless Mormons and hostile Indians."[6] When increased Indian activity and attacks along the Overland Mail Route followed the withdrawal of soldiers from Fort Crittenden, it soon became apparent that military action was required. President Young and territorial federal officials suggested that "a regiment of mounted men be raised"[7] to protect the mail, emigration, and telegraph routes. The government initially rejected their offer "because it is not supposed so large a force is necessary."[8] However, on April 28, 1862, by "express direction of the President of the United States," President Young was authorized to "raise, arm, and equip one company of cavalry for ninety days' service."[9] The government's request specified that "the company will be employed to protect the property of the telegraph and overland mail companies in or about Independence Rock, where depredations have been committed, and will be continued in service only till the U.S. troops can reach the point where they are so much needed. . . . It will not be employed for any offensive operations other than may grow out of the duty hereinbefore assigned to it."[10]

The requested soldiers were quickly mustered. Under the command of Captain Lot Smith, who had won fame during the Utah War, the company left Salt Lake City in early May 1862 for three months of active duty military service. In late August 1862, after the Utah volunteer company had returned to Utah, General James Craig, who was responsible for the overland mail and telegraph lines from the Missouri River to the Utah Territory, telegraphed Edwin M. Stanton, secretary of war, requesting either reinforcements from the States or permission to "re-enlist the Utah troops for a limited time."[11] Secretary Stanton answered the following day, "You are authorized to raise 100 mounted men in the mountains and re-enlist the Utah troops for three months as requested."[12] No action was apparently taken on the reenlistment offer. Military leaders determined that dispatching volunteer units from California would be a more permanent military solution to protecting commerce and traffic along the overland trail. The State of California was asked to recruit 16,000 soldiers—some of whom would be sent to Utah.[13]

In May 1862, Brigadier General George Wright, commander of the army's Department of the Pacific, appointed Colonel Patrick Edward Connor to command several companies of California Volunteers (or CVs as they were often called) to travel from Stockton, California, "to the vicinity of Salt Lake."[14] His stated mission was "to guard effectively the Overland Mail Route"[15] and "also the telegraph stations."[16] Connor's command arrived at Fort Churchill (near Reno, Nevada) in August 1862, where Colonel Connor assumed command of the military District of Utah, which included the Utah and Nevada Territories.[17]

Establishment of Camp Douglas

Utah residents had dismantled Fort Crittenden too well. Many buildings were sold or moved, with the remainder being left to the elements. Little did they know that the army would return in strength at the end of the following year, and the poor condition of Fort Crittenden would help influence the selection of the army's new encampment.

In the fall of 1862, Colonel Connor traveled, in advance of the army, to the Salt Lake Valley from Fort Ruby (Nevada Territory) in order to select a route and scout out the best location for a military campsite near the city. Wearing civilian clothing, he "took a stroll about town and looked around with an air of familiarity that indicated that after all Salt Lake City was something of a place, and might not be unpleasant notwithstanding, its desert surrounding."[18]

When word reached Utah that the army would soon be returning, there was great concern. A *New York Times* report from Salt Lake stated, "There may be still another jurisdiction conflict in our midst, and perhaps a very pretty quarrel. . . . Let us hope for the best, particularly in the present juncture of affairs, and that peaceable counsels will prevail."[19]

Patrick Edward Connor was a soldier, contractor, mining entrepreneur, and political leader. He founded the Liberal Party in Utah, is remembered as the Father of Utah Mining, and also established Utah's first daily newspaper, the Daily Union Vedette, *at Camp Douglas. (Used by permission, Utah State Historical Society. All rights reserved.)*

After visiting Fort Crittenden, Colonel Connor shared several reasons against reopening it. First, the fort was "in ruins" except for a few buildings (for which the owner wanted $15,000). Second, most of the few remaining buildings "would have to be torn down and removed." Third, "the post is badly located." His fourth, and most important, reason was that "I found another location, which I like better." The location was "on a plateau about three miles from Salt Lake City; in the vicinity of good timber and saw-mills, and at a point where hay, grain, and other produce can be purchased cheaper than at Fort Crittenden." Colonel Connor also revealed an additional unofficial purpose for the new location—keeping an eye on the Mormons: "It is also a point which commands the city, and where 1,000 troops would be more efficient than 3,000 on the other side of the Jordan. If the general decides that I shall locate there, I intend to quietly intrench my position, and then say to the Saints of Utah, enough of your treason; but if it is intended that I shall merely protect the overland mail and permit the Mormons to act and utter treason, then I had as well locate at Crittenden. The Federal officers desire and beg that I will locate near the city."[20]

On October 1, 1862, a few days before entering the Utah Territory with his soldiers, Colonel Connor reported, "The people of Utah are under the impression that I am to winter at Fort Crittenden."[21] He also informed his superiors that he had been "credibly informed by letter this morning that the flag-staff at Fort Crittenden was cut down since my visit and hauled away by Brigham's orders."[22] Connor quite likely viewed this as an affront to federal authority and a misuse of federal property.

Colonel Connor and his command (five infantry and two cavalry companies) camped at Fort Crittenden on October 17, 1862, and marched down State Street into Salt Lake City on October 22, 1862. The soldiers halted and formed two lines in front of territorial governor Stephen S. Harding's residence. After being introduced by Colonel Connor, Governor Harding addressed the troops while standing in a carriage:

> It is with pleasure that I meet you all here to-day. . . . The individual, if any such there be, who supposed that the Government has sent you here, that mischief might come out of it, knows not the spirit of our Government, and knows not the spirit of the officers who represent it in this Territory. . . .
>
> I confess, that I have been disappointed, somewhat, in your coming to this city.
>
> I do not know now what disposition is to be made of you, but I suppose you will be encamped somewhere, I know not where, but within a short distance of this city. I believe the people you have now come amongst will not disturb you if you do not disturb them.[23]

Following the governor's speech, the soldiers marched to the base of the mountains east of the city "between Red Bute and Emmigration Kanyons [*sic*]."[24] On October 26, 1862, Colonel Connor formally announced, "Pursuant to orders from department headquarters a military post is hereby established at this camp, to be called Camp Douglas." The boundaries of the camp began "at a post due north one mile distant from the garrison flag staff, and running thence west one mile, thence south two miles, thence east two miles, thence north two miles, and thence west one mile, to the place of beginning, containing 2,560 acres more or less."[25]

Tensions between Salt Lake City and Camp Douglas began almost immediately. Knowingly or unknowingly, Patrick Connor had agitated Salt Lake residents even in the selection of the name for the new installation—Camp Douglas.[26] Senator Stephen A. Douglas had been an early friend to the Latter-day Saints, but in the last years of his life he became quite outspoken against Mormonism. In 1857, he commented that "it will become the duty of Congress to apply the knife and cut out this loathsome, disgusting ulcer."[27] Shortly after Senator Douglas's death in June 1861, a *New York Times* correspondent reported from Salt Lake City: "Last Wednesday the Pony [Express] told us of the death of Senator Douglas. The Mormon portion of the community entertain certain hard recollections of the Senator, on account of his 'loathsome ulcer' recommendations. So there are no flags at half mast, no mourning appears, no tears are shed, no tokens of respect for the memory of the illustrious Illinoisan are visible, though an old neighbor in Nauvoo days."[28]

In the months following the establishment of Camp Douglas, the "Overland Mail Company, the Post-Office Department, and Department of the Interior" all urged Connor's superiors, including General Henry Halleck (President Lincoln's military general-in-chief), to move Connor's soldiers from Salt Lake City to Fort Bridger "as a check upon the Indians."[29] As a compromise, Connor was ordered to detach one or two companies from his command to occupy Fort Bridger. Echoing Colonel Connor's anti-Mormon sentiments, General Wright informed his superiors in Washington, DC, "Without entering into details I am well convinced that prudential considerations demand the presence of a force in that country [Salt Lake] strong enough to look down any opposition."[30] Governor Harding also recommended that Colonel Connor's command should remain at Camp Douglas: "I have not a doubt but that it will be the last time that U.S. soldiers will have the privilege of entering this Territory peaceably if Colonel Connor is now ordered away. I do not say that Mormons would meet our troops openly in such an attempt, although there are strong reasons for believing that they would, yet I have no doubt but the Indians would be encouraged to do so, and all possible succor would be given them by the powers here. . . . The base of operations should be here. . . . In the withdrawal of the troops the General Government virtually abandons her sovereignty over this Territory."[31]

The army's late arrival required them to work hard throughout the winter building the new camp. By February 1863, Colonel Connor reported they had built thirteen small officers' quarters, a guardhouse, a bakehouse, a commissary, quartermaster offices, stores, stables, a blacksmith shop, and a hospital. The enlisted soldiers lived in "temporary shelters of tents placed over excavations four feet deep, with good stone and adobe fireplace."[32]

Camp Douglas proved to be a source of welcome income for many local residents. While many supply items were received from the States, the military purchased tons of locally produced hay, barley, oats, potatoes, and cattle, among other products. In accordance with Colonel Connor's strong Unionist views, all contractors supplying items to Camp Douglas were "required to take the oath of allegiance to the United States Government."[33] Soldiers found Salt Lake City the obvious location to spend their monthly pay. In December 1862, the army "disbursed among them the snug sum of $74,000, so that they can now rejoice in being paid up. . . . The shopkeepers of this city are doing a heavy business. The stores are thronged most of the day, and 'green-backs' are more plentiful than blackberries in this Territory."[34] Businesses, some of a questionable nature, also began to spring up around the borders of the camp: "As is usual elsewhere, thanks to the weakness and wickedness of poor human nature, accommodating persons and institutions cluster around Camp Douglas, . . . and it is really too much to suppose that every officer and private is entirely unimpressible when Bacchus and Venus hang out their colors. So to prevent, as far as possible, any little accidents derogatory to discipline and military efficiency, Col. Connor at a dress parade on Monday, declared, by special order, that the military reserve connected with the post above-named, was extended to embrace an area of four miles square."[35]

There were apparently few, if any, discussions between Colonel Connor and Salt Lake civic authorities regarding either the original location or expanded dimensions of Camp Douglas. Much of the newly extended camp boundaries were within the corporate limits of Salt Lake City; this did not sit well with city authorities, but there was little they could do. Other problems arose during the next few months as the city and camp struggled to accommodate each other. Camp Douglas was just six months old when a grand jury of the US district court for the Third Judicial District of Utah Territory (with Latter-day Saint Apostles George A. Smith and Franklin D. Richards serving as the foreman and a jury member, respectively) was impanelled in Salt Lake City to consider Camp Douglas's "notoriously offensive or . . . obnoxious and revolting" water usage policies. The grand jury declared that Camp Douglas was abusing Red Butte Creek—the primary water supply for at least three thousand Salt Lake City residents: "Camp Douglas, where have since been stationed a large body of troops, . . . have placed obstructions in the stream; have built privies on or close to one of said streams of water, and in divers other ways have the said troops and those following them . . . fouled the water thereof, and rendered it extremely filthy and nauseous, to the great inconvenience of the people of the said city, and deleterious to their health."[36]

Friction between Church and State

Economic tensions were exacerbated by historical and philosophical differences between the Church and the US government. Relations between the two parties had been mixed since the Church's founding in 1830. Latter-day Saints viewed themselves as loyal Americans with a firm dedication to and belief in the Constitution of the United States. Several federal actions, though, especially military actions against the Saints, were not viewed favorably. A March 1863 article in the *Deseret News* proclaimed: "Ever since we as a people were driven from our homes in Illinois; traversed an almost trackless desert and settled in these distant valleys; a constant effort has been made by wicked and designing men to disturb our peace and interfere with those religious rights secured to us by the Federal Constitution. We have neither time, space, nor inclination to review the wrongs and insults that our bodies, and we as a people have suffered. They are all matters of history; delineating them will present one of the darkest pages ever recorded of any religious people."[37]

The early history of Camp Douglas boils down, in large measure, to the interaction between two strong personalities—President Young and Colonel Connor. Connor was seen by himself and many others as a true patriot. An Irish immigrant, he voluntarily left his family and a very comfortable life in California to serve his nation. President Young's feelings regarding soldiers being sent again to Utah might be summed up in the opening words of the proclamation he issued to the citizens of Utah five years earlier, on September 15, 1857:

> For the last twenty-five years we have trusted officials of the government, from constables and justices to judges, governors and presidents, only to be scorned, held in derision, insulted and betrayed. Our houses have been plundered and then burned, our fields laid waste, our principal men butchered while under the pledged faith of the government for their safety, and our families driven from their homes to find that shelter in the barren wilderness and that protection among hostile savages, which were denied them in the boasted abodes of christianity and civilization.

The Constitution of our common country guarantees unto us all that we do now, or have ever claimed. If the constitutional rights which pertain unto us as American citizens were extended to Utah, according to the spirit and meaning thereof, and fairly and impartially administered, it is all that we could ask, all that we have ever asked.[38]

As he had done during the Utah War, President Young sought to demonstrate his loyalty to the Constitution and the Union. When the transcontinental telegraph reached Salt Lake City in October 1861, for example, one of the first messages sent by Brigham Young affirmed that "Utah has not seceded, but is firm for the Constitution and laws of our once happy country."[39]

General Wright, Colonel Connor's superior, reported that "Brigham Young was exceedingly anxious that the troops should reoccupy Camp Crittenden or some point remote from the city, but after mature consideration I came to the conclusion that the site of the present camp was the most eligible for the accomplishment of the objects in view. It is a commanding position, looking down on the city, and hence has been dreaded by the Mormon chief."[40]

Colonel Connor saw it as his responsibility to do something about the Mormons. As early as September 1862, his official reports began to include complaints about Mormons and Mormonism. According to Connor, Mormons were "a community of traitors, murderers, fanatics, and whores"[41] who were "composed chiefly of the very lowest class of foreigners and aliens, . . . hesitating at the commission of no crime." He said that the Church was an "unholy, blasphemous, and unnatural institution" and that "if the crimes and designs of this people were known and understood by the people of the United States as I understand and know them, it would cause such a burst of indignation as would result in the utter annihilation of this whole people. . . . The sooner we are rid of the evil, and the nation of the stigma [of Mormonism], the better it will be for us. . . . Individually I would prefer to serve in another field.

At the same time there is much to do here, and it would give me great pleasure to contribute my humble services to blot out this stigma on our national honor."[42]

It was not just the tenets of Mormonism that bothered Patrick Connor. He saw Mormons as "disloyal almost to a man, and treason, if not openly preached, [was] covertly encouraged."[43] In Connor's eyes, "the so-called President Young" was "engaged in mounting cannon for the purpose of resisting the Government."[44] He reported that the Mormons were "hard at work making cartridges" and that President Young had placed a "guard of 300 men" at his home with which, from Connor's perspective, he could resist federal authority.[45]

Camp Douglas was a thorn in President Young's side, and Colonel Connor knew it. In December 1862, Connor reported, "My present position [at Camp Douglas] was selected for its availability, and commanding as it does not only all the avenues to but even the town itself, it is an important one, and I am not surprised that Brigham Young considers its occupancy dangerous to his interests."[46] Connor's view was that "Mormonism as preached and practiced in this Territory is not only subversive of morals, in conflict with the civilization of the present age, and oppressive on the people, but also deeply and boldly in contravention of the laws and best interests of the nation." Therefore, he "sought by every proper means in [his] power to arrest its progress and prevent its spread."[47] He initially believed there were but two ways to resolve the problems and influence of Mormonism: "First, by dividing the Territory into four parts and adding the parts to the four adjoining Territories; second, by declaring martial law."[48] By subdividing the territory, he hoped to weaken both Brigham Young's and Salt Lake City's influence on the surrounding regions. A few months later, he came to see a third way—"inviting into the Territory large numbers of Gentiles to live among and dwell with the people."[49] To accomplish this end, he "considered the discovery of gold, silver, and other valuable minerals in the Territory of the highest importance," and he "instructed commanders of posts and detachments to permit the men of their commands to prospect the country in the vicinity of their respective posts, whenever such course would not interfere with their military duties, and to furnish every proper facility for the discovery and opening of mines of gold, silver, and other minerals." Connor, who is recognized today as the "Father of Utah Mining,"[50] believed that by encouraging Gentiles to settle and mine in Utah, "the Mormon question will at an early day be finally settled by peaceable means, without the increased expenditure of a dollar by Government."[51] His belief in this policy was so strong that by spring 1864, he directed some of his subordinate commanders to "devote the most of [their] attention" to the discovery of new mines.[52]

The military blamed increasing tensions with Salt Lake inhabitants on "the open declarations of hostility to the Government on the part of their public men and their bold, continued, and unceasing teachings of disloyalty," which Colonel Connor stated "time and again tended to produce excitements leading to collision, which have only been avoided by the most temperate and moderate course of the officers and men of my command."[53]

March 1863 was a particularly tense period in the relationship between Salt Lake City and Camp Douglas. Several events and beliefs contributed to the heightening of tensions—chief among them was concern that the army was planning to arrest President Young.[54] Colonel Connor became alarmed on March 3 and again on March 4 when "Brigham caused to be removed from the Territorial arsenal to his residence all the ordnance and ordnance stores, and placed a large body of armed men in his yard, which is inclosed with a high stone wall."[55] Connor was uncertain whether Young's actions and intent were defensive or offensive. On March 8, President Young spoke in the Tabernacle and discussed the loyalty of the Saints, relations with the federal government, the Civil War, and Camp Douglas:

> But if the Government of the United States should now ask
> for a battalion of men to fight in the present battle-fields of the

nation, while there is a camp of soldiers from abroad located within the corporate limits of this city, I would not ask one man to go; I would see them in hell first. What was the result a year ago, when our then Governor . . . called for men to go and guard the mail route? Were they promptly on hand? Yes, and when President Lincoln wrote to me requesting me to fit out one hundred men to guard the mail route, we at once enlisted the one hundred men for ninety days. On Monday evening I received the instruction, and on Wednesday afternoon that hundred men were mustered into service and encamped ready for moving. But all this does not prove any loyalty to political tyrants.

We guarded the mail route. . . . We do not need any soldiers here from any other States or Territories to perform that service, neither does the Government, as they would know if they were wise. . . .

What can we do? We can serve God, and mind our own business; keep our powder dry, and be prepared for every emergency to which we may be exposed, and sustain the civil law to which we are subject. . . .

Now, as we are accused of secession, my counsel to this congregation is to secede, what from? From the Constitution of the United States? No. From the institutions of our country? No. Well then, what from? From sin and the practice thereof. That is my counsel to this congregation and to the whole world.[56]

On March 9, Colonel Connor reported that President Young "raised the national flag over his residence for the first time I am told since his arrival in the Territory, but not, however, from motives of patriotism or for any loyal purpose, but as a signal to his people to assemble armed, which they immediately did, to the number of about 1,500."[57] The following day, Colonel Connor reported that the Mormons "are determined to have trouble, and are trying to provoke me to bring it on, but they will fail."[58]

On March 12, the flag at President Young's residence was raised again—causing 1,500 Mormon militia members to assemble. As before, the unofficial militia was dismissed, but Latter-day Saint guards patrolled the city each night. Connor clearly recognized the friction that existed but apparently felt he was not responsible for it. He notified General Wright:

> The only excuse his adherents give for this extraordinary proceeding is that he feared I would arrest him for uttering treasonable language. . . . There has been nothing in my conduct or language which could be construed so as to induce that belief. . . . Since my arrival the people of the Territory have been treated kindly and courteously by both my officers and men, who have never given one of them cause for complaint, which the people freely acknowledge. But notwithstanding this, the courtesy we have given is returned with abuse. They rail at us in their sermons in which we are also classed with cutthroats and gamblers, our Government cursed and vilified in their public speeches and meetings.[59]

After noting that his command was "in no immediate danger," Colonel Connor explained, "If the present preparations of the Mormons should continue I will be compelled for the preservation of my command to strike at the heads of the church. . . . If I remain in my present position (although a strong one) for them to attack me, I am lost, as they have about 5,000 men capable of bearing arms and cannon of heavier caliber than mine. . . . I will do nothing rashly or hastily, and my intercourse with them will be, as heretofore, courteous and firm."[60]

After hearing of the increased tensions in Salt Lake City, General Wright admonished Colonel Connor, "Be prudent and cautious. Hold your troops well in hand. A day of retribution will come."[61] On March 29, 1863, with the approval of Secretary Stanton,[62] Connor was promoted to brigadier general for his "heroic conduct and brilliant victory on Bear River" over the local Indian population.[63] By the end of the month, General Wright notified Washington DC that "the excitement at Great Salt Lake City, brought about by the treasonable acts of Brigham Young and his adherents, has somewhat subsided, yet I am fully satisfied that they only wait for a favorable opportunity to strike a blow against the Union."[64]

Continuing distrust and tensions between Salt Lake residents and soldiers caused General Wright to inform army headquarters during July 1863 that he was seriously considering "the propriety of removing the troops from the immediate vicinity of Great Salt Lake City to the old position at Camp Floyd. . . . It would obviate the irritations and complaints which are constantly arising between the soldiers and citizens." The district's headquarters would remain in Salt Lake City, even if the soldiers were relocated, and no plans were entertained regarding the complete removal of soldiers from the Utah Territory. According to Wright, "The presence of the force now there is indispensable for the protection of the Overland Mail Route and the general safety of the country."[65]

That same day, July 31, 1863, General Wright notified General Connor that he was contemplating reoccupying Camp Crittenden and ordered Connor "to make immediate preparations to this end, . . . advise the general by telegraph . . . when the command at Camp Douglas can be moved to Camp Crittenden."[66] Any responses to this order from General Connor have apparently been lost, but something caused General Wright to change his mind. On August 19, General Connor received new orders: "To the extent that if, in your judgment, the withdrawal of the troops from Camp Douglas would produce an impression on the minds of the Mormons that the removal was in consequence of disapprobation of your course while in command, or in any manner injurious to the interests of the Government, you will retain Camp Douglas as your principal station,"[67] which he did.

Tension and misunderstanding between the Mormons and the military continued throughout the Civil War. In August 1863, James D.

Doty, Utah's territorial governor, noted, "Many of those difficulties arise from the mistaken notion that the interests of this people and those of the Government are at variance. I think they are not."[68] The Latter-day Saint perspective was probably adequately summarized after the war ended in a correspondent's November 1865 *New York Times* report:

> As to the graver matters of disloyalty and threatened difficulties, we may say that such accusations against the Mormons are not new, and perhaps are not now, any more than formerly, altogether without foundation. There may be two reasons for this—firstly, because more than half of the population of Utah consists of recent emigrants of foreign birth, gathered from all the lands under the sun, and from all the islands fixed in the sea; and secondly, because the long and terrible persecutions of the Mormons in Illinois and Missouri in the early days of the Church, have left behind them bitter memories of the power that failed to afford protection. Then, again, there have always been annoying quarrels in progress with the Mormons, which reached the very verge of war eight years ago, and the embers of which have been smouldering ever since. We do not see, however, from anything that has been published, that there have been any new or menacing developments of late, or that things are in any worse condition than that in which they have been for the last eighteen or twenty years.
>
> Is it necessary for the government to take any action in the premises?
>
> We decidedly think not.[69]

Fort Douglas after the Civil War

In the years following the Civil War, relations between Camp Douglas and Salt Lake City gradually softened from antagonism to grudging acceptance and finally to an embrace. In the space of a few short years, Camp Douglas became an important and noncontroversial part of Salt Lake City. Reflecting a personal example of the widespread change of attitude that occurred, General Connor returned to Salt Lake City in the later years of his life and lived there until his death on December 16, 1891, when, as he had requested, he was buried in the military cemetery at Fort Douglas.[70]

In 1878, the year after Brigham Young's death, Camp Douglas was officially renamed Fort Douglas and designated as an army regimental post. Soldiers from Fort Douglas played a contributing role in American history from the Civil War through the Korean War. Prisoners of war were housed at Fort Douglas during both World War I and World War II. The fort was officially closed in 1991, although a small section of the original grounds continued to support elements of the Utah National Guard and Army Reserve for several years. During the 2002 Salt Lake Winter Olympic games, part of Fort Douglas was used as the Olympic Village, housing visiting athletes from many continents. Visitors to Fort Douglas today can visit a military museum and several historic buildings that help preserve its historic past.

Notes

1. Orson Hyde, in *Journal of Discourses* (London: Latter-day Saints Book Depot, 1854–86), 6:12.

2. There are numerous sources for additional reading on this subject; for example, see William P. MacKinnon, ed., *At Sword's Point, Part 1: A Documentary History of the Utah War to 1858* (Norman, OK: Arthur H. Clark, 2008); LeRoy R. Hafen and Ann W. Hafen, eds., *Mormon Resistance: A Documentary Account of the Utah Expedition, 1857–1858* (Lincoln: University of Nebraska Press, 1958); and Norman F. Furniss, *The Mormon Conflict, 1850–1859* (New Haven, CT: Yale University Press, 1960).

3. "The Secession Rebellion," *New York Times*, May 24, 1861, 1.

4. "Affairs in Utah," *New York Times*, August 2, 1861, 5.

5. Gilbert Clements to W. G. Mills, August 25, 1861. Mills was then serving as a missionary in England, in B. H. Roberts, *A Comprehensive History of the Church of Jesus Christ of Latter-day Saints* (Provo, UT: Brigham Young University Press, 1957), 4:544n17.

6. "Secession Rebellion," 1.

7. *The War of the Rebellion: A Compilation of the Official Records of the Union and Confederate Armies*, Series 1, Vol. 50, Part 1 (Washington DC: Government Printing Office, 1897), 1023 (hereafter *WOTR* 1.1).

8. L. Thomas to George Wright, April 8, 1862, in *WOTR* 1.1, 1023.

9. *The War of the Rebellion: A Compilation of the Official Records of the Union and Confederate Armies*, Series 3, vol. 2 (Washington DC: Government Printing Office, 1899), 27 (hereafter *WOTR* 3.2).

10. L. Thomas to Brigham Young, April 28, 1862, in *WOTR* 3.2, 27.

11. James Craig to Edwin M. Stanton, August 23, 1862, in *WOTR* 3.2, 449.

12. Edwin M. Stanton to James Craig, August 24, 1862, in *WOTR* 3.2, 453.

13. Richard H. Orton, ed. *Records of California Men in the War of Rebellion, 1861–1867* (Sacramento: State Office, 1890), 2.

14. Special Orders No. 115, Headquarters Department of the Pacific, San Francisco, CA, July 5, 1862, Richard C. Drum, in *The War of the Rebellion: A Compilation of the Official Records of the Union and Confederate Armies*, Series 1, Vol. 50, Part 2 (Washington DC: Government Printing Office, 1897), 5–6 (hereafter *WOTR* 1.2).

15. Special Orders No. 115, in *WOTR* 1.2, 5–6.

16. George Wright to L. Thomas, December 15, 1862, in *WOTR* 1.1, 181.

17. P. E. Connor to Richard C. Drum, August 5, 1862; R. C. Drum to Colonel Connor, August 5, 1862; and Orders No. 1, Fort Churchill, August 6, 1862, in *WOTR* 1.2, 53–55.

18. "Memoranda in relation to Camp Douglas, U. T. furnished by Gen. P. E. Connor," in Brigham D. Madsen, *Glory Hunter: A Biography of Patrick Edward Connor* (Salt Lake City: University of Utah Press, 1990), 65.

19. "Affairs in Utah," *New York Times*, September 7, 1862, 3.

20. Patrick Edward Connor to Richard C. Drum, September 14, 1862, in *WOTR* 1.2, 119.

21. Patrick Edward Connor to Richard C. Drum, October 1, 1862, in *WOTR* 1.2, 143. Stenhouse states, "There is no truth in this." See T. B. H. Stenhouse, *The Rocky Mountain Saints* (London: Ward, Lock, and Tyler, 1874), 602.

22. The historian B. H. Roberts reported that Colonel Philip St. George Cooke, the last commander at Fort Crittenden, "presented to Brigham Young the flag staff of Camp Floyd–Camp Crittenden. . . . After the remnant of the army was departed, the flag staff was removed from Fort Crittenden, and planted on the hillcrest immediately east of the Beehive House," but Roberts did not mention the date when the actual removal occurred. See Roberts, *Comprehensive History of the Church*, 4:543.

In a 1907 address to the Daughters of Utah Pioneers, Hiram B. Clawson provided additional details regarding President Young's flagpole. "One evening, while sitting in front of the general's tent [at the Camp]," he said, "I was attracted by a beautiful flag and staff and I was asked by the commanding officer [Colonel St. George Cooke], if I thought President Young would accept it. I assured him that he would not only accept it, but place it on his Salt Lake home, the 'White House,' and that on all national occasions the flag would be unfurled. They presented it; it was accepted and placed as stated." George D. Pyper, *The Romance of an Old Playhouse* (Salt Lake City: Seagull Press, 1928), 75. For details regarding why Clawson was at Camp Floyd/Crittenden, please see the chapter in this book entitled "The Salt Lake Theatre: Brigham's Playhouse."

23. "Affairs in Utah," *New York Times*, November 15, 1862, 2.

24. "Arrival of Col. Connor's Command," *Deseret News*, October 22, 1862.

25. Orders, No. 14, Headquarters District of Utah, October 26, 1862, in *WOTR* 1.2, 195.

26. Colonel Connor's admiration for Senator Stephen A. Douglas was apparently deep-seated. While living in California, he had "established a subscription office in Agricultural Hall seeking donations for a new monument to be erected to the late Senator Stephen A. Douglas" (Madsen, *Glory Hunter*, 49).

27. This statement was made in a remarks delivered in the State House in Springfield, Illinois, on June 12, 1857. The speech was published in the *Missouri Republican* on June 12, 1857, and republished in the *Deseret News*. See "Comments," *Deseret News*, September 2, 1857.

28. "Affairs in Utah," *New York Times*, July 8, 1861, 2.

29. Henry Halleck to George Wright, December 9, 1862, in *WOTR* 1.2, 244.

30. George Wright to L. Thomas, December 9, 1862, in *WOTR* 1.2, 245.

31. Stephen S. Harding to George Wright, February 16, 1863, in *WOTR* 1.2, 315.

32. Patrick Edward Connor to Richard C. Drum, February 26, 1863, in *WOTR* 1.2, 326.

33. "Affairs in Utah," *New York Times*, November 23, 1862, 5.

34. "Affairs in Utah," *New York Times*, December 21, 1862, 2.

35. "Affairs in Utah," *New York Times*, February 8, 1863, 2.

36. "Third District Federal Court," *Deseret News*, April 15, 1863.

37. "Arrest of Brigham Young for Polygamy," *Deseret News*, March 11, 1863.

38. Roberts, *Comprehensive History of the Church*, 4:273.

39. "The Pacific Telegraph Line," *New York Times*, October 19, 1861, 5.

40. George Wright to L. Thomas, March 30, 1863, in *WOTR* 1.2, 369.

41. Patrick Edward Connor to Richard C. Drum, September 14, 1862, in *WOTR* 1.2, 119.

42. Patrick Edward Connor to Richard C. Drum, February 19, 1863, in *WOTR* 1.2, 319–20.

43. Patrick Edward Connor to Richard C. Drum, February 19, 1863, in *WOTR* 1.2, 319.

44. Patrick Edward Connor to Richard C. Drum, December 20, 1862, in *WOTR* 1.2, 257.

45. Patrick Edward Connor to Richard C. Drum, March 8, 1862, in *WOTR* 1.2, 342.

46. Patrick Edward Connor to Richard C. Drum, December 20, 1862, in *WOTR* 1.2, 257.

47. Patrick Edward Connor to Richard C. Drum, October 26, 1863, in *WOTR* 1.2, 656.

48. Patrick Edward Connor to Richard C. Drum, February 19, 1863, in *WOTR* 1.2, 320.

49. Patrick Edward Connor to Richard C. Drum, October 26, 1863, in *WOTR* 1.2, 656–57.

50. "Utah: The Treasure House of the Nation," Utah Mining Association, http://www.utahmining.org/brochure.htm.

51. Patrick Edward Connor to Richard C. Drum, October 26, 1863, in *WOTR* 1.2, 657.

52. M. G. Lewis to N. Baldwin, May 11, 1864, in *WOTR* 1.2, 846.

53. Patrick Edward Connor to Richard C. Drum, October 26, 1863, in *WOTR* 1.2, 656.

54. See Stenhouse, *Rocky Mountain Saints*, 422; James F. Varley, *Brigham and the Brigadier* (Tucson, AZ: Westernlore Press, 1989), chapter 6, for information about the "March Madness," as Varley called it. For additional insights into the relationship between Brigham Young and Patrick Connor, see E. B. Long, *The Saints and the Union* (Urbana: University of Illinois Press, 1981).

55. Patrick Edward Connor to Richard C. Drum, March 15, 1863, in *WOTR* 1.2, 371.

56. Brigham Young, in *Journal of Discourses*, 10:107, 109, 111.

57. Patrick Edward Connor to Richard C. Drum, March 15, 1863, in *WOTR* 1.2, 371. This may have been the first time that Colonel Connor saw the national flag flying at Brigham Young's residence, but it was clearly not the first time a flag had flown there. See, for example, "Affairs in Utah," *New York Times*, April 6, 1862, which reports, "The Stars and Stripes were flung to the breeze from Brigham's bee-hive mansion."

58. Patrick Edward Connor to Richard C. Drum, March 10, 1863, in *WOTR* 1.2, 344.

59. Patrick Edward Connor to Richard C. Drum, March 15, 1863, in *WOTR* 1.2, 371.

60. Patrick Edward Connor to Richard C. Drum, March 15, 1863, in *WOTR* 1.2, 372.

61. George Wright to Patrick Edward Connor, March 11, 1863, in *WOTR* 1.2, 347.

62. Edwin M. Stanton to Henry Halleck, March 29, 1863, in *WOTR* 1.2, 185.

63. Henry Halleck to Richard C. Drum, March 29, 1863, in *WOTR* 1.2, 369. The Battle of Bear River occurred January 29, 1863, about 150 miles north of Camp Douglas. With Colonel Connor personally commanding, his soldiers killed at least 224 Indians and lost only fourteen soldiers. See Report of P. Edward Connor, February 20, 1863, in *WOTR* 1.1, 184–87. By July 1964, General Connor reported, "The policy pursued toward the Indians has had a most happy effect. That policy, as you are aware, involved certain and speedy punishment for past offenses, compelling them to sue for a suspension of hostilities, and on the resumption of peace, kindness and leniency toward the redskins. They fully understand that honesty and peace constitute their best and

safest policy" (Patrick Edward Connor to Richard C. Drum, July 1, 1864, in *WOTR* 1.2, 887). Yet by February 1865, General Connor was again reporting that Indians "have again returned in increased force. The troops are insufficient to contend with them" (Patrick Edward Connor to Richard C. Drum, February 10, 1865, in *WOTR* 1.2, 1131).

64. George Wright to L. Thomas, March 30, 1863, in *WOTR* 1.2, 369.

65. George Wright to Adjutant General U.S. Army, July 31, 1863, in *WOTR* 1.2, 546.

66. Richard C. Drum to Patrick Edward Connor, July 31, 1863, in *WOTR* 1.2, 547–48.

67. Richard C. Drum to Patrick Edward Connor, August 19, 1863, in *WOTR* 1.2, 581.

68. James Duane Doty to George Wright, August 9, 1863, in *WOTR* 1.2, 584.

69. "The Mormon Question—Its Easy and Peaceful Solution," *New York Times*, November 28, 1865, 4.

70. "Death and Funeral of General P. E. Connor," *Deseret News*, December 26, 1891.

Reunion of the Saints, *by C. C. A. Christensen. (Courtesy of Daughters of Utah Pioneers.)*

Chapter 11

The Arrival of Nineteenth-Century Mormon Emigrants in Salt Lake City

Fred E. Woods

A number of articles, books, and lengthy essays have been written during the past century and a half on Mormon immigration and emigration by land and sea.[1] However, in nearly every instance, the reader is left to wonder what happened once the Latter-day Saint converts reached their destination in the West. Before steam vessels replaced sailing ships as the most popular passenger carriers, European Mormon converts were propelled by wind across the Atlantic and then traversed the plains by wagon, on foot, or by handcart. During the trail years (1847–68), it took several months to reach the Salt Lake Valley. Often, European converts who left early in the year did not complete their journey until fall. The average time to reach the East Coast from Liverpool was estimated at thirty-eight days, and the journey from Liverpool to New Orleans typically took fifty-four days.[2]

Fred E. Woods is a professor of Church history and doctrine at Brigham Young University.

Yet regardless of the time it took to reach Utah by sail, rail, or trail, the moment these emigrant converts reached Salt Lake City appears to have been the high point for most of them, the culmination of their journey.[3] Having left the boundaries of Babylon and now reached the borders of Zion, these foreign converts frequently felt a flood of emotions caused by the impact of arrival and the challenge of assimilation. Although assisted in most instances by trustworthy missionaries returning home from their fields of labor, the new arrivals were still on the threshold of a new life in an unfamiliar territory. What were their thoughts when they entered the city of the Saints? What did they experience when the journey came to an end? Where exactly did that journey end, and how did it change during the latter decades of the nineteenth century? Who met the emigrants at those junctures? What did the Church do to aid assimilation? Did the process change during the peak period of Mormon emigration during the trail years (1847–68) and rail years (1868–90)? This study explores these questions and offers an overview of what most Latter-day Saint converts likely experienced upon arrival in the Salt Lake Valley in the latter half of the nineteenth century.

Arrival at the Old Fort (1847–49)

During the first two years of arrival in the valley, many early Mormon sojourners made contact with the Old Mormon Fort, and a number of them also found lodging in or near there.[4] One major reason this fort had been built was to protect the early pioneers from Native Americans in this desolate region. One week after Brigham Young arrived in the Salt Lake Valley, vanguard camp historian William Clayton noted that Elder Heber C. Kimball proposed that a corral (or fort) be erected and "that the houses form a stockade or fort to keep out the Indians that our women and children be not abused, and that we let Ute Indians alone."[5]

Less than a week later, the Quorum of the Twelve Apostles issued an epistle which noted, "We are also laboring unitedly to build a stockade of houses around a ten acre block. This also will be a greater blessing to others." Further, "We are engaged in other improvements here in like manner, but when we come here with our families and the inhabitants begin to spread abroad in the city, we expect that every family will have a lot on which they may build, plant and also farm, as much land as they can till, and every man may be a steward over his own."[6]

Several accounts provide a glimpse of the life of the pioneers as they arrived in the Great Basin from 1847 to 1848, experienced immediate blessings, and soon thereafter prospered. For example, J. C. Ensign recalled, "I drove the first Ox team into the valley under the direction of Daniel Spencer landing on the grounds of old Fort square. September 23rd. 1847."[7] Apparently Ensign, starting his Salt Lake sojourn with very humble beginnings, reached out to others who found themselves in the same situation or worse. His situation a year later is discernible from the account of Rachel Emma Woolley Simmons: "We went to Brother Ensign's who kindly offered us the hospitality of their one room until we could do better."[8] Other early pioneers, not so fortunate on arriving in the Valley, found themselves in a position where rental payment was needed. Ann Cannon Woodbury wrote, "Uncle Taylor rented a room of the old fort from some of the Mormon Battalion boys who got to the valley ahead of some of the pioneers. They build some houses in the pioneer fort and rented them to some of the folks that came later. We got into the fort on October 6, 1847."[9]

When Daniel Davis entered the Salt Lake Valley the following year, he noted, "Went down towards the fort or temple Block & as We drew near the Saints came out to meet us with cheers[.] Bro Brigham Met us to bade Welcome[,] also Parley P Pratt & Bro Jediah [Jedediah] M. Grant."[10] Aroet Lucious Hale remembered that as he came into the Valley the same year, "We camped around the Old Fort that the Poyneers [pioneers] of 47 built." Further, "In the fawl [fall] of 48 all the Saints had liberty to Scatter out . . . and Settle on their City Lots."[11]

Arrivals at Union Square (1850s)

Journals during the 1850s frequently mention arrivals at Union Square, or Public Square,[12] as it was called. William Goforth Nelson wrote, "We reached Salt Lake City, Sept. 9, 1850, and camped on the public square for two days."[13] Peter McIntyre recalled, "We arrived in Salt Lake City on Sept. 22nd 1853 and camped on the Public Square."[14] One distinctive group who entered Union Square during this decade was the Abraham O. Smoot company, arriving in early September 1852. Isaac Brockbank remembered, "On first taking a view of the city, our hearts were filled with gratitude to God that we had been enable[d] to complete our journey. . . . This being the first company that had arrived direct from Europe under the auspices of the Perpetual Emigration Fund Co., considerable interest was taken by the Saints of the City in visiting the company on their arrival on Union Square. Pres. Brigham Young, Heber C. Kimball, and others of the leading authorities of the Church visited and counseled the new arrival[s]."[15]

William Woodward recalled his experience of receiving help and guidance from a new acquaintance he met shortly after his arrival in September 1851: "How beautiful Salt Lake City appeared after crossing the plains. Here we met acquaintances and were greeted with kindness. I was now looking for something to do. After my arrival in the city I met an acquaintance on Main Street, who asked what I was thinking of doing." This person said, "'Come across the street and see our Bishop.' This was N. [Nathaniel] V. Jones, of the Fifteenth Ward. He introduced me to Brother Jones and told my business. Said Brother Jones, 'My brother-in-law, Robert Burton, wants a hand.' This brother took me to Brother Burton's and I engaged to work for him, and went there the next day."[16]

Two years later, Ann Gregory Wilkey would give birth to a little girl shortly before reaching the Salt Lake Valley. Although Ann was tired, hungry, and exhausted, teams and provisions sent from the valley enabled her and her company to successfully reach their destination. Ann wrote, "We were then placed on the public square in Salt

Lake City, with no shelter, but the blue sky above us and the ground beneath[,] no home and nothing to eat and in October. My baby was then ten days old. I was very sick and tired and very weak having had not much food and being sick . . . but dear friends came. Bro. and Sis. Theabald took us to their home. They had been in Utah two years. We remained with them a few weeks."[17]

During this same year, Joseph W. Young led a company into the valley. Hugh Pugh, who served as the company clerk, is an example of what must have taken place many times as various companies were dismissed from Union Square. Pugh notes that the company had arrived there at 5:00 p.m., October 10, 1854:

> Tuesday Oct. 11. This morning the company was aroused by Trumpet Sound at 6 o'clock to prepare for dismissing[.] About 9 A.M. a meeting was called when president J. W. Young spoke well to the saints enjoining upon them faithfulness, diligence &c[.] they were also addressed by President Brigham Young with power and the manifestation of the Holy Ghost, teaching the saints that which was essential for their future destiny, also welcoming them to this delightful vale. By request of the company's Prest. [president] he then broke up the organization, blessed the people in the name of the Lord Jesus and retired. Good counsel was afterwards given by Elders J. C. Haight, Wallace and Lorenzo D. Young.[18]

Ann Lewis Clegg, who reached the Salt Lake Valley in 1854, recalled her memorable entrance into the city of the Saints and expressed gratitude for the splendid reception she and her company received at the time of arrival:

> We came through Emmigration Canyon through the valley and on to the public square, where we camped with hundreds of others for a few weeks until we could get located. How little

Salt Lake City seemed to us. The square was full of people to welcome us in. Brigham Young was there first and gave us a hearty welcome. . . . Some were expecting their loved ones in the company and I tell you it was a grand reunion, a time of rejoicing together. I was glad our journey was ended, but I was very lonesome for awhile. We had been 3 months on the road and arrived in Salt Lake Sept. 30, 1854, just in time to attend the great October conference.[19]

Though it was not uncommon for family and friends to meet the incoming emigrants, some who had no one to meet them felt lonely. Watkin Rees and his wife were one such couple who also entered the Valley in 1854 at conference time. "Here on the Public Square many of the emigrants ware met by friends[;] others had places to go to and it was not long befor[e] the whole camp was disposed of[.] it happened that I and the wife and baby was left till last and we felt somewhat Lonesome without money without friend and all gone but us it looked blue."[20]

John Crook, who journeyed by wagon in the Philemon C. Merrill company (1856), recalled his initial impressions of the Salt Lake Valley: "There was the scene before us that we had long looked for, and read and sung about, the city of the Saints. Oh what a joy filled each bosom at the sight. About noon the 15th of August we rolled into Salt Lake City and went into camp on Emigration square."[21]

During most of the handcart years (1856–59), Union Square continued to be used as the arrival point, and Church leaders continued to welcome some of the arriving emigrants. Wilford Woodruff wrote that he was particularly impressed with the behavior of the leader of the first handcart company, Edmund Ellsworth, as Ellsworth returned to Salt Lake from a mission to England with his cart in hand on September 26, 1856. According to Woodruff, "Brother Ellsworth . . . passed by his lovely home and saw his wives and children standing in his door, he made no halt, only gave a passing salute, continuing with his company until he reached the public square and saw them all comfortably encamped and fed." Woodruff further recalled, "I felt that his position was far more honorable and lovely in the eyes of God and Angels and good men, than it would have been, had he been mounted upon the best steed that ever trod the earth, clothed with ermine and gold."[22]

Mary B. Crandal, who arrived the same day as Ellsworth but in the Daniel D. McArthur handcart company, recalled, "Bands came out to meet us, and the First Presidency came. What a beautiful sight met our eyes after our long journey. . . . What cheering and shouting as we came. . . . The streets were thronged with men, women and children. . . . When we got to the Public Square there were plenty of victuals cooked up for the two companies. We were the second company and Brother Edmund Ellsworth's was the first; but we came into the Valley at the same time."[23] Such assistance is further evident in individual ways, as attested by Robert McQuarrie, who came into view of the Salt Lake Valley in the early fall of 1857 and recorded the following entry in his journal on September 12: "Robert Baxter met us on the top of the little mountain, we went into Salt Lake City and camped on the public square at 2 O'clock. bro Baxter took us (my fathers family) to his house and kindly entertained us for one week. during which time I went to Ogden and bought a farm of R.G. Golding for $1000.00."[24]

Arrivals at Eighth Ward Square (1859–65)

Commencing in 1859, during the latter part of the handcart era, it appears the emigrants first gathered and camped on what is referred to as the Eighth Ward Square, Washington Square, and Emigration/Immigration Square.[25] Ellen Wasden, then age ten, remembered, "When we came into Salt Lake City, it was a small 'city' then, we camped on 8th Ward Square, where the City and County Building now is. We drew our wagons into a circle and the Saints hailed our coming by the band playing, 'Home, Sweet Home.' . . . I shall never forget how my tired and weary body and soul responded to that song. We had reached our goal, worn and hungry, with nothing but the strength of a mighty purpose to support us. There were no comrades we had known before and the solemn primal curse, 'Earn thy bread by the sweat of thy brow,' was upon us."[26]

Robert Bodily wrote concerning his arrival, "[We] finally arrived on the 5th day of Oct. 1860. We camped on the lot where now stands the City & County Building S L City. The next day we went to Conference and heard that great man President Brigham Young and other good men whom we had never heard before. . . . After Conference my father bought a place in the 6th Ward."[27]

In subsequent years, Mormon converts continued to record their arrival in the Salt Lake Valley. For example, in 1861, Eli Wiggill came to Zion from South Africa. In his autobiography, he recalled the following about his day of arrival in Salt Lake City: "Found an old acquaintance from Africa by the name of Charles Roper, who lived in the Seventh Ward. . . . Stay at his house untill our Company came into the City who came in the Next day and we campted on the Emigration Square."[28]

In 1862, Hannah Harrison crossed the plains with the James Wareham company and recalled, "After 13 long weeks on the plains we reached Salt Lake City, September 30, and camped for the night on what was then known as Immigration Square. This was then the camping ground of all immigrant trains."[29] Arriving the following year, Charles Henry John West remembered, "We were in all 10 weeks on the plains, when we arrived at Salt Lake City on the camping grounds of the 8th Ward Square. The friends and relations of different ones would come and take them away to their homes."[30]

Although new arrivals were often met by family and friends, many of the newcomers would also need assistance from Church leaders, and of course all appreciated the support of their fellow Church members, especially on the day of arrival in the city of the Saints. World traveler and celebrated writer Richard F. Burton, an eyewitness to one handcart company's arrival in 1860, described from a non-Mormon point of view the impressive Mormon manner for rendering support and immediate assistance to the joyful newcomers at the public square: "We saw the smoke-like column which announced the emigrants were crossing the bench-land; and people were scurrying from all sides to greet and get news of friends. Presently the carts came. . . . All the new arrivals were in clean clothes, the men washed and shaved, and the girls, who were singing hymns, habited in Sunday dresses. The company was sunburned, but looked well and thoroughly happy." In addition, Burton provided the observant detail that "when the train reached the public square . . . of the 8th ward, the wagons were in line for the final ceremony. . . . On this occasion the place of Mr. Brigham Young was taken by [Edward] Hunter, a Pennsylvanian, whom even the most fanatic and intentionally evil-speaking anti-Mormon must regard with respect. Preceded by a brass band." Finally, Burton observed, "In a short time arrangements were made to house and employ all who required work, whether men or women."[31]

A most impressive report was also published in the *Deseret Weekly News* in the late fall of 1864. A lengthy excerpt from this article, "Home Items," is provided below for its rich detail and keen observations concerning Mormon assimilation and arrival in downtown Salt Lake City:

The last of this season's emigration has arrived, mostly in good health and fine spirits. Cap. Wm. Hyde's train, which reached the Public Square on the afternoon of the 26th ult; was unusually well provided for by the donations of the people through their Bishops. Early on that day brother Jesse C. Little, one of Bishop Hunter's counselors, Bishop John Sharp, together with those appointed at the regular Bishop's meeting viz. Wm. A. McMaster, of the 11th Ward, Samuel Turnbow and Martin Lenzi of the 14th Ward, Father Booth of the 10th and brother Leach of the 2d Ward, got some tents from the General Tithing Store and put them upon the 8th Ward Square preparatory to the reception of the company.

Immediately on the arrival of the train, the brethren and sisters came forward with soup, beef, potatoes, pies, sugar and coffee, to supply the wants of those who had just come in from their long and tedious journey across the plains. The above named brethren saw to the plentiful distribution of the food among the passengers. They also provided for the sick, and had them made comparatively comfortable in the 8th Ward School House. Sister Sluce was on hand to wait upon the sisters, several of whom were in a delicate state of health.

Dr. Hovey was called in to give medical advice and to administer such remedial agents as could best be applied; and, from the arrival of the train to the time that all found places to go to, the best that could be done was done, to alleviate suffering, to comfort, to bless and render happy the poor of God's chosen people, and in this none seemed remiss in their duty to God and their brethren and sisters.

It has always been customary for the Saints to assist the incoming emigration, but this season has seemed to call for an extra and additional effort, because of the lateness of the season before the last two companies got in. This call for assistance, therefore, was made upon every Ward in the city, and, to their praise be it spoken, every Ward, and almost every family freely responded to the Bishops' call. . . . We think great credit is due to Bishop Hunter and his assistants for the promptness and energy with which they have carried out the wishes of our President in providing food and homes for these large companies of Saints. This is

Donations were provided through bishops such as Bishop Edward Hunter. (Courtesy of Church History Library.)

the way the Latter-day Saints treat their poor brethren when they come here from distant nations, ignorant of our manners and customs, ignorant of our mode of procuring the necessities of life, and many of them ignorant of the language we speak. Can this be the result of fanaticism? or is it the fruit of that pure and undefiled religion of which the apostle speaks? We ask, can the Christian world show its equal? Our religion teaches this maxim, "By their fruits ye shall know them."[32]

Tithing Yard (1866 to the End of the Nineteenth Century)

By 1866, there is evidence that incoming emigrants were being temporarily housed at the Tithing Yard (located at the northeast corner of South Temple and Main Street), where the Joseph Smith Memorial Building now stands. A *Deseret News* article titled "Commendable" announced, "There is a very comfortable structure erected in the yard of the General Tithing Store, for the incoming immigrants, with other accommodations for their use. Bishop [Edward] Hunter and Counsel have been energetically preparing for their comfort. Bishop J. [Jesse] C. Little aiding, counseling, directing and laboring with his accustomed zeal."[33] Yet, when Hans J. Zobell arrived three years later, it appears there was not enough room in this structure, and evidently the hospitality he longed for in the city of the Saints was also absent. Notwithstanding, he found inner contentment, as surmised from this penetrating account:

> We therefore arrived in Salt Lake City on August 11, 1869 and were dumped out in the tithing yard, and made our bed on the ground with high heaven for roof. So this was Zion. We all felt to praise our God for our safe delivery but it seemed that it was Zion in name only, because there were none to welcome or give us a brotherly handshake; no one paid the least bit of attention to us.

We soon found out that we were to be more or less upon our own resources and the familiar words of the song came to me when I was pondering over these things, namely: "Think not when to Zion you arrive that your troubles are over" and so on. I realized at once that my troubles had come to an end—the first end, because I had left a goodly home, with a roof over it to shelter me, a nice soft bed to rest myself, and plenty of food to eat; and here I am in Zion, with no home, no bed, and no food. But still I was happy and my very soul went up in praise to my Heavenly Father because I stood here in Zion, under the stars, with empty hands, a mother, two sisters and a betrothed sweetheart to look after, in a strange land, strange people and customs, and no work of the kind that I was trained in. And still I knew within my heart that I had obeyed the voice of the one who had said: "Get ye up out of Babylon and get ye to the tops of the mountains, where you can walk in my paths and keep all of my statutes," so I felt an assurance that if God had given me the call to come here, he would not leave me here to starve, and to be without shelter. So I was satisfied with my lot.[34]

Just three months earlier, the transcontinental railroad had been completed, which meant the entire journey across America would be by rail instead of trail, and thousands would pour into Utah at a much faster pace. However, several accounts indicate that a number of incoming Saints got off the train at various locations before reaching the Salt Lake Valley. By the 1880s, the Salt Lake Valley was filling up with Saints, and thus a number of converts had dispersed to expand the periphery of Zion's core. For example, in 1882, William George Davis wrote, "We arrived at Evanston in the afternoon and at Echo about dusk. Several of our company left us at these places, they having friends who met them and took them to their homes." He later noted, "We arrived in Ogden about midnight. . . . Many of the Saints left us at Ogden and went with friends who came to meet them. . . . We

A nineteenth-century photograph of the Deseret Store and Tithing Office. (Courtesy of Church History Library.)

arrived in Salt Lake City about noon and found the depot crowded with friends and old acquaintances."[35]

Arriving at the edge of Utah's border in the fall of 1885, Samuel R. Bennion recorded, "Quite a number got off at Evanston."[36] Anthon H. Lund, who presided over this same company, observed, "At Evanston 14 emigrants left our train." Another Scandinavian convert wanted to be dropped off soon thereafter, as "he did not like to be oxen." Still another was asked to leave the train at Uintah.[37]

During the late nineteenth century, improved facilities in Salt Lake City were provided for these newcomers, who generally traveled on the transcontinental railroad; on the other hand, a number of companies that passed through New York to Norfolk, Virginia, journeyed on the Denver and Rio Grande Railroad, heading to Salt Lake City from the South.[38] In the spring of 1873, the *Millennial Star* issued an article titled "For Emigrants," which announced the following: "A new and substantial building is in course of erection in the Tithing Office yard [Salt Lake City], which is to be used for the accommodation of emigrants arriving here without any home to go to, until they are in a position to provide for themselves. The building will be 43 by 20 feet, two storeys high, and will have a porch on the south side."[39]

Just a few months later, Jens A. Weibye, on his arrival in Salt Lake City in late September, wrote, "The Saints scattered to different places. Some of us to the Emigrant House in the Tithing Yard."[40] About this same time, William Kilshaw Barton recalled, "The Saints who had no relatives or particular friends, went [to] the Tithing yard where they stayed until homes were provided for them in Salt Lake City or in the other towns south."[41] One company had no one there to meet them when they arrived one fall night in 1880 because news had gone forth that the train would arrive the following morning. James Samuel Page Bowler explained, "We passed the night in the tithing house as best we could, but even that was better than thousands of others who came to this country in early days."[42]

The Tithing Yard was not just a place of dispersion and a dwelling where incoming converts temporarily lodged at the Emigrant House. The yard was also a place for instruction, and such timely tutorials proved invaluable, especially to those vulnerable foreign converts who did not speak any English. In 1874, company leader Peter C. Carstenson reported, "A meeting was held in the tithing yard, in the afternoon, when Brother [Erastus] Snow gave many good counsels and instructions to the newly arrived Saints, and spoke in the Danish language. After meeting was closed the company separated, the Saints going with their relations and friends to their homes."[43]

During the following decade, immigrant accounts reveal that the incoming Saints continued to gather to and disperse from the Tithing Yard. For example, James H. Hansen, who reached Salt Lake City in 1882, wrote, "A great many people was at the station to meet their friends and teams came to take all the emigrants up to the Tithing Yard where some provisions were brought for them."[44] The following

Image shows the Salt Lake City tithing office and yards. It was located on the corner of Main Street and South Temple where the Joseph Smith Memorial Building is now. In the early years of the Church, members would rarely pay their tithing with money. More often, it was paid in livestock, dry goods, or a portion of their crop. This was all stored at the tithing office yards and distributed through the Deseret Store. (Used by permission, Utah State Historical Society. All rights reserved.)

year, Andrew Christian Nielson arrived and later recalled, "Got to Salt Lake City, stopped in the Tithing Yard, and emigrants scattered."[45] The front page of the *Deseret Evening News* for November 12, 1883, carried the headline "Immigrants Arrived." The editor then explained, "Those who came down to the city were met, as usual, by their immediate friends and relatives, conveyed by the teams provided by the Bishops to the Immigrant House in the Tithing Yard."[46]

Additional articles from the *Millennial Star* provide evidence that the Tithing Yard was used to temporarily house the incoming converts throughout the 1880s. For example, in 1885, C. J. Arthur explained in the *Star*, "Most of the company have left, a few only remain, and they will soon find some friends who will provide them labor and a home for the time being. At present they remain in the Emigrants' Home, in the Tithing Yard."[47] The following year, Edwin T. Wooley reported, "Our company went forward to their various destinations without delay, and by nine o'clock of the morning following our arrival in Salt Lake City but very few were left at the emigrant quarters in the Tithing Yard."[48] That same year, C. F. Olsen recounted the dispersive activity when his company arrived in Ogden in mid-July: "Those going north remained in Ogden over night, and those bound for Salt Lake City and the south proceeded to the city the same evening, where many received a hearty welcome and warm greeting from their friends and relatives, while those who were going still further were made comfortable at the Tithing Yard."[49]

In 1889, another *Star* article appeared in which John William Craven also wrote of his company's safe arrival: "We went to the Tithing Office, and were very soon enjoying the good things which are temporarily provided free of expense to all members of the Church. Before going on to our destination we stayed one week, visiting former friends whom we knew in England."[50]

Temporary Lodging in the City of the Saints

Immigrants arriving in the late nineteenth century not only visited friends but on many occasions stayed with fellow Saints until they could be permanently situated. Charlotte Ann Bates, who entered Salt Lake City in the summer of 1871, vividly remembered, "We arrived in Salt Lake City about the 20th of July. It was in the evening after dark. I remember passing on South Temple and looking down Main Street. They had boardwalks and a small ditch on each side of the street with water running down it. They had lamp posts with lamps lit up all the way down the street." Bates further recalled with gratitude that Milford Bardship, one of the missionaries, "took us to his home for a day or two until we could get located some place. The next day some friends of father's and mother's named Smith came to see us and said they had a house we could live in as long as we wanted it. There was a log room and a lumber room, so we moved in."[51]

Others were filled with a profound sense of thanksgiving as they entered the city of Zion and met its inhabitants. One who felt this way was Alma Ash, who arrived in Salt Lake City in 1885. As Ash reflected upon this sacred occasion, he remembered with great intensity:

> Never shall I forget how our hearts throbbed gratitude filled with emotion as we peered all around us to catch a glimpse of the place and the people as silently our little company trudged long South Temple Street towards the tithing yard where we expected to stay until morning. Oh, how reverently we regarded everything and everybody and so sacred did everything appear to us. . . . We wondered almost how people could be rude or light-minded in such a sanctified city. We gazed up at the temple . . . with the towers just commenced and silently in our hearts we resolved to begin a new life with new ambitions. . . . We spoke in a quiet manner, I may say in a whisper, for fear of appearing boisterous or in any manner unbecoming.[52]

While Ash's company was being kindly fed at the Tithing Yard, he received a message from a friend who had emigrated six years before and desired to take him to his home. Upon arriving at the home of his friend's parents, Ash was surprised to see the prosperity of the family as they comfortably conversed while reclining in their rocking chairs. On this occasion, Ash recalled, "We were received kindly and were soon answering questions about the folks in Birmingham [England] Branch. . . . They invited us to sleep outside and [we] readily consented. . . . This was the first time in my life that I had slept outside. Of course such a thing would hardly be possible in England except upon very rare occasions when a dry spell would occur in the summer time." Ash then concluded, "I confess that I enjoy the novelty of sleeping outside in the open air the first night in Zion. . . . My prayer was that I would or might be faithful to God and his people."[53]

Church Leaders Meet Rail Pioneering Saints and Assist with Assimilation

Like the Saints who crossed the plains by handcart or covered wagon, the Saints who journeyed by rail also enjoyed visiting with friends and were impressed with Church leaders who greeted them as they entered Utah. As noted, Apostle Erastus Snow met the Danish Saints and provided needful instructions in their native tongue to help ease them into assimilation, and visits from other Church leaders no doubt helped with the transition into Zion.

The month after the transcontinental railroad was finished, Thomas Meikle Forrest met President Young shortly after arriving at the railroad terminus in Ogden, Utah: "Saturday, June 26, 1869 . . . We had the privilege of seeing Brigham Young this morning at 4:30. He shook hands with all who were awake." Forrest also described Young as "a fine looking man, heavy and tall with gray whiskers."[54]

Just eight months after the transcontinental railroad was finished, the Utah Central Rail, which ran from Ogden down to Salt Lake City, was completed. Commencing in 1870, Church leaders met incoming converts on this route before the newcomers even reached Salt Lake. For example, John MacNeil wrote home to his family in Scotland, "When we were about half way to the City we had shunt to let a train past that came from the City. When they were passing they stopped and let out Brigham Young, George A. Smith & Daniel H. Wells. They stepped into our train and went right through shaking hands with everyone as they went along through the cars."[55] About six weeks later, another company of incoming Saints traveling by train was blessed to meet prominent Church leaders. Jesse N. Smith recalled this memorable event: "At Kaysville we were met by the First Presidency of the Church and some others. . . . The brethren passed through the cars shaking hands

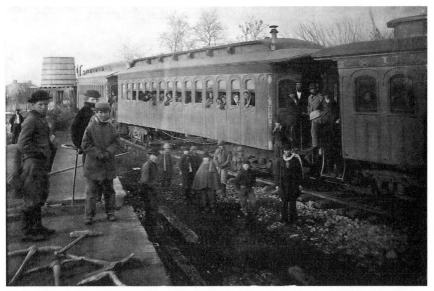

First train from Ogden at Salt Lake City Depot on January 10, 1870. (Courtesy of Church History Library.)

with the passengers. At Woods Cross we were met by Bishop [Edward] Hunter. . . . Our train was the largest that had ever come to the City there being in all eleven passenger and five baggage cars."[56]

George Goddard recalled meeting the Brethren once his party reached the City of the Saints: "We arrived in Ogden after dark, and remained in the cars until morning. . . . [In Salt Lake City] we found Presidents [John] Taylor and [George Q.] Cannon, and a host of warm hearts and cheerful faces, to welcome us as we met them in the street or visited them in their offices."[57]

Finding Zion from the Inside Out

The cost to get to the Salt Lake Valley and to settle was significant, especially for the Europeans, who bore the high expense of crossing the Atlantic before their journey across the plains. However, for most the cost was worth it, and Church leaders had established the Perpetual

221

Emigrating Fund, which provided temporary assistance to the poor. Yet all who partook of the aid knew that inasmuch as it was a revolving loan, they needed to repay their debts as soon as possible after reaching the Salt Lake Valley. The word *perpetual* served as a constant reminder that the Fund needed to be replenished for others. Although some were not able to repay their loans, most did so through a variety of employment opportunities, including labor on public work within the boundaries of Salt Lake City.[58] Others would have opportunities to launch immediately into various colonies. This was influenced in many cases by the skills of the immigrants and the needs of the colonies. For example, Silas Richards, writing from Union, Utah, to President Young in 1860, noted, "As the immigration will begin to arrive soon . . . I wish to employ a Tanner and currier, and a boot and shoemaker that are first-rate workmen. I also want a farmer with a small family that has not the necessary means to carry on the business himself." Richards further noted that "there are a number of small tracts of land on the creek for sale of good quality . . . also houses and lots in Union very low from one hundred to six hundred dollars. This would be a good location for a black Smith; common laborers can get employment."[59]

Notwithstanding, for many Europeans it was a trial to find employment to match their skills, as well as to know how best to live. Church leaders were keenly aware of such challenges, which continued over the remaining decades of the nineteenth century, but over time the Saints grew stronger as colonies were established and Zion extended her borders in several directions.

"Knowing how to live" seems to be symbolic of whether the Mormon converts who entered the Salt Lake Valley and vicinity ever really found Zion. Zion is defined in Latter-day scripture as both a spiritual state as well as a temporal or actual place where one dwells. Zion was not only places where the Saints gathered, such as Independence, Missouri (D&C 57:4); Nauvoo, Illinois; or the Salt Lake Valley, but it was also defined as the abode of "the pure in heart" (D&C 97:18)—people who "were of one heart and one mind, and dwelt in righteousness; . . . [with] no poor among them" (Moses 7:18).

Some immigrants discovered this concept of Zion, yet others did not. It was certainly to be perceived not only with the eyes, but also with the heart—something that was not just talked about but required implementation to be fully realized. Joseph Smith had warned incoming converts who gathered to Nauvoo, "They must not expect to find perfection, or that all will be harmony, peace, and love; if they indulge these ideas, they will undoubtedly be deceived."[60] There would be those who did not abide this counsel and thus never found the Zion they sought, while others found a promised land by making it so. This concept seems best captured in the experience of a fifteen-year-old Swiss convert named Frederick Zaugg, who asked a penetrating question as he entered the Salt Lake region in August 1885. When he came to the end of his long journey and climbed a hill to view Park Valley,[61] he "drew a long breath" and asked, "Is this Zion?" A wise man named Mr. Hirschi, there to greet and guide him, responded, "Yes, when you make it [so]." Zaugg later wrote, "These words left a deep impression in my mind. 'If you make it,' became my mot[t]o. Things we like to live in and enjoy, we have to make. If we want a friend, we must love him. If you want a favor of the Lord, we must serve him and keep his commandments and the blessings will come by going after them."[62]

Conclusion

As the Saints reached the Salt Lake Valley, they were often met immediately by Church leaders, family, and fellow members at various locations where immigrants congregated. Although the lodging was varied and improved as the decades rolled on, whether the Saints traveled by rail or trail, there was a steady flow of caring and accommodation that persisted throughout the latter half of the nineteenth century. Most immigrants assimilated quickly into the city and scattered communities where they found employment. For those who did not secure immediate housing with family or friends, there was always temporary shelter at the Emigrant House or in the Tithing Yard. Furthermore, although all Saints did not wear halos, evidence reveals that most appeared to be kind and hospitable to the newest arrivals. And those individuals who came seeking Zion may have discovered it faster by looking in a mirror rather than through a window at the unfinished City of the Saints.

Notes

1. For a list of publications from 1830 to the present on Mormon immigration and emigration, see the website http://www.lib.byu.edu/mormonmigration/ under Sources. This website is based on research the author has conducted on this topic for the past fifteen years. See especially Philip A. M. Taylor, *Expectations Westward: The Mormons and the Emigration of Their British Converts in the Nineteenth Century* (Edinburgh: Oliver & Boyd, 1965); William Mulder, *Homeward to Zion: The Mormon Migration from Scandinavia* (2000; repr., Minneapolis: University of Minnesota Press, 1957); and Wallace Stegner, *The Gathering of Zion: The Story of the Mormon Trail*, American Trails Series (New York: McGraw-Hill, 1964).

2. Conway B. Sonne, *Saints on the High Seas: A Maritime History of Mormon Migration, 1830–1890* (Salt Lake City: University of Utah Press, 1983), 69, 126. With steam power, ocean vessels could reach America in only eleven days, and the transcontinental railroad made it possible to go from coast to coast in about a week and a half instead of six months.

3. For additional sources treating Salt Lake City in the nineteenth century, see Edward W. Tullidge, *The History of Salt Lake City and Its Founders* (Salt Lake City: Edward W. Tullidge, 1886); and Thomas G. Alexander, *Mormons and Gentiles: A History of Salt Lake City*, Western Urban History Series, vol. 5 (Boulder, CO: Pruett Publishing, 1984). For an outsider's view, see Sir Richard Francis Burton, *The City of the Saints, and Across the Rocky Mountains to California* (Niwot, CO: University Press of Colorado, 1990).

4. The Old Fort was located about three blocks west and three blocks south of modern Temple Square in what is now known as Pioneer Park.

5. "Diary of William Clayton," August 1, 1847, Church History Library, The Church of Jesus Christ of Latter-day Saints, Salt Lake City. See also "Letter of Thomas Bullock," written from the "Camp of Israel, Winter Quarters, Council Bluffs, January 4, 1848," *Millennial Star*, April 15, 1848, 118.

6. Cited in Nicholas Groesbeck Morgan Sr., "The Old Fort: Great Salt Lake City, Great Basin, North America: As Constructed by the Pioneers upon Their Arrival in the Salt Lake Valley in 1847," 1950, cartographic material, 14, Special Collections and Archives, Utah State University, Logan, UT.

7. Reminiscences of J. C. Ensign, in Utah Semi-Centennial Commission, "The Book of the Pioneers" (unpublished manuscript, ca. 1897). Most accounts used in this article for the crossing the plains period (1847–68) were first identified from this online resource: http://www.lds.org/churchhistory/library/ pioneercompanysearch/1,15773,3966-1,00.html. It was created by LDS Church senior librarian Melvin S. Bashore and is hosted by the Church History Library. However, most of these accounts were also checked against the originals to ensure accuracy.

8. "Brief Biography of Rachel Emma Woolley Simmons," Pioneer History Collection, 11–14, Pioneer Memorial Museum, Salt Lake City.

9. "Autobiography of Ann Cannon Woodbury," in *Cannon Family Historical Treasury*, ed. Beatrice Cannon Evans and Janath Russell Cannon (Salt Lake City: George Cannon Family Association, 1967), 167–69.

10. "Diary of Daniel Davis," September 24, 1848, 101, Church History Library.

11. "Diary of Aroet Lucious Hale," 17–18, typescript, Church History Library. Archivist and Salt Lake City historian W. Randall Dixon noted that the Old Utah Fort was the primary gathering place for the arrival of the Mormon pioneers in the late 1840s and that some Saints continued to settle there until it was torn down in 1851. Dixon also explained that during the 1850s the next arrival place for the incoming emigrants was Union Square, also known as the Public Square and referred to as the Sixteenth Ward. Phone conversation with W. Randall Dixon, March 12, 2010.

12. Dixon also noted that the Old Fort in Salt Lake City once stood at what is now known as Pioneer Park, between Third and Fourth West and Third and Fourth South. He further explained that Union Square was also located near downtown Salt Lake City where West High School now stands, between Third and Fourth

West and between Third and Fourth North. The author thanks Dixon, senior archivist at the Church History Library, for his assistance with this article. Randy is recognized for his expert knowledge of early Salt Lake City. Phone conversation with W. Randall Dixon, March 12, 2010.

13. "Reminiscences of William Goforth Nelson," in Journal History of The Church of Jesus Christ of Latter-day Saints, Church History Library, September 9, 1850, 7.

14. "Autobiography of Peter McIntyre," ca. 1850–1854, 40, typescript, Church History Library.

15. "Autobiography of Isaac Brockbank," in Stephen W. Brockbank, "Isaac Brockbank, Jr., 1837–1927: Autobiography" (unpublished manuscript, 1997), 9–15, Family History Library, Salt Lake City. Leonard J. Arrington, *Great Basin Kingdom: An Economic History of the Latter-day Saints 1830–1890* (Cambridge, MA: Harvard University Press, 1958), 64, explained that the Perpetual Emigrating Company, also known as the Perpetual Emigrating Fund or PEF, was launched in Salt Lake City in 1849, following an economic windfall from the California gold rush, which brought tens of thousands of overlanders through the Mormon mecca. John D. Unruh Jr., *The Plains Across: The Overland Emigrants and the Trans-Mississippi West, 1840–1860* (Chicago: University of Illinois Press, 1993), 253, maintains that "at least 10,000 forty-niners detoured via the Mormon oasis." The PEF assisted nearly one-third of the European Mormon converts who gathered to the Salt Lake Valley during this period. See Fred E. Woods, "Perpetual Emigrating Fund," in *Encyclopedia of Latter-day Saint History*, ed. Arnold K. Garr, Donald Q. Cannon, and Richard O. Cowan (Salt Lake City: Deseret Book, 2000), 910. Arrington, *Great Basin Kingdom*, 98–99, also explained that there were three types of immigrants who came to Zion in the nineteenth century. One group was the PEF, who were the poor that needed their entire way paid. Another group was known as "ten-pound companies," who paid a portion of their own transportation. A third group, known as "cash companies," paid all of their own costs to Utah.

16. William Woodward, "In Early Days," *Juvenile Instructor*, July 15, 1896, 415.

17. "Autobiography of Ann Gregory Wilkey," 2, Church History Library.

18. "Joseph W. Young Emigrating Company, Journal," October 10–11, 1853, Church History Library.

19. "Autobiographical Sketch of Ann Lewis Clegg," ca. 1911, 2–3, Church History Library.

20. "Reminiscences of Watkin Rees," 8–12, in Watkin Rees, "Papers," ca. 1880–1905, Church History Library.

21. "[Autobiography] of John Crook," in "Utah Pioneer Biographies," 7:252–56, Family History Library.

22. Wilford Woodruff, "Correspondence from Utah," *Mormon*, November 15, 1856, 3.

23. Mary B. Crandal, "Autobiography of a Noble Woman," *Young Woman's Journal*, June 1895, 427.

24. "Journal of Robert McQuarrie," September 12, 1857, Church History Library.

25. The Eighth Ward Square is located in downtown Salt Lake City. "It is bounded by 4th and 5th South and State [1st East] and 2nd East Streets." E-mail from W. Randall Dixon to the author, January 14, 2011.

26. "[Autobiography] of Ellen Wasden," in "Two Pioneer Stories," 2–5, Church History Library.

27. "Journal of Robert Bodily," typescript, 11, Church History Library.

28. "Autobiography of Eli Wiggill," 484–85, Church History Library.

29. "[Autobiographical sketch] of Hannah Harrison Snow," in Archibald F. Bennett, Ella M. Bennett, and Barbara Bennett Roach, *Valiant in the Faith: Gardner and Sarah Snow and Their Family* (Murray, UT: Roylance Publishing, 1990), 316.

30. "Reminiscences of Charles Henry John West," 7, Church History Library.

31. Richard F. Burton, *The City of the Saints, and Across the Rocky Mountains to California*, ed. Fawn M. Brodie (New York: Knopf, 1963), 249–50.

32. "Home Items," *Deseret Weekly News*, November 9, 1864, 44.

33. "Commendable," *Deseret News*, August 30, 1866, 309.

34. "Reminiscences of Hans J. Zobell," 73, translated from Danish by Albert L. Zobell, copy in possession of Elgarda Zobell Ashliman, Rexburg, Idaho. It is not known why Zobell experienced this lack of hospitality. However, it is possible that there was an abundance of incoming emigrants, which affected the normal care given in such transitional circumstances. There is also evidence that during the trail years of the mid-nineteenth century, members of a few Mormon companies reported that there was no one to greet them upon their arrival in Salt Lake City or simply did not mention any reception upon entrance into the Valley. See, for example, the "Mormon Pioneer Overland Trail, 1847–1868" website (http://lds.org/churchhistory/library/pioneercompany), which notes several such references,

including the following culled from companies who arrived in the early fall of 1850: Tamma D. M. Curtis, who traveled in the Benjamin Hawkins company of 1850, recalled, "The first of September we landed in Salt Lake City without any home or anyone to hunt us one, we were very lonesome indeed." About this same time, the David Evans company arrived in the Salt Lake Valley. Abram Hatch, a member of the company, remembered, "On September 15th, 1850 we entered the Salt Lake Valley. . . . The company disbanded and our three wagons passed on to the banks of the Jordan River." The Warren Foote Emigrating Company recorded, "The first Fifty passed through Salt Lake City in the afternoon of the 26th of Sept [1850] and camped on the Jordan bottom west of the City. Many of the brethren were anxious to get counsel, where they had better locate." Whether arriving by trail or rail, these accounts noted above seem to be the exception to the rule of incoming emigrants being generally welcomed by family, friends, or Church leaders.

35. "Diary of William George Davis," June 3–4, 1882, 48–49, Church History Library. Don Strack, "Railroads in Utah," in *Utah History Encyclopedia*, ed. Allan Kent Powell (Salt Lake City: University of Utah Press, 1994), 451, notes, "The growth of a network of railroads in Utah began with the completion of the Utah Central between Ogden and Salt Lake City in January 1870." Thus Davis and those traveling with him would have taken the Utah Central to Salt Lake City in 1882.

36. "Diary of Samuel R. Bennion," November 9, 1885, Church History Library.

37. "Diary of Anthon H. Lund," November 10, 1885, Church History Library. Although Lund recorded the date as November 10 and Bennion noted it as November 9, both also recorded that Tuesday was the day of arrival.

38. High cost of rail travel in 1887 led to route changes. Instead of departing from New York City, incoming immigrants now commenced their rail travel from Norfolk. See Fred E. Woods, "Norfolk and the Mormon Folk: Latter-day Saint Immigration through Old Dominion (1887–1890)," *Mormon Historical Studies* 1, no. 1 (Spring 2000): 72–92.

39. "For Emigrants," *Latter-day Saints' Millennial Star*, April 8, 1873, 221.

40. "Reminiscences and Journals of Jens C. A. Weibye," September 29, 1873, Church History Library.

41. "Diary and Missionary Journal of William Kilshaw Barton, Pioneer of 1852," November, 1873, 33, privately printed, Church History Library.

42. "Autobiography of James Samuel Page Bowler," 41, Church History Library.

43. P. [Peter] C. Carstenson to Joseph F. Smith, July 23, 1874, *Millennial Star*, August 25, 1874, 538–39. Erastus Snow was the Apostle who opened up LDS missionary work to Scandinavia in 1850, and therefore he was beloved by the Danish Saints.

44. "Daybook of James H. Hansen," July 10, 1882, 29–30, Church History Library.

45. Andrew Christian Nielson, "[Autobiography]," *Our Pioneer Heritage*, comp. Kate B. Carter (Salt Lake City: Daughters of Utah Pioneers, 1968), 11:300–301.

46. "Immigrants Arrived," *Deseret News*, November 12, 1883.

47. Letter of C. J. Arthur dated November 12, 1885, "The Last Company," *Millennial Star*, December 7, 1885, 778.

48. E. [Edwin] T. Woolley, letter, May 22, 1886, "Home in Zion—Incidents of Travel—Labors and Experience," *Millennial Star*, June 21, 1886, 398–99.

49. C. F. Olsen, letter, July 20, 1886, "Correspondence," *Millennial Star*, August 16, 1886, 524.

50. John William Craven, "Correspondence," *Millennial Star*, May 20, 1889, 310.

51. "The Life of Charlotte Ann Bates," 3, Church History Library.

52. "Autobiography of Alma Ash," 30–31, Church History Library.

53. "Autobiography of Alma Ash," 30–31, Church History Library.

54. "Diary of Thomas Meikle Forrest," 6, submitted to author by Keith Forrest.

55. John MacNeil to David and Ann MacNeil, September 27, 1870, in Frederick S. Buchannan, ed., *A Good Time Coming: Mormon Letters to Scotland* (Salt Lake City: University of Utah Press, 1988), 100.

56. "Autobiography and Journal of Jesse N. Smith," August 10, 1870, 262, Church History Library.

57. Elder George Goddard, "Incidents of Travel," *Millennial Star*, December 15, 1884, 798.

58. See Arrington, *Great Basin Kingdom*, 108–12, on public works in Salt Lake City.

59. Silas Richards to Brigham Young, August 11, 1860, Correspondence of Brigham Young, Church History Library.

60. Joseph Smith, Sidney Rigdon, and Hyrum Smith, "A Proclamation to the Saints Scattered Abroad," *Millennial Star*, March 1841, 274.

61. Park Valley is located about seventy-five miles west of Brigham City, near Promontory Point, where the transcontinental railroad was joined together.

62. Frederick Zaugg, "[Autobiography] of Frederick Zaugg," 33; copy in author's possession.

A front view of the Church Administration Building. (© Intellectual Reserve, Inc.)

Chapter 12

A House for the Presidency: The History of the Church Administration Building

Matthew O. Richardson

The completion of the Church Administration building in 1917, located at 47 East South Temple in Salt Lake City, was the culmination of plans and hopes dating almost from the foundation of the Church. As early as 1833, the Church was commanded by revelation to erect such a building. However, a variety of circumstances, including persecution, movement of Church headquarters, and financial difficulties, precluded the fulfilling of the commandments. Now, however, the building stands as monument not only to those who finally accomplished its erection but also to much of what the Church itself stands for.

In August 1833, the Lord revealed to Joseph Smith that a "house for the presidency" should be built on the first lot south of the temple in Kirtland, Ohio.[1] This house was intended to be a place for the First Presidency of the Church to do their work, which included

Matthew O. Richardson is a professor of Church history and doctrine at Brigham Young University.

"obtaining revelations" and ministering to "all things pertaining to the church and kingdom" (D&C 94:3). It was revealed that the building would include an upper and lower court, measuring fifty-five feet in width by sixty-five feet in length. This would have been a structure of considerable size, matching the measurements proposed for the Kirtland Temple (see D&C 95:15).[2] The Lord also instructed that this house for the presidency would be "dedicated unto the Lord for the work of the presidency" (D&C 94:7). Like any other dedicated building, care should be taken to keep the building clean both temporally and spiritually so it could accommodate the Lord's presence (see D&C 94:8–9).

Unfortunately, the Kirtland Temple consumed the funds of the Saints, making it difficult to begin construction on a house for the presidency. On October 10, 1833, however, Church leaders decided to build a single building that would accommodate a printing press and a space for the School of the Prophets.[3] That building was completed in November 1834 and the presidency held meetings there.[4] This model of having a building for multiple uses set the standard for the next several decades. The First Presidency used locations such as the Kirtland Temple, schoolhouses, Joseph's home, and the Red Brick Store in Nauvoo for their administration meetings. Even after the Saints arrived in the Salt Lake Valley, the affairs of President Brigham Young and his presidency were transacted mostly in his residence, known as the Beehive House. John Taylor and Wilford Woodruff used the Gardo House, located on South Temple just opposite the Beehive House, as their administrative offices and as a place for entertaining guests and dignitaries.[5] When Lorenzo Snow became President of the Church, he returned to the Beehive House for his administrative office, as did Joseph F. Smith. Other General Authorities and officers were housed in a variety of cramped, unsuitable quarters during this time.[6]

During John Taylor's administration, the Church considered building proposals that included new administrative office space. In 1884, the newly called Presiding Bishop, William B. Preston, formally commissioned Joseph Don Carlos Young, a local architect, to create a plan for Block 57 in Salt Lake City.[7] Joseph Don Carlos Young (born May 6, 1855, in Salt Lake City) was the son of Brigham Young and Emily Dow Partridge (daughter of Edward Partridge). Best known as Carl or identified by his initials J. D. C., he graduated from Rensselaer Polytechnic Institute in Troy, New York, in 1879 with degrees in architectural engineering.

The area known as Block 57, located just east of the Salt Lake Temple near the Lion House and Beehive House, was also referred to as the administration block. Young's ambitious plans incorporated a series of buildings that included administrative offices, meeting rooms, business space, and places for public gatherings that would stretch along Main Street and South Temple Street.[8] Paul Bradford Westwood, in his master's thesis on J. D. C. Young, described these early designs as "a proto-modern American corporate campus located on what was then considered the fringes of American civilization."[9] The scope of his plans was so large that it would have required razing both the Beehive and Lion Houses to make room for the new structures. The buildings resembled French chateaus with a flare of Romanesque Revival, a popular architectural design during the 1870s and 1880s.[10] Young estimated that it would cost fifty thousand dollars to build his administrative complex, a projection that was not only too low but also impractical because the Church was facing severe financial difficulties.[11] Even a bargain bid could not tempt Church leaders to go ahead with the proposal.[12] As a result, the plan to create a new administrative hub was forgotten.

Ideas for structural changes resurfaced during President Joseph F. Smith's administration and it appeared that the timing to build a house for the presidency was more favorable than in times past. It was during this time that the Church began to enjoy enough prosperity to support and even encourage large-scale building projects in Salt Lake City. For example, the Dr. W. Groves Latter-day Saints Hospital, a state-of-the-art facility, was completed in January 1905. Two years later, a new office building for the Presiding Bishopric and General Auxiliary Presidencies was announced, and other building projects on the administration block such as the Deseret Gymnasium and the Hotel Utah were also under way.[13] But even though financial means were more readily available at the beginning of President Smith's presidency, a structure for the First Presidency did not seem to be part of the expansion plans. Elder Joseph Fielding Smith explained that "it was not . . . until all other needs, seemingly, had been provided for, before President [Joseph F.] Smith determined that better quarters for the Presiding Authorities and the Historical Department of the Church should be prepared."[14] As the existing building projects neared completion, the First Presidency considered the possibility of building a new administrative headquarters.

Although the improved financial affairs of the Church were a motivating factor for a new administrative building, the pressing need for adequate administrative space to conduct the affairs of the growing Church could no longer be ignored. Elder Joseph Fielding Smith described the administrative situation of the time. "In the early days in the Salt Lake Valley, the headquarters, perhaps, were serviceable," he observed, "but as the Church grew and the need of greater and better quarters became necessary, no such accommodations were available. The offices of all departments were cramped and unserviceable."[15] The time had come when the First Presidency could seriously reconsider building the structure that Joseph Fielding Smith would later refer to as "one of the most important of all the structures" built during his father's administration.[16]

The site selected for the Church Office Building was at 47 East South Temple nestled between the newly constructed Hotel Utah and the Lion House. It was designed for the distinct purpose of administering the affairs of the Church as outlined in the Prophet Joseph Smith's revelation received over eighty years earlier.

Designing the Building

Once again, the Church turned to J. D. C. Young for help. Since his initial 1884 sketches of the administrative block, Young had gained valuable experience that greatly influenced his work. He worked on the Salt Lake Temple as an assistant to the Church architect, Truman O. Angell, and when Angell died in October 1887, Young was called to be the new Church architect. Consequently, Young redesigned some exterior parts of the temple—changing the spires from wood covered in metal to matching granite masonry—and then redesigned the entire interior of the temple.[17] While Young was working on the Salt Lake Temple, Karl G. Maeser asked him to design the Brigham Young Academy Building in Provo, which was completed in 1892. When the Salt Lake Temple was completed in 1893, Young was released as Church architect and started an architectural firm, called Young & Son, with his son, Don Carlos Young.

When Church leaders approached Young & Son, there were at least three important expectations for the design of the new building. They included (1) a functional building to serve as the administrative headquarters of the Church, (2) a building that provided the best possible security and protection from natural disaster, and (3) a building that served as a visible marker portraying a growing, vibrant, modern, and legitimate organization.

A useable administrative headquarters. Since 1833, it had long been a desire of both the Lord and officers of the Church to have a house dedicated for the presidency to administer "all things pertaining to the church and kingdom" (D&C 94:3). In 1917, President Joseph F. Smith said, "A couple of years ago . . . we concluded that we would build a house that would furnish suitable accommodations for the Presidency and others."[18] At another time, President Smith provided more details, saying that the new structure would "provide offices for the First Presidency, the Council of the Twelve, the Presiding Patriarch, the Historian's office, the Genealogical Society, and other Church organizations."[19]

Importantly, the vision of the building had expanded from an administrative office solely for the First Presidency to a building for the leading officers of the Church. This provided a central location and headquarters of the presiding administrative body. It also meant that the new structure needed to be large enough to accommodate office space and other facilities needed to meet the needs of the administrative affairs for the entire church. After Young & Son accepted the commission to design the building, Young began sketching his ideas in a notebook. On February 24, 1913, he sketched preliminary drawings in his personal sketchbook that he labeled as the "L.D.S. Church Administration Building."[20] Young completed three different sketches of a multilevel building that ranged in size from 150 to 200 feet long and from 80 to 124 feet wide. When compared with the 1833 Kirtland house for the presidency, Young's varied designs for an administrative house or headquarters were eight to sixteen times larger.

A secure and protective building. One critical aspect in the design of the building was the need that it be secure and impervious to natural elements, especially fire and flooding. Since it was intended that the building contain the valuable historical documents of the Church, there was great concern that it should adequately protect its contents from any foreseeable disaster. Upon completion of the new Church Office Building, Anthon H. Lund, first counselor in the First Presidency, told of his earlier worries about the Church's historical documents. "I have often been anxious about the precious documents, letters and books that we have in the Historian's office," he said. "If we should have been unfortunate enough to have had a fire and to lose them we could never have restored the loss, and I am therefore happy now that we have these splendid collections of historical matters pertaining to the Church placed in a safe building."[21]

President Lund's worries about protection and safety were shared by other officers of the Church, so Young & Son made security and protection an important aspect of their design. As a result, they designed what they referred to as a "Class 'A' construction."[22] They later explained that this class of construction called for a steel frame skeleton that is fireproofed with reinforced concrete. In addition, the building was designed to resist all lateral wind pressure, and the windowless basement was designed to be constructed of steel, granite, and reinforced concrete, making it both fireproof and waterproof. The architects designed the building to be built on a grade that was considerably higher than the normal street grade to provide additional protection from the periodic floodwaters of City Creek.[23]

A monument to a growing, vibrant, and modern church. President Joseph F. Smith yearned for an administrative building that would be "a monument of the real character of the work" of the Church and its leaders.[24] Rather than simply requiring a functional and secure administration building, President Smith wanted an edifice that would also inspire and make a lasting impression fitting of the mission of the Church. As a result, the façades in Young's 1913 sketches were quite different from his 1884 French and Romanesque revival designs. This time his drawings reflected the American Renaissance period (1878–1917). Many of the government and civic buildings designed and built during this period neatly fit into neoclassical designs that evoke a sense of power and stability commonly associated with Greek and Roman architecture.

On April 2, 1913, Young showed the First Presidency two draft sketches of the new building. President Lund recorded in his diary that the Presidency "liked it very much."[25] Just nineteen days later, the First Presidency publicly announced their intention of building a Church office building. On April 26, 1913, an announcement of the "Design of General Church Office Building" appeared in the *Deseret Evening News* with an architect's drawing of the building.[26] The announcement described the proposed building as "an imposing structure, designed to be a monument not only to the Church, but to Salt Lake City and Utah."[27] The printed perspective of the building was very similar to one of Young's 1913 preliminary sketches made in his notebook earlier in February. Although the detailed perspective was printed in the newspaper announcement, the appearance and details of the building were yet to be finalized. For example, the announcement stated that the finished building would "be a modification of the one shown in the above cut" and that "the new building [would] not be as large as that specified in this drawing."[28] Clearly, though, the proposed building was going to be built and would be an imposing and a fitting monument to the Church.

On August 12, 1913, Presidents Anthon H. Lund and Charles W. Penrose of the First Presidency reviewed the current plans for the new administration building.[29] The final plans were completed in October 1913, and Young took out a patent on the blueprints.[30] As anticipated, the final design was altered from the original drawings in both appearance and size. While the building design clearly fits the neoclassical style of architecture, J. D. C. Young characterized the building's design as Grecian Ionic.[31] Young felt this design style was "one of the most graceful and pleasing of all architectural styles."[32] The building would extend five stories above a basement and would measure 101 feet and 11 inches wide by 165 feet and 3 inches long.

President Smith's desire for the building to be designed as a monument was also embraced by others involved with the building. Elder Junius F. Wells, for example, proposed that the building should explicitly honor the legacy of Church leaders by inscribing their names into the exterior granite walls. Wells worked with Pope and Guptull, architects from the Pratt Institute in Brooklyn, to complete blueprints showing the name of the Church, important historical dates and locations, and all the names of latter-day prophets, apostles, the Three Witnesses, and all other General Authorities along with the dates of their service inscribed in the building's granite exterior.[33] Obviously, this particular plan did not come to fruition.

Building Construction

With Young & Son leading the design and engineering on the building, J. W. Mellen, a prominent local contractor, was selected as the lead contractor.[34] Excavation began on September 3, 1913, and it was anticipated that the construction of the building would take only two years barring any significant complications or delays.[35] During the first year of construction, Young reported that the recently poured concrete for the foundation froze in the severe winter conditions. Upon initial inspection and testing, the concrete crumbled to dust and could not support the weight of the five-story building. Due to poor weather conditions, it was determined to wait until warmer weather to remove the foundation. It was not until spring 1914 that the weather warmed sufficiently to rectify the faulty concrete. Prior to removing the foundation, the concrete was retested. Much to the shock of the architects, engineers, contractors, and builders, the foundation was deemed to be structurally sound and could be left intact. Young and others felt the change in the condition of the foundation was nothing short of miraculous providence, for it saved time and precious funds.[36]

In October 1914, President Smith described work on the building as "progressing slowly but satisfactorily."[37] He attributed the lack of progress not to construction delays but to financial difficulties. "I might add possibly without inconsistency," he said, "that the progress of this building might have been a little more rapid if we had seen clearly our way to supply the means necessary to force it along a little faster."[38] The Church had used $128,663 of tithing funds to support the construction of the administration building but this amount was obviously insufficient to keep the project on schedule.[39] To help subsidize the cost of construction, it was determined that the proceeds from the sale of Church Historian Andrew Jenson's 1914 edition of *Church Chronology: A Record of Important Events Pertaining to the History of the Church of Jesus Christ of Latter-day Saints* would be used to help meet the financial needs of the new building.[40] Even with financial assistance from other sources, President Smith felt that the real solution to meeting the obligations of the growing Church would be for members of the Church to pay their tithing.[41]

The basement, which would support the entire superstructure of the building, was far enough along to construct the steel skeleton by November 1914.[42] The basement extended twelve feet below grade and was constructed of reinforced concrete and a "projecting plinth" of solid granite.[43] With the basement and main floor complete, most of the six hundred tons of steel used in the building was used to erect a fireproof framework designed to carry the load for the entire building.[44] With this in place, the exterior stonework could begin.

All of the exterior walls were composed of Utah granite taken from the same quarry in Little Cottonwood Canyon that supplied the granite used to build the Salt Lake Temple.[45] By early spring 1915, two rows of granite were laid, and a cornerstone-laying ceremony was scheduled for May 19, 1915, at 10:00 a.m. The ceremony was delayed to 3:00 p.m. because the inscription for the copper plate on the memento box was not completed.[46] President Smith was in Hawaii at the time and unable to attend the ceremony so his counselors presided in his place. Francis Lyman, President of the Quorum of the Twelve, opened the ceremony with prayer after which the stone was hoisted up and set in place. The cornerstone is the largest stone in the exterior walls, weighing about eight tons, and is located at the southwest corner of the building.[47] As soon as the cornerstone was set in place, President Lund, first counselor, declared the stone as being laid according to "rule & plummet" and stated that he hoped "the building would all be as well and solidly laid as this stone."[48] Following President Lund's declaration, President Penrose, second counselor, dedicated the cornerstone.[49]

The Exterior

The exterior was constructed of 4,517 granite block stones diagrammed by individual weight, cubical contents, and cost—totaling 73,000 cubical feet of granite weighing 6,025 tons.[50] The distinctive feature of Young's Grecian Ionic design was twenty-four columns and capitals forming a colonnade on each side of the building between the granite masses at each corner. Each column was forty-eight feet tall and measured five feet in diameter at the base. True to the classic Ionic order, each capital is a carved volute, creating a spiral scroll.[51] Above the columns rests a massive granite entablature described by J. D. C. Young as "consisting of a beautifully carved architrave, heavy dentils, the water leaf course and the egg and dart moldings."[52] The only other exterior decorative symbols carved of stone are the two stone wreaths above every window portal and the granite lion heads appearing over each column on the corona. At the crown of the building is a solid granite parapet.[53]

The building had two entrances, the main entrance and a private entrance located in the northeast corner of the building. The main entrance is found on the south and is reached by climbing sixteen solid granite steps flanked by granite pedestals on either side. A decorative bronze tripod bearing an inverted glass bowl was perched on the threshold of each pedestal with a high powered lamp placed inside each bowl that was "so arranged as to throw a flash of light upon the Ionic columns flanking it."[54] The main doors are made of solid bronze with glass panels. In front of these doors is a pair of bronze grills that slide out from inside the exterior walls to enclose the entrance at night. Like the front entrance, the rear door is also made of bronze and glass. True to the neoclassical styling, a pediment was placed over the main entrance and the tympanum contained the blocked letters "LDS."[55] Directly under the pediment in block letters was inscribed "CHURCH OFFICES," which designated the official name for the building as the "LDS Church Offices" at the time.

The Interior

By 1916, the building's exterior was nearing completion, and the interior construction was under way. The primary purpose of the basement was to provide the best possible security against any foreseeable natural disasters. Consequently, the concrete walls were reinforced and waterproofed. A vault to store the most prized historical documents of the Church was installed in the basement. The remainder of the basement was unfinished and used for storing files, records, and maintenance equipment.

Main floor. The first, or main, floor was designed to accommodate public receptions, large meetings, and the administrative work of the First Presidency, the Patriarch of the Church, and the administrative staff. Every effort was made to make the interior of the building as stately and grand as its exterior, especially on the first floor. The entry was floored in white marble, and the walls were veneered with large blocks of golden travertine marble—both extracted from Utah quarries. A white marble staircase with treads of white Tennessee marble, balusters and handrails made of Utah marble and travertine of varying tints curve upward connecting the upper floors. Two elevators with bronze doors are opposite the staircase and service all floors of the building including the basement.

North of the entry, through two large glass doors, lay a thirty-foot by forty-foot reception hall of white marble floors and marble-veneered walls. Four marble standards set into the walls extended seven feet to an entablature and had an inverted glass dome fixture attached. While the building was still under construction, the First Presidency met with members of the Presiding Bishopric to discuss details concerning the design of the reception hall. Presiding Bishop Charles W. Nibley felt that sixteen fluted Doric columns should be purchased for forty thousand dollars and placed in the room.[56] Nibley's second counselor, David A. Smith, however, favored having marble pedestals with the busts of the Presidents of the Church over the columns. Anthon H. Lund expressed his preference of not using either option, feeling that the costly marble veneering on the walls and the existing columns in the building would be sufficient.[57] In the end, the reception room was ultimately flanked with sixteen fluted marble monoliths taken from the Bird's Eye Quarry in Thistle Canyon.[58]

Interior of the Church Administration Building in Salt Lake City. (© Intellectual Reserve, Inc.)

These columns were arranged to support an entablature that created a floating ceiling made of art glass, creating a light court in the reception area. Light wells, or large open areas in each upper floor, allowed natural light to cascade vertically through the building from the open roof behind the parapet.

Two large conference rooms are accessible from the reception area. To the west is a twenty-eight-foot by ninety-eight-foot room running north to south with deep mahogany-paneled walls and a marble fireplace carved with sego lilies on its eastern wall. This conference room was designated for use by General Authorities, general officers, and members of the various general boards of the Church.

The other conference room is located just north of the reception hall through a small waiting room often referred to as the Onyx Room, named because of the light-colored Utah onyx walls and white marbled floor.[59] Through the doors of the Onyx Room is a twenty-seven-foot by forty-seven-foot conference room running east to west that is used by the First Presidency for receiving dignitaries and holding business meetings. The walls are warmed by rich panels of Circassian walnut where the panels are mounted in an intricate pattern known as the butterfly effect.[60] The ceiling is blocked with walnut, and a white travertine marble fireplace lines the east wall of the room.

Another large area (twenty-nine feet by ninety-eight feet) on the east side of the main floor running north and south was provided as general office space for the administrative staff. This room was divided by "screens and counters" (cubicles) to create private working spaces for staff assignments. A "fire- and burglar-proof vault" for the use of the First Presidency was also located in this area.[61]

Private offices for the members of the First Presidency were located on the main floor in the northeast, northwest, and southwest corners of the building. Each office was furnished with personal facilities and had an adjoining secretary's office. The First Presidency's administrative secretary and the office for the Patriarch of the Church were located in the southeastern corner of the main floor.

The upper floors. The second floor originally housed the offices for the Council of the Twelve, Council of the Seventy, and staff. All private offices aligned with the exterior walls, providing each office with at least one window. A storage room, restrooms, closets, stairwells, elevators, and a light well used the rest of the inner floor space.

The third and fourth floors had nearly identical floor plans. Each was designed with nine offices, an open twenty-foot by forty-eight-foot work room, and an open stack room that was used for storage, shelving, reading, and reference work. The third floor was allocated to the Church historian. The Genealogical Society of Utah was housed on the fourth floor; instead of having a work room, a classroom was built on the east side for class instruction in genealogy and temple recording.

The fifth floor was primarily designed to serve as a "stack room" for the records and files of the Church Historian and the Genealogical Society. This floor was almost entirely open space filled with shelving.[62]

Completion of the New Church Office Building

Church leaders expected the building to be ready for dedication by April 1917. Occupancy of the building took place in stages as construction was completed during 1917. The Genealogical Society and business offices for the First Presidency's staff, for example, began moving into the building on February 28, and the First Presidency begin moving into their private offices on April 4. The building was officially deemed complete on October 2, 1917, when an eight-foot mantelpiece of white travertine marble was installed on the fireplace in the First Presidency's conference room.[63] The cost of the building was announced as approximately nine hundred thousand, although some estimates had the building costing more than one million dollars.[64]

During the October general conference of 1917, President Joseph F. Smith stated that a dedication date for the building had not yet been set but would "take place in the near future."[65] During the same conference, President Lund expressed his gratitude for the completion of the "new office quarters" and invited the public to "come and see them."[66] Visitors toured the building for decades after President Lund's invitation. Tours were organized, and in the 1920s a handsome brochure of the building was created to be distributed to guests touring the building.[67] These tours continued well into the late 1960s, when it was reported that "at general conference time, the building literally overflows with members of the Church who find occasion to enter it. At other times, groups of seminary students and others may be found touring the building and seeing for themselves some of the historic records stored there."[68] Due to heightened security needs, public tours were discontinued during the 1970s.

Continued Improvement to the Building

In October 1947, it was announced that the building would be remodeled to create more usable space as well as to improve the building's efficiency. Before remodeling, the basement was used as a makeshift storage area and vault. The new changes split the basement into thirds with a receiving and supply area, a suitable storage area for documents and files (stack room), and a mechanical section to meet the needs for the publicity and radio functions of the Church.

The most dramatic change of this remodeling, however, was covering the natural light wells on the second, third, and fourth floors to create usable space for additional offices and storage. As a result, a missionary assembly room, once located on the fourth floor, was moved to the newly created space on the third floor which, in turn, made ample room for the Presiding Bishopric and their staff to occupy the fourth and fifth floors on November 27, 1949.[69]

Renovation and remodeling, 1975–77. In addition to regular maintenance, several changes were made to the building over the next twenty years to facilitate administrative changes of the Church. For example, a private branch exchange (PBX)—a switching station for telephones—was installed to handle growing communication needs. By 1969, the light well on the fifth floor was covered, creating additional space.

With the announcement of the new multistoried Church Office Building to be built on the administrative block at 50 East North Temple in the early 1960s, confusion over the appropriate nomenclature for the new headquarter complex surfaced. A simple but important change to the façade of the building on 47 East South Temple clearly resolved any question on this matter. The letters "LDS" on the building's tympanum were removed, and the words "Church Offices" above the main entrance were replaced with "Administration Building." In addition, "The Church of Jesus Christ of Latter-Day Saints" was added in large bronze block letters to the architrave over the main entrance.[70]

In the early 1970s, Church architect Emil B. Fetzer was working on plans to add a fire escape to the Administration Building when he determined that while the foundation and exterior walls of the building were in excellent condition, the interior needed a drastic renewal.[71] After approaching the First Presidency with the idea, Fetzer was given permission to proceed but was counseled that the building "should be brought to the character and quality of the original building, with the present-day standards."[72]

Around this same time, Relief Society general president Belle S. Spafford began looking for an appropriate rug for the reception room on the main floor.[73] She contacted William Pera, who secured a large rug, thirty-nine by eighteen feet, that was woven in the 1920s. The rug was reportedly made in Bulgaria and originally placed in a Bulgarian palace, but it was removed when the Communists took over the government at the end of World War II. President Spencer W. Kimball said three families worked together for seven years to create the rug.[74] The colors of the rug beautifully matched the hues of the marble in the reception room, and the rug's cypress tree motif fittingly matches the tree of life symbolism from the Book of Mormon.[75] The rug was purchased and presented to the Church as a gift from the Relief Society.[76] It still adorns the main floor reception room.

By 1972, Emil B. Fetzer completed his early designs for the renovation and remodeling of the Administration Building.[77] Although the project only involved the interior of the building, the size and scope was so extensive that Bishop H. David Burton later described the building as being "torn apart and restructured."[78] The building was vacated during the remodeling. The First Presidency, Quorum of the Twelve Apostles, other General Authorities, their staffs, and those affiliated with other departments housed within the building moved their offices in July 1975 into the new church office building at 50 East North Temple.[79]

Architect Fetzer's plans called for both a renovation and a remodeling of the building's interior. The renovation included completely modernizing the electrical, mechanical, fire sprinkler, plumbing, heating, and air-conditioning systems throughout the building. Most carpets, draperies, and other furnishings were also replaced and updated.[80]

The remodeling was bold and drastic. The entire basement was redesigned to include a cafeteria for General Authorities, an exercise room, dressing rooms, an efficient mechanical room, and an office for the building manager. New private elevators for General Authority use were installed in the northern end of the building as was an additional stairwell.[81] Another entrance to the Administration Building was created in the basement by making an opening in the north wall of the basement and connecting it with the underground parking level created for the Church Office Building in 1965.[82]

The private offices of the First Presidency on the main floor were updated, and the northwest corner office was enlarged for the President of the Church.[83] Offices and work rooms were created from the open general office space in the east portion of the building. Members of the Council of the Twelve occupied all four corner offices of the second, third, and fourth floors. Other General Authorities occupied offices on the upper floors. The administrative offices are paneled in either cherry or walnut.[84] In all, the newly remodeled Administration Building offered ninety-three offices on the upper four floors for General Authorities and their staff. Other additions to the building included a library on the fourth floor and a large meeting room for the Council of the Twelve, Presiding Bishopric, and other General Authorities on the fifth floor.[85] The General Authorities began moving back into the newly completed Church Administration Building during September 1977.[86]

When the project was completed, plans for rededicating the building were discussed. Soon, though, a question arose as to whether or not the building was ever dedicated in the first place. After careful examination, the Historian's Office determined that the building had never been dedicated, making a rededication impossible. When considering why the building was not dedicated when first completed, President Kimball felt it was most likely due to a series of events rather than single event. He explained that President Joseph F. Smith fell ill during the fall of 1917 and on January 23, 1918, his forty-five-year-old son, Hyrum Mack Smith, died. This event greatly affected him for quite some time. In April, President Smith suffered a stroke that hampered him until his death on November 19. Finally, the Spanish flu epidemic limited public gatherings and even caused the postponement of the general conference in 1919 from April until June. President Kimball concluded that the "dedication of this Administration Building was postponed and left to be taken care of at another date."[87]

It is rather ironic that this particular building had never been dedicated. After all, its inception was by divine revelation in 1833 and the Savior specifically stated that the house for the presidency would be "dedicated unto the Lord" (D&C 94:7). On February 8, 1978, President Kimball gathered the Church leaders and staff in the west conference room of the newly refurbished building to "properly dedicate this magnificent building." He said, "It now becomes our pleasure and satisfaction to offer this building, even at this late date, and dedicate it to the Lord for the carrying on of all his work, particularly for the growth and development of the kingdom here on the earth."[88]

Post-1980 changes. Only two other significant changes have taken place since the dedication of the building in 1978. The first was a remodeling of the basement entrance that was added in 1977. A new entrance extended into the underground parking facility, creating a gracious room that complimented the interior styling found throughout the building. The new entrance also afforded General Authorities privacy and the convenience to enter the building from the parking entrances while creating an efficient security room for screening visitors and assessing possible threats.

In July 2006, the Administration Building underwent a life-safety or seismic renovation. The crews worked double shifts six days a week for one month so that the renovation would disrupt the busy schedules of the General Authorities as little as possible.[89]

Conclusion

True to its prophetic conception, the Church Administration Building has been a place dedicated to the Lord for the presidency to do their work in ministering to "all things pertaining to the church and kingdom" (D&C 94:4). More than just an administrative facility, this building has been a place of tribute to those who have, as President Kimball prayed, "served . . . and who loved this building . . . and brought credit to it."[90] The bodies of Presidents Heber J. Grant, George Albert Smith, David O. McKay, Joseph Fielding Smith, Harold B. Lee, Spencer W. Kimball, Ezra Taft Benson, and Howard W. Hunter have all lain in repose in the reception hall.[91] The Administration Building has welcomed prominent individuals, governmental and religious leaders, and dignitaries visiting Salt Lake City. It is a stately building that will continue to serve the Church in the decades ahead.

The Administration Building continues to fulfill President Joseph F. Smith's desire that it would be "a monument of the real character of the work."[92] Upon its completion in 1917, it was reported that "the first impression one receives of the building is its massiveness, coupled with its striking beauty, richness and harmony in every detail." Another visitor called the structure "a poem in stone."[93] Oscar Wenderoth, supervising architect of the US Treasury Department, said that the Administration Building was "equal to anything he has seen in the East or in Europe, and that it will be a lasting monument to the Church that is erecting it."[94]

The lasting monument of the Administration Building, however, is not found in its strength, security, functionality, or even in its impressive beauty. This building is a monument to something far more significant, as was expressed in an *Improvement Era* article commemorating its fiftieth anniversary: "Third and even fourth generations of Church members are receiving direction and guidance that come from within this beautiful granite building."[95] This statement affirms the Lord's original intention that such a building truly would be "for the work of the presidency, in obtaining revelations; and for the work of the ministry of the presidency, in all things pertaining to the church and kingdom" (D&C 94:4).

Notes

1. The heading for Doctrine and Covenants 94 states that this revelation was received by Joseph Smith on May 6, 1833. The Kirtland Revelation Book, however, shows that the D&C 94 was actually the last portion of the revelation known as D&C 97. See Kirtland Revelation Book, 64, Church History Library, The Church of Jesus Christ of Latter-day Saints, Salt Lake City.

2. When completed, the outside walls of the Kirtland Temple measured 59 feet by 79 feet 2 inches, and the inside walls measured 57 feet by 77 feet 2 inches.

3. *History of the Church of Jesus Christ of Latter-day Saints*, ed. B. H. Roberts, 2nd ed. rev. (Salt Lake City: Deseret Book, 1957), 1:418.

4. *History of the Church*, 2:379.

5. John P. Livingstone and others, *Salt Lake City: Ensign to the Nations* (Provo, UT: Religious Studies Center, Brigham Young University, 2009), 48. The Gardo House was also known as Amelia's Palace and was used until 1891, when it was taken from the Church by the Edmunds-Tucker Act; see also Journal History of The Church of Jesus Christ of Latter-day Saints, November 13, 1891, Church History Library.

6. James B. Allen and Richard O. Cowan, *Mormonism in the Twentieth Century* (Provo, UT: Brigham Young University Press, 1967), 26.

7. Paul Bradford Westwood, "The Early Life and Career of Joseph Don Carlos Young (1855–1938)" (master's thesis, Brigham Young University, 1994), 90, Church History Library. Westwood concluded that while Bishop Preston is credited with commissioning the plan, the First Presidency would have known about the project or "jointly commissioned" Young to the work. Westwood reasons this must have been the case since George Q. Cannon, First Counselor in the First Presidency, was Joseph Don Carlos Young's brother-in-law.

8. See Joseph Don Carlos Young, "Sketches for a Church Block: Block Development in Salt Lake City One Hundred Years Ago" (master's thesis, Brigham Young University, 1990), L. Tom Perry Special Collections, Harold B. Lee Library, Brigham Young University, Provo, UT.

9. Westwood, "Early Life and Career," 90, 92. Westwood is currently the manager of collection development, Church History Library.

10. Westwood, "Early Life and Career," 93.

11. Westwood, "Early Life and Career," 90.

12. Westwood, "Early Life and Career," 94.

13. The Deseret Gymnasium was considered to be one of the best-equipped gymnasiums of the time and was an adjunct of the Church school system. The Hotel Utah, situated on South Temple and Main Street, was completed in June 1911. President Joseph F. Smith described it as being "one of the most magnificent hotels that existed on the continent of Americas, or in the old continent either." In Conference Report, October 1911, 129.

14. Joseph Fielding Smith, *The Life of Joseph F. Smith: Sixth President of the Church of Jesus Christ of Latter-day Saints* (Salt Lake City: Deseret Book, 1969), 427.

15. Smith, *Life of Joseph F. Smith*, 427.

16. Smith, *Life of Joseph F. Smith*, 427.

17. For additional information on the construction of the Salt Lake Temple, see Richard O. Cowan's article herein.

18. Joseph F. Smith, in Conference Report, April 1917, 8.

19. Journal History, August 20, 1913, 2. See also Joseph F. Smith, in Conference Report, October 1914, 4.

20. Joseph Don Carlos Young Family Papers, 1873–1978, February 24, 1913, J. Willard Marriott Library, University of Utah, Salt Lake City.

21. Anthon H. Lund, in Conference Report, October 1917, 10.

22. J. D. C. Young, "The Latter-day Saints Church Office Building," *Utah Genealogical and Historical Magazine*, April 1917, 57.

23. Paul L. Anderson, interview by George Cannon Young, Salt Lake City, 1973, 35, Church History Library.

24. Joseph F. Smith, in Conference Report, April 1917, 8.

25. *Danish Apostle: The Diaries of Anthon H. Lund*, ed. John P. Hatch (Salt Lake City: Signature Books, 2006), April 2, 1913, 496.

26. "Design of General Church Office Building," *Deseret Evening News*, April 26, 1913, 1.

27. "Design of General Church Office Building," 1.

28. "Design of General Church Office Building," 1. Even with the disclaimer that the building would be smaller than the design provided, no actual dimensions of the building were given in the announcement.

29. *Danish Apostle*, August 12, 1913, 511.

30. The original blueprints were dated October 1913. Gary L. Phelps, "The Church Administration Building," August 1969, 3, L. Tom Perry Special Collections, Harold B. Lee Library.

31. There are three ancient orders of classical architecture, known as the Doric, Ionic, and Corinthian. All of these orders were invented by the Greeks, although the Romans (and others) recast the orders according to their own tastes.

32. Young, "Latter-day Saints Church Office Building," *Utah Genealogical and Historical Magazine*, 57.

33. Junius F. Wells papers, 1867–1930, Church History Library.

34. *Deseret Evening News*, April 14, 1917, 9.

35. Smith, *Life of Joseph F. Smith*, 428; *Deseret Evening News*, Saturday, April 26, 1913, 1.

36. Phelps, "Church Administration Building," 3–4.

37. Joseph F. Smith, in Conference Report, October 1914, 4.

38. Smith, in Conference Report, October 1914, 4.

39. Joseph F. Smith, in Conference Report, April 1915, 8.

40. "Church Chronology," *Improvement Era*, June 1915, 752.

41. Smith, in Conference Report, October 1914, 4.

42. Harry Shipler, "Bransford Apartments, Eagle Gate and Hotel Utah," Shipler Commercial Photographers, November 1914, photograph, Collection MSS C 275; Shipler #15691, Utah State Historical Society.

43. A plinth is a continuous course of stones (or other solid material) supporting a structural wall. A plinth negotiates the space between a structure and the ground—a footing. Young, "Latter-day Saints Church Office Building," *Utah Genealogical and Historical Magazine*, 57–58.

44. "L.D.S. Church Office Building—A Poem in Stone: New Church Offices Open to Public Inspection," in *Deseret Evening News*, Saturday, April 14, 1917, 9.

45. Spencer W. Kimball, "Dedication of the Church Administration Building," 1978, Church History Library; "Fiftieth Anniversary of the Church Office Building," *Improvement Era*, November 1967, 64.

46. *Danish Apostle*, 578; Smith, *Life of Joseph F. Smith*, 428.

47. Young, "Latter-day Saints Church Office Building," *Utah Genealogical and Historical Magazine*, 58.

48. *Danish Apostle*, 578. A plummet is a plumb bob, used for measuring verticality in construction.

49. *Danish Apostle*, 578.

50. Young, "Latter-day Saints Church Office Building," *Utah Genealogical and Historical Magazine*, 58.

51. A volute is a spiral or scroll-like ornament set atop a column.

52. J. D. C. Young, "The Latter-day Saints Church Office Building," *Juvenile Instructor*, March 1916, 147. An entablature is a part of a building resting on columns. A classical entablature consists of an architrave, a frieze, and a cornice. The architrave is the main beam resting on top of a column or row of columns. A dentil is one of a series of small, rectangular blocks arranged like a row of teeth. These blocks are used as ornaments, typically on the molding of a cornice. The design included a pattern of egg-shaped ovals, arrows (darts), and leaves.

53. A parapet is a low wall running along the edge of a roof or balcony. Young said that by using a parapet, he was "enabled to get a fine room out of a space that is usually lost." Young, "Latter-day Saints Church Office Building," *Juvenile Instructor*, 147. Because there were no windows in the parapet, lighting was accomplished by having windows on the interior walls or in the light well.

54. Young, "Latter-day Saints Church Office Building," *Utah Genealogical and Historical Magazine*, 58.

55. In Greek architectural styling, a pediment is the triangular section above the entablature on the front of a building. The pediment is usually placed over an entrance. The tympanum is the recessed area within the pediment.

56. Doric columns are the oldest and simplest of the Greek design and usually stand flat on the ground with a smooth, flared capital.

57. *Danish Apostle*, 606.

58. The term "bird's eye" came from small, round fossil corals found in the marble that resemble the eye of a bird. The columns are made of golden travertine marble.

59. Brooks Hale, secretary of the First Presidency, Church Office Building notes, June 2010; notes in author's possession.

60. Circassian walnut is a rare wood from the area between the Black and Caspian Seas known as Circassia. When the wood was purchased for the First Presidency's room, it was the only log of Circassian walnut in the United States and was purchased for five hundred dollars. The commercial value of the log at the time was

estimated to be about ten thousand dollars. Don Carlos Young Family Papers, 1873–1978, box 8, folder 4. J. Willard Marriott Library, University of Utah. See also Young, "Latter-day Saints Church Office Building," *Utah Genealogical and Historical Magazine*, 60.

61. Young, "Latter-day Saints Church Office Building," 60. When Joseph Fielding Smith became the President of the Church, he placed a large safe that was used to store historic documents and sacred artifacts that had "been under his exclusive control for years" in the First Presidency's vault on the main floor. Gibbons reported that the contents of this safe "provided grist for numerous and unfounded rumors and speculations" over the years. Francis M. Gibbons, *Joseph Fielding Smith: Gospel Scholar, Prophet of God* (Salt Lake City: Deseret Book, 1992), 459; see also Young, "Latter-day Saints Church Office Building," *Juvenile Instructor*, 149.

62. Young, "Latter-day Saints Church Office Building," 60.

63. Journal History, October 2, 1917, 3. Andrew Jenson also recorded the completion date of the Church Office Building as October 2, 1917, in the *Encyclopedic History of the Church.*

64. The *Herald Republic* reported the building cost as about nine hundred thousand. See Journal History, April 22, 1917, 10. The million-dollar figure was reported in Janie L. Rogers, "The Life and Work of Joseph Don Carlos Young: Utah's Architectural Heritage," December 10, 1986, 10–11, Church History Library.

65. Journal History, October 2, 1917, 3.

66. Anthon H. Lund, in Conference Report, October 1917, 10.

67. "Latter-day Saints Church Office Building," Church History Library.

68. "Fiftieth Anniversary of the Church Office Building," *Improvement Era*, November 1967, 65.

69. "The Church Moves On," *Improvement Era*, October 1947, 632; Church Office Building fourth floor (blueprints), 1948, CR 126 99, Church History Library.

70. Photographs of the Administration Building in 1967 bear the changes. See photo in "Fiftieth Anniversary of the Church Office Building," *Improvement Era*, November 1967, 64; Phelps, "Church Administration Building," 4. See also building photographs PH 4397, folders 1 and 2, Church History Library.

71. "Church Leaders Move Offices," *Church News*, September 10, 1977, 7.

72. "Church Leaders Move Offices," 7.

73. Douglas Coy Miles, "Persian Rugs in the Church Administration Building," MS 14563, Church History Library.

74. Spencer W. Kimball, "Dedication of the Church Administration Building, 1978," First Presidency, photocopy of typescript, CR 1 80, Church History Library.

75. Peter Scarlet, "LDS Church Administration Building Rug Is Swept Up in Royal History All Its Own," *Salt Lake Tribune,* Saturday, November 2, 1991, A8.

76. Kimball, "Dedication of the Church Administration Building, 1978." According to a letter written by Douglas Miles Coy, he and his wife, Blanche Miles, purchased the rug and donated it the Church. Douglas Coy Miles, "Persian Rugs in the Church Administration Building," MS 14563, Church History Library.

77. "Remodeling and Addition to the Church Administration Building, 1972," CR 103 386, fd.1, Church History Library.

78. Lynn Arave and Scott Taylor, "For 35 years, Church Office Building Has Been Symbolic Mormon Headquarters, Operational Center for Church Growth," *Deseret News*, April 1, 2010.

79. "First Presidency to Move Offices," *Church News*, June 14, 1975, 3.

80. "New Insides for a Grand Old Building," *Ensign*, November 1977, 108; "Church Leaders Move Offices," *Church News*, September 10, 1977, 7.

81. "First Presidency to Move Offices," 3; Emil B. Fetzer's blueprints reveal the many changes during this remodeling, See "Remodeling and Addition to the Church Administrative Building," Church History Library.

82. "Remodeling and Addition to the Church Administrative Building, 1972."

83. Prior to this change, the Church President's office was located in the northeast corner.

84. "New Insides for a Grand Old Building," 110.

85. "Remodeling and Addition to the Church Administration Building 1972."

86. "Church Leaders Move Offices," *Church News*, September 10, 1977, 7.

87. Kimball, "Dedication of the Church Administration Building, 1978."

88. Kimball, "Dedication of the Church Administration Building, 1978."

89. "LDS Church Administration Building Seismic Upgrade," www.jacobsen construction.com/portfolio/religious/lds-church.

90. Kimball, "Dedication of the Church Administration Building, 1978."

91. President Joseph F. Smith did not lie in repose in the building because the flu epidemic limited public participation in his funeral.

92. Joseph F. Smith, in Conference Report, April 1917, 8.

93. "L.D.S. Church Office Building—A Poem in Stone," 8.

94. Young, "Latter-day Saints Church Office Building," *Utah Genealogical and Historical Magazine*, 58.

95. "Fiftieth Anniversary of the Church Office Building," *Improvement Era*, November 1967, 65.

President Harold B. Lee, considered the father of modern Church correlation.
(© Intellectual Reserve, Inc.)

Chapter 13

Correlation: The Turning Point (1960s)

Michael A. Goodman

Correlation has a long history of starts and stops, successes and setbacks. Often misconstrued as solely related to curricular issues, correlation has had a much broader focus from the beginning. President Harold B. Lee stated that one of the primary purposes of correlation was to place "the Priesthood as the Lord intended, as the center core of the Kingdom of God, and the auxiliaries as related thereto; including a greater emphasis on the Fathers in the home as Priesthood bearers in strengthening the family unit."[1]

Though the vision has been large as eternity, the work of the kingdom for the first century was largely local in focus and readily directed by the presiding brethren at Church headquarters. Though missionaries were sent throughout the world starting as early as 1830, most converts were encouraged to emigrate soon after their conversion. Though some converts stayed in their native lands, the Church's international

Michael A. Goodman is an associate professor of Church history and doctrine at Brigham Young University.

presence was relatively small. The work became far more challenging as the Church continued to expand both numerically as well as geographically. The auxiliary organizations were created in an effort to better serve the needs of an ever-expanding membership. Relief Society, Sunday School, Young Men, Young Women, and Primary became vital organizations to help the presiding authorities meet the needs of the members worldwide.[2] By the end of the nineteenth century, the administration of the Church had grown much more complex, and at times the leaders struggled to minister to and manage the growing membership and organizations meant to serve them. Correlation in the twentieth century served as one of the primary means of helping the presiding authorities in Salt Lake City guide the Lord's work.

Early Attempts at Correlation

President Joseph F. Smith began the work of correlation at the beginning of the twentieth century. He created the General Priesthood Committee on Outlines on April 8, 1908, and appointed recently called Apostle David O. McKay as the chair.[3] The committee's major assignment was to write the curriculum for priesthood quorums and groups. The committee was also tasked to help the priesthood "understand its duty, . . . assume its own responsibility, . . . magnify its calling, and fill its place in the Church, to the uttermost."[4] In 1912, President Smith organized the Correlation Committee and once again assigned Elder McKay as the chair.[5] "The purpose of the committee was to prevent the unnecessary and undesirable duplication of work [of all kinds] in the various auxiliaries of the Church. . . . and for the general purpose of unifying the work and advancing the cause of each organization."[6] By 1916, the Social Advisory Committee was formed with Elder Stephen L Richards as chair.[7] The work of this committee overlapped with the work of the Correlation Committee. As a result, by the beginning of 1921, these two committees were merged to form the

President David O. McKay, chair of the General Priesthood Committee and Church correlation. (© Intellectual Reserve, Inc.)

Amalgamated Correlation–Social Advisory Committee. The committee members worked for several more years before being released in 1922.

The next effort at correlation focused largely on Church curriculum and again involved Elder McKay. In 1928, while serving as both Apostle and the general superintendent of the Sunday School, Elder McKay announced that the curricula of all quorums and the Sunday School would be reviewed and authorized by a common committee.[8] In 1938, the First Presidency organized the Committee of Correlation and Coordination and asked three members of the Twelve (Elder Joseph Fielding Smith, Stephen L Richards, and Albert E. Bowen) to take the lead.[9] This committee worked together for only a few years, and little was documented regarding the work they accomplished.

March 29, 1940, proved to be a watershed moment in the correlation efforts of the Church. President J. Reuben Clark Jr., under assignment by President Heber J. Grant, called the leaders of the Relief Society, Sunday School, Young Men, Young Women, Primary, and the Genealogy Society together and presented detailed instructions on correlation principles. A follow-up letter entitled the Memorandum of Suggestions and signed by all three members of the First Presidency was sent thereafter.[10] This memorandum largely summarized past and current correlation challenges and outlined suggestions on how best to address each of them. The principles contained in this document still guide correlation work today. At this meeting, President Clark announced the formation of the Union Board of the Auxiliaries with President George Q. Morris, then general superintendent of the Young Men Mutual Improvement Association, as the president.

Four years later, the First Presidency again set up a committee to evaluate all Church publications. In a letter dated August 9, 1944, the First Presidency formed the Committee on Publications, made up of Elders Joseph Fielding Smith, John A. Widtsoe, Harold B. Lee, and Marion G. Romney. "The function of this Committee is to pass upon and approve all materials . . . to be used by our Church Priesthood, Educational, Auxiliary, and Missionary organizations in their work of instructing member of the Church."[11] The First Presidency also named a Reading Committee to assist the Committee on Publications. The First Presidency gave strict guidelines that were to be used to evaluate all published materials.

One of the final attempts at correlation in the first half of the twentieth century began on December 15, 1947. The First Presidency assigned Elder Lee to head a committee of Apostles to look at work in the Melchizedek Priesthood quorums and the auxiliaries and recommend changes.[12] In 1948 and again in 1949, Elder Lee suggested a redesign of the ward teaching program to bring it under the supervision of the Quorum of the Twelve.[13] Nothing was changed at the time, however. With the end of World War II, the Church began to expand internationally at a dramatically faster rate. This expansion further exacerbated the challenges facing the Church. As Elder Lee once stated, "The problem of correlation becomes more acute as the Church grows and develops."[14]

Though many correlation ideas would have to wait until the 1960s and 1970s to come to full fruition, the principles were taught as early as the first decade of the 1900s. And when the needs became acute, the work of correlation was set to proceed on the foundation laid over the first sixty years of the twentieth century.

Beginning of the Modern Era of Correlation

On March 24, 1960, the modern era of correlation officially began. With the continued national and international growth of the Church, the challenges of ministering to an ever-increasing membership from Church headquarters in Salt Lake City also continued to grow. The First Presidency and Quorum of the Twelve sent a letter authorizing the General Priesthood Committee, directed by Elder Lee, to begin a study of the curriculum of both priesthood and auxiliary organizations. In September 1961, Elder Lee and the General Priesthood Committee organized the All-Church Coordinating Council (ACCC) made up of several members of the Twelve, the Presiding Bishop, the heads of each auxiliary, secretaries, and ultimately the heads of each of the four standing priesthood committees.[15] Elder Lee, the members of the Twelve who would be chairs of three age-group correlation committees, and their secretaries formed the Correlation Executive Committee (CEC).[16] Antone K. Romney, brother of Marion G. Romney and a BYU education professor, served as secretary.[17]

At the first meeting of the ACCC on October 11, 1961, Elder Lee announced the creation of three age-group correlation committees headed by a member of the Twelve, each supported by a staff-level secretary.[18] The children's committee was to direct the correlation of all curriculum for members from birth to age eleven; the youth committee, age twelve to roughly twenty; the

President Marion G. Romney, member of the All-Church Coordinating Council. (© Intellectual Reserve, Inc.)

adult committee age twenty and older. Marion G. Romney was named chairman of the adult committee, with Reed H. Bradford as secretary, Richard L. Evans was named as chairman of the youth committee with Daniel H. Ludlow as secretary, and Gordon B. Hinckley was named chairman of the children's committee with B. West Belnap as secretary. These committees, functioning under the guidance of the CEC and ACCC, became the primary mechanism to bring about a correlated curriculum in the Church. Their stewardship included correlating all curriculum developed for the priesthood quorums and the auxiliaries.

In June 1962, Elder Lee stressed the importance of fully defining the priesthood and its scope. He said, "When you get the priesthood fully defined it is going to be comparatively easy for us to define where [each auxiliary] fits in."[19] Defining and promoting the work of the priesthood largely became the responsibility of four standing priesthood committees: the home teaching committee, the missionary committee, the genealogy and temple committee, and the welfare committee. These committees were created and staffed between March and June 1963. Early on it was made clear that these committees were actually subcommittees of the General Priesthood Board, made up of the Quorum of the Twelve Apostles.[20] Their day-to-day work, though, was strongly associated with correlation and specifically with Elder Lee—both in his role as the chair of the General Priesthood Committee and as the CEC chair. In fact, the chairs of each priesthood committee became standing members of the CEC in January of 1964, and the managing directors who served under them attended when invited.[21] Each committee consisted of about twenty-five members and a chair.

These correlation councils and priesthood committees played a central role in the correlation effort. The three main goals of correlation were to place the priesthood where the Lord directed in the revelations, to put the family back at the center of the Church's efforts, and to correlate the material used by organizations to teach the gospel to both members and nonmembers. To achieve these goals, the CEC focused on four major initiatives throughout the sixties: home teaching, family home evening, priesthood training and enrichment, and curriculum correlation. This history will discuss these four major initiatives.

Home Teaching

Though correlation would ultimately entail many aspects of Church governance, in the early 1960s it centered on what would come to be known as home teaching. The original name of the home teaching program was the Priesthood Correlation Program.[22]

Home teaching actually dates back to the very beginning of the Church. From the days of Joseph Smith, teachers have visited the homes of members.[23] They have been called teachers, acting teachers, block teachers, ward teachers, and ultimately home teachers. Their duties have been defined by the scriptural injunction "to watch over the church always, and be with and strengthen them; and see that there is no iniquity in the church, neither hardness with each other, neither lying, backbiting, nor evil speaking; and see that the church meet together often, and also see that all the members do their duty" (D&C 20:53–55). The efforts and effectiveness of these programs, however, have varied greatly. By the mid-1900s, ward teachers were largely supervised by the Presiding Bishopric because the program was considered an Aaronic Priesthood responsibility.

Church authorities had long seen a need for greater correlation between the Quorum of the Twelve and the Presiding Bishopric.[24] A main issue was the lack of priesthood quorum oversight of the various versions of home teaching. By the 1950s, ward teaching had largely moved away from the concept of watching over and having responsibility for the welfare of families to simply going into the homes of members and sharing a message. This is not to suggest that ward teachers did not offer a meaningful service. However, the brethren were desirous of strengthening the efforts of the priesthood in watching over and ministering to the families of the Church. In November 1960, the

Presiding Bishopric was asked to work with the Quorum of the Twelve to develop a "vigorous ward teaching program."[25]

On March 22, 1961, Elder Lee presided over a meeting of the General Priesthood Committee in which they reviewed the final draft of the revised ward teaching program entitled "Priesthood Correlation Program."[26] That year fourteen stakes tested the new program under the guidance of a committee made up of the members of the Twelve. This program was turned over to the Correlation Executive Committee, who further fine-tuned it in preparation for Churchwide implementation. The program was first presented privately to President McKay and then to the combined First Presidency and Quorum of the Twelve, who gave their approval on August 30, 1962.[27] After several months, the final program was approved by members of both the Correlation Executive Committee and the All-Church Correlation Council (on January 9 and 25, 1963, respectively).[28] In the General Priesthood Meeting in October 1962, President Romney gave an excellent overview of the new program:

> Now, priesthood correlation, as we are using the term here, contemplates all that is now being done in ward teaching and much more. It unites under one undertaking many activities. It requires that attention be given to every member of every family, particularly to those who need special encouragement to live the gospel. It means much more than a perfunctory visit once a month. It includes:
>
> 1. Periodic visits to every family by two priesthood bearers;
> 2. Laboring with Melchizedek Priesthood bearers to build spiritual and temporal "strength";
> 3. Laboring with inactive and overage members of the Aaronic Priesthood under 21;
> 4. Activating and bringing into full church participation senior members of the Aaronic Priesthood and their families;
> 5. Fellowshipping and bringing into full activity recent converts, new arrivals, and all inactive church members;

6. Encouraging all parents and other family heads to maintain genuine Latter-day Saint homes in which are practiced and taught the sanctifying principles of the gospel.[29]

After the program was presented to the First Presidency and the Quorum of the Twelve, President McKay is reported to have said, "The program has been refined, and it is now the job of the various organizations of the church to make it work, not to say that this or that cannot work, but to see that those parts of any program which are affected will fit in and correlate with the Home Teaching Program. It is a home-centered, priesthood-centered program which embodies all."[30]

The name of the program was officially changed in March 1963 to the "Home Teaching Program."[31] This initiative was at the heart of the correlation effort to restore the priesthood to the center of the work of the ministry and to focus on the family. The home teachers were to be the means of supporting the family and connecting them to the priesthood. All other programs, whether priesthood-based or auxiliary-based, were to be correlated through the home teachers to the individual families. Home teachers were to be assigned by the Melchizedek Priesthood quorums under the direction of bishops or branch presidents. Home teachers would then report any needs they could not personally meet to their quorum leaders, who would share these concerns with the bishop. The bishop could then access all of the resources of the ward council to help the family.

Family Home Evening

The concept of setting apart one night as a family night has a long history. Most historians point to a program in the Salt Lake City Granite Stake directed by President Frank Y. Taylor as the formal beginning of the practice. For some years before the official inauguration of this program, the Granite Stake leadership had prompted stake members to devote at least one night a week to the "gathering of their children around their own fireside to teach them the principles of the gospel."[32] On October 16, 1909, President Taylor formally initiated the family night program within his stake. President Joseph F. Smith was one of the keynote speakers at that meeting. In April 1915, the First Presidency formally introduced the program to the entire Church. In the First Presidency letter, family night was recommended as a once-a-month practice.[33] Following this introduction, several Church leaders, including Heber J. Grant and George Albert Smith, periodically commended family night to the Saints. Sometimes family night was referred to as a monthly program and sometimes as a weekly program.[34] The name also changed periodically. In the late 1940s, it was referred to as the family hour. Up through the early 1960s, leaders struggled to get the majority of Church members to hold family home evening on a consistent basis.[35]

Home night was first formally discussed by the Correlation Executive Committee on December 12, 1962.[36] The program was seen as a perfect opportunity to fulfill all three major correlation objectives by putting the correlated curriculum directly into the hands of parents to enable them to teach the gospel to their families. Also, family night was thought to be closely tied to home teaching, the centerpiece of correlation at that time. On January 29, 1963, an assignment was made to undertake a study of the history of family night in the Church. Discussions also began regarding the development of a formal home-based curriculum.[37]

Elder Lee noted that at the time the First Presidency and Quorum of the Twelve approved age groupings and curriculum outlines, it was decided that there should be a formal plan for teaching the gospel in the home.[38] In April 1964, the correlation committee secretaries requested approval to develop a formal family night curriculum to be used beginning in January 1965. Forty-eight lessons—about one per week—were planned.[39]

In addition to developing a family night curriculum, the Correlation Executive Committee planned several steps to introduce and promote family night. A film entitled *Of Heaven and Home* was approved to reintroduce the program to the Church. An instructional filmstrip was planned and announcements were included in Church periodicals during the last quarter of 1964. Plans were made to develop lessons for priesthood and Relief Society meetings as well as for home teachers to bring into the home that would provide support to parents in their efforts to hold regular family nights. It was suggested that one sacrament meeting a month could be dedicated to a monthly family night theme.[40] As can be seen, the priesthood and auxiliaries were seen as aids to help parents more fully bring the gospel into their homes. Family night was the first attempt to bring the Church curriculum into the home, with the support of priesthood and auxiliary programs.[41]

In August 1964, the official name of the family night program was changed to family home evening.[42] Leaders suggested that each ward, under the direction of the stake president, designate one night a week as the official night for family home evening. The following month Elder Lee expressed a concern with holding family home evening on a weekly basis. He agreed it was ideal but worried that with so few members holding family home evening on a monthly basis, it may be a better idea to start with a monthly schedule and then move toward a weekly schedule later. They agreed to delay any public announcement until Elder Lee could counsel with President McKay. In the meantime, the correlation secretaries were asked to do further research on previous First Presidency statements regarding family home evening to make sure they were in line with what the First Presidency had counseled. The following month Elder Lee reported that President McKay wanted family home evening held on a weekly basis from the very beginning and asked correlation to proceed with their original plans.[43] Forty lessons had already been written, and they planned to finish the last lessons within two weeks. The 1965 family home evening lesson manual contained forty-six lessons and was distributed to families through home teachers.

With the home evening program officially initiated, the correlation committee worked to ensure that new curriculum would be ready for 1966–69. The goal of the curriculum was to help members develop closer relationships with their families and with Heavenly Father. A set of guidelines in accordance with the Blue Book—the committee's guidebook to a correlated curriculum—were proposed to guide the production of curriculum manuals each year.

Exactly who would be responsible for writing the family home evening manuals was a question which the Correlation Executive Committee wrestled with for several years. From 1965 through 1968, lessons were written by a three-member committee supervised by Elder Bruce R. McConkie with the assistance of Daniel Ludlow. Each year, to provide continuity, one member was released and another added. As early as 1966, the proposal was made to place family home evening under the priesthood home teaching program, then supervised by President Romney.[44] This recommendation was ultimately approved, and the family home evening committee was placed under the direct supervision of the priesthood home teaching committee in January 1969.[45] Leaders recommended that each stake set aside one evening every week for family home evening for the entire stake. Finally, in September 1970, a priesthood bulletin statement announced that family home evening would be held on Monday night throughout the Church.[46]

Priesthood Training and Enrichment

From the very beginning of correlation, Church leaders recognized the need for the priesthood to assume its proper place in the Lord's kingdom. At the April 1906 general conference, President Joseph F. Smith prophesied:

We expect to see the day, if we live long enough (and if some of us do not live long enough to see it, there are others who will), when every council of the Priesthood in the Church of Jesus Christ of Latter-day Saints will understand its duty, will assume its own responsibility, will magnify its calling, and fill its place in the Church, to the uttermost, according to the intelligence and ability possessed by it. When that day shall come, there will not be so much necessity for work that is now being done by the auxiliary organizations, because it will be done by the regular quorums of the Priesthood. The Lord designed and comprehended it from the beginning, and He has made provision in the Church whereby every need may be met and satisfied through the regular organizations of the Priesthood.[47]

Thus the instruction to direct the work of correlation was given to the General Priesthood Committee, with Elder Lee as its chairman.

Besides general Church governance, the work of the priesthood was divided into four areas of focus, as explained previously. The missionary, genealogy and temple, home teaching, and welfare committees were formed in March of 1963. Apostles chaired the first three and the Presiding Bishop chaired the welfare committee. The chairman and managing directors of each priesthood committee were added to the CEC to make sure that the priesthood curriculum and other training would be in line with the overall correlation program. This meant that by January of 1964, six of the Quorum of Twelve and the Presiding Bishop were members of the CEC.

These priesthood committees were tasked with creating curriculum for priesthood instruction as well as providing specific training and direction to help priesthood leaders fulfill their responsibilities. As early as 1964, these committees were already providing written curricula for the priesthood quorums in each of the four areas.[48] By 1965, a Melchizedek Priesthood manual was completed that was designed to teach priesthood holders their duties in all four areas. These committees continued to provide the curriculum for both the Melchizedek and Aaronic Priesthood groups and quorums throughout much of the decade. They also were charged to help develop the Melchizedek Priesthood handbook. This handbook was updated regularly and included instruction in the four focus areas. It also included information on ordinances and ceremonies and a large section on ward councils.[49] This handbook became a model that Elder Lee said was to be used by every curriculum writer.

Priesthood committees also provided general, regional, and stake training and instruction. As early as April 1963, the priesthood committees were assigned to attend stake conferences on an alternating basis to provide instruction in their areas of responsibility. Though it was recognized that all priesthood holders had some responsibilities for each of the four areas, the brethren also saw some specialization by priesthood quorums. Home teaching was the responsibility of all Melchizedek Priesthood quorums, missionary work was associated with the Quorums of the seventies, genealogy with high priests, and welfare with elders quorums.[50]

Regional representatives. Though progress was made in revitalizing the priesthood, the challenge of how to deal with the geographic and numeric growth of the Church remained. In 1941, there were 138 stakes in the Church. By 1967, there were 435 stakes and 1,200 more stake conferences.[51] This growth would only accelerate in the future, making it even more difficult to provide training and leadership. Elder Lee spent May 7, 1967, at home recovering from surgery and pondering how to address this challenge.[52] The Church had previously been regionalized for welfare and other purposes into seventy regions (with as many as twelve stakes per region). With this concept in mind, Elder Lee recorded the basic concept of regional representatives of the Twelve in his journal.[53] On May 16, Elder Lee dictated a memo "relative to the future role of priesthood committee representatives and the desirability of vesting them with a designated priesthood authority by naming 'regional coordinators' in the seventy regions of the Church."[54] By May 30, the First Presidency and Quorum of the Twelve approved the concept. Two days later, correlation leaders met to discuss the need

Elder Thomas S. Monson, member of the Adult Correlation Committee. (© Intellectual Reserve, Inc.)

for a new level of Church leadership. Elder Lee asked the CEC members for ideas regarding how to most effectively organize the change.[55]

By the October 1967 general conference, the First Presidency and Quorum of the Twelve unanimously approved the calling of regional representatives of the Twelve. These leaders were called on a service basis. They continued to work and live in their homes, but were asked to train and help direct the work within their geographic areas. The leaders determined that most of the priesthood committee members would be released by the end of the year, with many being called as regional representatives.[56] The official announcement was given by the First Presidency in general conference. There would be two regional conferences held each year. General auxiliary leaders would conduct training at regional conferences and would no longer attend stake conferences.[57]

Under the direction of the First Presidency and Quorum of the Twelve, the CEC and ACCC became the main bodies used to implement these changes. For the next three years, the committees worked out the details regarding how regional representatives would function and be trained. At first, their training was developed by the Adult Correlation Committee under the leadership of Elder Thomas S. Monson.[58] By September 1967, Elder Lee created a leadership committee, separate from the Adult Correlation Committee but still chaired by Elder Monson, to continue developing priesthood leadership training for regional representatives and local leaders.[59] Wendell J. Ashton, James E. Faust, Neal A. Maxwell, Hugh W. Pinnock, and Rex A. Skidmore ultimately served on this committee under Thomas S. Monson. The regions would be reconstituted to more evenly divide stakes throughout the church. Instead of 70 regions, there would be 108 regions composed of one to six stakes.[60] A letter was sent to all stake presidents inviting them to attend the October 1967 general conference to receive training on the concept of regional representatives and to be introduced to their new regional representative.

By January 1968, the authority and responsibility of regional representatives was clarified. Regional representatives were not responsible for every aspect of Church work within stakes and wards, and they held no direct-line authority. They were also not to attend stake conferences unless authorized to do so by the Twelve. However, they were explicitly asked to provide training and leadership in the four priesthood programs and to conduct regional meetings.[61] In April 1968, Elder Lee explained that regional representatives worked on three separate levels. They had administrative responsibility over the four priesthood programs and, by appointment of the Twelve, were to attend and train at stake conferences. They were to be a training resource, though not a line authority, when working with stake presidents. And finally, they had no responsibility in some areas, such as temples and patriarchs. In summary, they were representatives of the Twelve for the purpose of training and providing priesthood leadership, especially as it pertained to the four priesthood areas.

Curriculum

Since the early 1900s, there had been at least eight attempts made by different committees to correlate the curriculum of the Church.[62] In 1960, Antone K. Romney, secretary to the CEC, was asked to lead a research committee to study the past correlation attempts and each organization's current curriculum throughout the entire Church. Their final study and recommendations were presented in July 1961.[63] They recommended that all curricula be correlated according to three age-groups by three correlation committees. These committees would work with, but not supplant, the existing organizations. The suggestion to correlate curriculum by age cannot be originally attributed to the research committee: that recommendation first came from the First Presidency in 1940 to the Union Board of the Auxiliaries, the correlation organization at that time.[64] However, it had not yet been implemented.

Each organization was told to proceed with their planned 1962 curricula but charged to have their proposed 1963 curricula reviewed by a correlation Reading Committee. The children's committee created the pamphlet *Curriculum for Children*, the youth committee created the pamphlet *Proposed Curriculum for Youth*, and the adult committee created the pamphlet *Instructional Curriculum for Adults*.[65] These would ultimately form the basis of the Blue Book, the term used to refer to the "Proposed Curriculum of Instruction by Age Group." Once approved, this document guided all future efforts by the CEC, ACCC, and Correlation Committees to correlate the curriculum. President McKay and members of the Quorum of Twelve Apostles unanimously approved the Blue Book on June 21, 1962.[66]

With these guidelines in place, writers were called to begin working on curricula for the priesthood while the auxiliaries continued to work on their own curricula. Elder Lee stressed the importance of having all curricula reviewed by the correlation committees in order to assure that the curricula fit the guidelines established by the Blue Book.[67] Though the hope was to have all curricula reviewed as early as 1963, the target date for a fully correlated curriculum was 1965.[68] Each committee was to review all curricula for its age-group. As a final check, the three secretaries of each age-group committee were to read all curricula from every age-group before it was brought to the CEC for final approval. If there were conflicts between any organizations (be they priesthood or auxiliary), the issue would be brought to the member of the Twelve who was the chairman of that age-group's committee. He would then resolve the conflict in conjunction with the originating organization or bring it to the CEC.[69]

In one of the correlation meetings, the committee shared an example of how the Primary would work through the correlation process. The writers for the Primary were to create a curriculum proposal based on the guidelines contained in the Blue Book. After the Primary president approved it, she would then send it to Elder Lee, who was the chair of both the CEC and the reading committee. Elder Lee would pass the proposal on to the correlation age-group secretaries. The secretaries would bring it to their respective committees for review. They would pass their recommendations back to the secretaries of each age-group committee, who would review the proposal one last time before resubmitting it to Elder Lee. Elder Lee would then instruct the Primary president to work with the Apostle who was the chair of the children's committee to resolve any differences before submitting the curriculum to the publications committee.[70]

As was the case in earlier attempts to correlate the curriculum, this did not always work flawlessly. There were constant struggles to produce curricula in a timely manner. In fact, fully correlated curricula for adults and youth did not appear until 1967. The children's curriculum took an additional year.[71] Often, the challenge was working everything through the review process in a timely fashion. Other times, there were differences of opinion between writers, leaders of organizations, and the correlation committees. In certain instances, organizations were given two or even three years to fully adopt correlation recommendations. Elder Lee constantly stressed the need for everyone to be involved in the process from the beginning in order to come up with the most effective curricula possible. By the end of the 1960s, this had largely been accomplished. It was also determined that curriculum would be written and used on a rotational basis rather than writing completely new curriculum for each organization every year.[72]

Conclusion

The changes to Church curriculum mirrored the other substantial changes brought about in the name of correlation. It took years for many of these changes to come to fruition, and it was difficult for some to accept them. Faithful members had labored for years on the early Church boards and in the auxiliaries. These members cherished their service, and some struggled to see things change.[73] The leaders right on up through Elder Lee and President McKay realized this. There was a constant theme throughout the meeting minutes of the need to proceed with caution. This caution sometimes meant that whole portions of the program were held off for substantial periods of time, not because of any known problem with the new program but out of sensitivity to those who would be affected by the changes. However, ultimately the changes the presiding brethren saw necessary were carried through.

At the October 1971 general conference, President Harold B. Lee, then serving as a counselor to President Joseph Fielding Smith, summarized many correlation accomplishments during the past decade:

> Even as I repeat them now it seems unbelievable that we have been able to do what we have done in this time: priesthood home teaching; family home evening; unified social services; the expansion and clarification of the missionary responsibilities of the seventies quorums; expansion of the home-study seminary course; bishops' training course; priesthood teacher development; libraries and how to use them; definition of a closer relationship between the Aaronic Priesthood and the MIA; improving and making more effective preparation, editing, translating, and distributing of teaching materials, and the distribution to meet the deadlines at seasonal beginnings; introduction of a Church-wide library program; the experimental study of the Church membership all over the world to achieve a feeling of closer relationship with the full Church program; the correlation and clarification

of the LDS Student Association role to meet the unmet youth needs using the existing structure rather than a separate professional staff; and the correlation of military relations programs using existing Church structure instead of professionals. So we go on and on, and all of this under the direction of the Twelve, as I have already explained, acting under the responsibility given by the First Presidency; and you, their brethren, are to carry this to the ends of the earth so that these things might be implemented in every part of the world—a tremendous responsibility.[74]

Even that list is not complete. The correlated music program, new schedules for Church meetings, stake and ward PEC and ward council meetings, the position of executive secretary at both the ward and stake level, Church athletics, the prospective elders program, consolidated and correlated reporting systems, priesthood bulletins and a new *General Handbook of Instructions*, consolidation of Church magazines, and a general Church budget could also be included.[75] So many things which we now take for granted were developed at this critical time.

Correlation encompassed much more than curricular issues. What had begun at the turn of the century under the leadership of Elder McKay truly came of age under the leadership of Elder Lee. In the middle of his efforts, Elder Lee once stated, "I have never seen the will of the Lord manifest itself more than in the last two years. President McKay has said on occasion that nothing more important has happened in his entire administration than this correlation work. May we not falter, and may we not grow weary, and may our task not become burdensome, but may we receive that divine assurance as we pursue our course step by step."[76] Elder Lee constantly reminded his fellow laborers that they worked under the guidance and direction of the First Presidency. On several occasions he admonished those who served under him to stay within the bounds which the First Presidency had set. Before every major initiative, the meeting minutes indicate that they did not move forward until after the First Presidency and Quorum of the Twelve had given guidance and approved their decisions.

Though correlation may have been the mechanism that helped to bring about the changes, the effort operated under the guidance and direction of the First Presidency and the Quorum of the Twelve. It was largely directed by Harold B. Lee throughout his service as an Apostle, member of the First Presidency, and Church President. As his biographer said, "Some historians may well argue that President Harold B. Lee's most significant lifetime work for the Church, though not generally understood by the membership, was the reorganization of the kingdom under the direction of President David O. McKay."[77]

The history of correlation clearly shows President McKay's, President Lee's, and other leaders' fingerprints. But to see correlation as they saw it is to see the hand of God moving his work forward. Almost all those who were associated with the changes created through correlation spoke of the divine direction they received. President Lee exclaimed: "We have been receiving as pertinent and important divine direction as has ever been given to the Church in any similar period in its history through the prophet and leader who now presides as the President of this Church. You may recognize it in some of the developments we know as the correlation program. You have seen it being unraveled bit by bit, and you will see and hear more of it."[78]

Referring to the correlation program, Marion G. Romney explained, "We know that it has been developed by assignment of the First Presidency under the spirit of revelation; those of you who have been close to use will know this is so. We will continue to work under the spirit of the Lord."[79]

The leaders often spoke of correlation as much more than a simple reorganization. They saw in correlation the Lord's preparation for the future of his kingdom. President N. Eldon Tanner expressed this view when he said, "Priesthood Correlation is the closest blueprint yet in mortality to the plan presented in the Grand Council of Heaven before the world was created and is the most effective utilization thus far of special keys given to the Prophet Joseph Smith in the Kirtland Temple."[80]

President Monson, who was part of the correlation process from the early 1960s, stated that "the battle plan whereby we fight to save the souls of men is not our own. It was provided . . . by the inspiration and revelation of the Lord. Yes, I speak of that plan which will bring us victory, even the Correlation Program of the Church.[81] Though the period from 1960 to 1972 saw some of the greatest achievements in this battle plan, history shows that those achievements came as a result of the inspired work that began at the turn of the century. It has been stated that Church correlation did not spring forth, Minerva-like, in the mid-1960s. It came line upon line, precept upon precept, born of necessity and from a long history filled with both inspiration and the best efforts of all involved.

Notes

1. Harold B. Lee, regional representatives seminar, 2–3, in Bruce C. Hafen, *A Disciple's Life: The Biography of Neal A. Maxwell* (Salt Lake City: Deseret Book, 2002), 325.

2. The Relief Society was organized in March 1842 by the Prophet Joseph. The Sunday School was organized December 9, 1849, by Brigham Young. The Young Women's Mutual Improvement Association was organized on November 28, 1869, as the Young Ladies' Retrenchment Society. The Young Men's Mutual Improvement Association was formed on June 10, 1875, also by Brigham Young. Finally, the Primary was organized on August 25, 1878, by John Taylor.

3. Dale Mouritsen, "Efforts to Correlate Mormon Agencies in the Twentieth Century: A Review," 1974, 6, Church History Library, The Church of Jesus Christ of Latter-day Saints, Salt Lake City.

4. Joseph F. Smith, in Conference Report, April 1906, 3.

5. Gregory A. Prince and Wm. Robert Wright, *David O. McKay and the Rise of Modern Mormonism* (Salt Lake City: University of Utah, 2005), 141.

6. Joseph F. Smith, in Marion G. Romney, "The Basics of Priesthood Correlation" (address, General Priesthood Board meeting, Salt Lake City, November 15, 1967), 2.

7. Minutes of the Social Advisory Committee, 1916–20, Church History Library.

8. Prince and Wright, *Rise of Modern Mormonism*, 142.

9. First Presidency of The Church of Jesus Christ of Latter-day Saints, letter, January 1939, in Antone K. Romney, "History of Correlation of L.D.S. Church Auxiliaries," F.

10. Grant, Clark, and McKay, "Memorandum of Suggestions," in Antone K. Romney, "History of the Correlation," G.

11. Heber J. Grant, J. Reuben Clark Jr., and David O. McKay to Joseph Fielding Smith, John A. Widtsoe, Harold B. Lee, and Marion G. Romney, August 9, 1944, in *Messages of the First Presidency of The Church of Jesus Christ of Latter-day Saints*, vol. 6, ed. James R. Clark (Salt Lake City: Bookcraft, 1975), 209.

12. First Presidency and Council of the Twelve, temple meeting minutes, January 22, 1948, in Antone K. Romney, "History of the Correlation," H.

13. L. Brent Goates, *Harold B. Lee: Prophet and Seer* (Salt Lake City: Deseret Book, 1985), 365.

14. Harold B. Lee, as quoted by Marion G. Romney in "Correlation Items," Church History Library, 3.

15. Minutes of the Correlation Executive Committee, 1961–65, volume 1, Church History Library, 7 (hereafter Minutes, Correlation Executive Committee, 1961–65). See also correlation chronology as reflected in Minutes of the Correlation Executive Committee, 1960–71, comp. Carol H. Cannon, Church History Library, 1 (hereafter Minutes, Correlation Executive Committee, 1960–71).

16. Minutes, Correlation Executive Committee, 1961–65, 14–15; see also Minutes, Correlation Executive Committee, 1960–71, 1.

17. Minutes, Correlation Executive Committee, 1961–65, 10; see also Minutes, Correlation Executive Committee, 1960–71, 1.

18. Minutes, Correlation Executive Committee, 1961–65, 9; see also Minutes, Correlation Executive Committee, 1960–71, 1.

19. Minutes, Correlation Executive Committee, 1961–65, 36. A similar but inferior paraphrase (although it is quoted, it varies from the meeting minutes) is found in Minutes, Correlation Executive Committee, 1960–71, 2: "Bring the priesthood

back where it should be, according to the revelations, and then determine the relationship of the auxiliaries to the priesthood."

20. Minutes, Correlation Executive Committee, 1961–65, 93.

21. Marion G. Romney was asked to chair the home teaching committee with Presiding Bishop John Vandenberg as vice-chair; Spencer W. Kimball was asked to chair the missionary committee; Howard W. Hunter, the genealogy and temple committee; and Bishop John H. Vandenberg, the welfare committee.

22. Minutes, Correlation Executive Committee, 1961–65, 46–47.

23. "Recollections of the Prophet Joseph Smith: Elder William Farrington Cahoon," *Juvenile Instructor*, August 15, 1892, 492–93.

24. Prince and Wright, *Rise of Modern Mormonism*, 142.

25. Goates, *Harold B. Lee*, 367.

26. Goates, *Harold B. Lee*, 367.

27. Goates, *Harold B. Lee*, 371.

28. Minutes, Correlation Executive Committee, 1961–65, 69–77; see also Minutes, Correlation Executive Committee, 1960–71, 4.

29. Marion G. Romney, in Conference Report, October 1962, 77–78.

30. Minutes, Correlation Executive Committee, 1961–65, 84.

31. Minutes, Correlation Executive Committee, 1961–65, 81; see also Minutes, Correlation Executive Committee, 1960–71, 4.

32. Robert E. Larson, "Factors in the Acceptance and Adoption of Family Home Evening in the LDS Church: A Study of Planned Change" (master's thesis, Brigham Young University, 1967).

33. "Home Evening," Editors' Table, *Improvement Era*, April 1915, 733–34.

34. George Albert Smith, in Conference Report, April 1926, 145–47.

35. Larson, "Factors in the Acceptance and Adoption," 19.

36. Minutes, Correlation Executive Committee, 1961–65, 65; see also Minutes, Correlation Executive Committee, 1960–71, 4.

37. Minutes, Correlation Executive Committee, 1961–65, 78.

38. Minutes, Correlation Executive Committee, 1961–65, 170.

39. Minutes, Correlation Executive Committee, 1961–65, 175.

40. Minutes, Correlation Executive Committee, 1961–65, 176; see also Minutes, Correlation Executive Committee, 1960–71, 12.

41. Minutes, Correlation Executive Committee, 1961–65, 194.

42. Minutes, Correlation Executive Committee, 1961–65, 207. In Minutes, Correlation Executive Committee, 1960–71, this date is incorrect. The minutes say that the name was changed in June 1964, but although it was suggested in June, it was not voted on and accepted until August.

43. Minutes, Correlation Executive Committee, 1961–65, 221; see also Minutes, Correlation Executive Committee, 1960–71, 12.

44. Minutes, Correlation Executive Committee, 1961–65, 141.

45. Minutes of the Correlation Executive Committee, 1966–72, volume 2, Church History Library, 295 (hereafter Minutes, Correlation Executive Committee, 1966–72); see also Minutes, Correlation Executive Committee, 1969–71, 27.

46. Minutes, Correlation Executive Committee, 1966–72, 382–83; see also Minutes, Correlation Executive Committee, 1960–71, 31.

47. Joseph F. Smith, in Conference Report, April 1906, 3.

48. Minutes, Correlation Executive Committee, 1961–65, 154–55; see also Minutes, Correlation Executive Committee, 1960–71, 9.

49. Minutes, Correlation Executive Committee, 1961–65, 138–39.

50. Minutes, Correlation Executive Committee, 1961–65, 130; see also Minutes, Correlation Executive Committee, 1960–71, 7.

51. Minutes, Correlation Executive Committee, 1966–72, 160.

52. Goates, *Harold B. Lee*, 373.

53. Goates, *Harold B. Lee*, 373.

54. Goates, *Harold B. Lee*, 373.

55. Minutes, Correlation Executive Committee, 1966–72, 160.

56. Hafen, *Disciple's Life*, 323.

57. Hafen, *Disciple's Life*, 323.

58. Hafen, *Disciple's Life*, 320–21.

59. Hafen, *Disciple's Life*, 320–21.

60. Minutes, Correlation Executive Committee, 1966–72, 211.

61. Minutes, Correlation Executive Committee, 1966–72, 229.

62. See Michael A. Goodman, "Correlation: Putting First Things First," in *A Firm Foundation: Church Organization and Administration* (Provo, UT: Religious Studies Center, Brigham Young University; Salt Lake City: Deseret Book 2011), 319–38.

63. Prince and Wright, *Rise of Modern Mormonism*, 149.

64. Grant, Clark, and McKay, "Memorandum of Suggestions," G.

65. Minutes, Correlation Executive Committee, 1961–65, 33–34.

66. Minutes, Correlation Executive Committee, 1961–65, 47; see also Minutes, Correlation Executive Committee, 1960–71, 3.

67. Minutes, Correlation Executive Committee, 1961–65, 148; see also Minutes, Correlation Executive Committee, 1960–71, 10–11.

68. Minutes, Correlation Executive Committee, 1961–65, 87.

69. Minutes, Correlation Executive Committee, 1961–65, 167.

70. Minutes, Correlation Executive Committee, 1961–65, 166–73.

71. Minutes, Correlation Executive Committee, 1966–72, 12–13; see also Minutes, Correlation Executive Committee, 1960–71, 19.

72. Minutes, Correlation Executive Committee, 1966–72, 348.

73. For further details on some of the struggles and how they were addressed, see Goates, *Harold B. Lee*; Hafen, *Disciple's Life*; Prince and Wright, *Rise of Modern Mormonism*.

74. Goates, *Harold B. Lee*, 368.

75. Goates, *Harold B. Lee*, 368–69.

76. Minutes, Correlation Executive Committee Meetings, 1961–65, 128.

77. Goates, *Harold B. Lee*, 363.

78. Harold B. Lee, in Conference Report, October 1964, 137.

79. Marion G. Romney, "Church Correlation" (address to seminary and institute of religion faculty, Brigham Young University, Provo, UT, June 22, 1964).

80. N. Eldon Tanner (speech, Priesthood Genealogy Committee training meeting, December 1963), quoted in *Encyclopedia of Latter-day Saint History*, ed. Arnold Garr, Donald Q. Cannon, and Richard O. Cowan (Salt Lake City: Deseret Book, 2000), 251.

81. Thomas S. Monson, "Correlation Brings Blessings," *Relief Society Magazine*, April 1967, 247.

Chapter 14

Historical Highlights of LDS Family Services

John P. Livingstone

Walking north on State Street in downtown Salt Lake City a block and a half southeast of Temple Square, one comes to the remodeled Promised Valley Playhouse. Not only has the exterior of the old playhouse been cleaned and refurbished, but the interior has also been changed dramatically. Where families used to enter for entertainment, they now enter for edification. The former playhouse now houses the world headquarters of LDS Family Services.

Just as pioneer trails changed from wagon roads to gravel thoroughfares to asphalt highways and finally to modern high-speed freeways, LDS Family Services has grown from humble beginnings into a major resource for priesthood leaders and members alike. The organization is now set to move forward internationally in order to bless Latter-day Saints all over the world much as it has in North America.

John P. Livingstone is an associate professor of Church history and doctrine at Brigham Young University.

As Salt Lake City grew into a cosmopolitan center at the latter end of the nineteenth century, social problems already common in other large American cities began to emerge. Out-of-wedlock pregnancy, family violence, various forms of abuse, and criminal activity, to name a few, tested the mettle of civic and Church leaders. These problems underscored the need for some kind of organized effort that would help individuals and families battle some of mankind's oldest ailments. By the end of World War I, Church leaders recognized a need for technical assistance with these social ills. The lay leadership of the Church came from all walks of life and voluntarily served Church members who brought issues and challenges to their ecclesiastical doors. While the vast majority of these problems could be solved in the office or home of a dedicated bishop who, more often than not, left his work in the field, the shop, or the office to listen and counsel as directed by spiritual promptings, some difficulties required time and resources not readily available to him. This need resulted in the organization of what is known today as LDS Family Services.

The history of LDS Family Services parallels the history of social work as it evolved in the United States. Amy Brown Lyman, who in 1940 became the eighth general Relief Society president, was familiar with social work. In the early 1900s, while her husband, Richard Lyman (who later served as an apostle), attended the University of Chicago, Amy Brown Lyman took social work classes that introduced her to the famous Hull House in Chicago. She was deeply impressed with the efforts of social work pioneer Jane Addams, the primary force behind the Hull House, where university students and other visitors could interact with troubled individuals or families to try to help them to work their way out of life's problems, and came away determined to help the needy back home in Utah. Indeed, this kind of social work seemed to typify true New Testament Christian living to both Jane Addams and Amy Lyman.

This article is a descriptive study and overview of the growth and development of LDS Family Services since its beginning within the

Relief Society and subsequently under several commissioners (all of whom are still living). Major participants in the organization as well as almost all of the commissioners were interviewed regarding their particular era.

The Pioneer Trail:
Relief Society Gives Birth to Social Services

Amy Lyman's short internship at the Hull House gave her ideas regarding how significant social ills might be approached and hoped that they could be rectified in a measured, organized fashion. Her subsequent call to the Relief Society General Board facilitated the creation of a social services department within the Relief Society. In 1917, Utah governor Simon Bamberger asked Sister Lyman to attend the

Amy Brown Lyman, founder of Relief Society social work programs and General Relief Society President, 1940–45. (Used by permission, Utah State Historical Society. All rights reserved.)

National Conference of Charities and Corrections as an official delegate to help Utah families displaced by World War I. At a follow-up six-week course in Denver, several Utah women receiving an intense institute, or seminar, laid the foundation for the development of social work in Utah. The instructors taught that "the principal values and methods of charity organizations were 1) rehabilitation through diagnosis and case treatment of families in need; 2) education of the public in correct principles of social welfare work and cooperation; and 3) gathering evidence through the first two principles and establishing volunteer networks to eliminate the causes of poverty and dependence."[1]

Utilizing what they had learned in Denver, these Relief Society women, in conjunction with the Red Cross, went about establishing social service organizations in several Utah cities. Sister Lyman took responsibility for following up with families assisted through the Red Cross that identified themselves as Latter-day Saints. She later met with President Joseph F. Smith, who suggested that she head up a social services department within the Relief Society. After returning to Denver for additional training, Sister Lyman established the Relief Society Social Services Department in January 1919. President Joseph F. Smith had passed away in November 1918 and was succeeded by Heber J. Grant.[2] Sister Lyman taught a six-week summer course on social services in 1920 in Aspen Grove, Utah. Sixty-five stakes (representing 78 percent of the Church) sent sisters to receive social work training at the event. The following year, the Relief Society began holding social service institutes to train local Relief Society women in family welfare work.[3] Over four thousand sisters received training to become "stake social service aids."[4] Additional Relief Society Social Service Department branch offices, staffed by professional social workers, were soon created in Los Angeles in 1934 and also in Ogden in 1940 to meet family welfare needs. Social services efforts, though, were primarily seen by many as a women's program.

An important supplement to social services work began in 1954, when the Indian Student Placement Program was formally initiated. That year, so many Indian children were placed in Latter-day Saint foster homes that it caught the attention of John Farr Larson, director of the Utah Department of Public Welfare, who "indicated his concern inasmuch as there was a law which required children placed for foster care to be placed through a licensed agency."[5] Not many records were kept of the earliest efforts, but in 1957 Elder Mark E. Petersen invited Clarence R. Bishop to meet with Elder Spencer W. Kimball, who headed the Lamanite Committee of the Church.[6] Because the Relief

Society Social Services Department was licensed with the State of Utah, Indian Placement headed by Bishop, was placed under its auspices and formal home evaluations were carried out for students arriving from the reservations. The Indian Placement Program burgeoned from the basement of the new Relief Society Building in the mid 1950s.[7]

In 1956, the Relief Society Social Services Department added a Youth Guidance Program, which was instigated to help troubled teens and children.[8] In the sixties, Allen J. Proctor was hired within the Youth Guidance Program to help with youth "camps." He told of initial youth groups meeting in the basement of the Relief Society building near the Salt Lake Temple. They were a lively and somewhat rough group of boys (referred to as delinquents) to be in such a stately new building. On one occasion, a young man escaped from the group, only to be brought back by the scruff of his neck by none other than general Relief Society president Belle Spafford. It was shortly after this incident that the youth groups were moved to the old Veteran's Hospital on 12th Avenue and E Street in Salt Lake City, where they had a beautiful view of the valley while they participated in therapy.[9] As these programs expanded, more Relief Society Social Services Department offices were opened in Phoenix and Las Vegas in 1962 and 1965 respectively.

Sister Spafford was a strong supporter of social work, especially while it was under the direction and responsibility of the Relief Society. Shortly after the establishment of the Brigham Young University law school, she remarked in a monthly meeting with social services workers, "Ernest Wilkinson got his law school, and I'm going to get my social work school . . . whatever it takes!"[10] Shortly afterward, it was announced that Brigham Young University would start a social work school.

The Trail Becomes a Road:
LDS Social Services under Priesthood Direction

In 1969, due to the Church correlation movement, a decision was made to bring the social services efforts under priesthood direction.

289

Unified Social Services took all aspects of social services from the Relief Society. Elder Marvin J. Ashton said: "I was called in September 1969 to act as managing director for the Social Services program. The First Presidency at that time directed that President Spencer W. Kimball, Acting President of the Council of the Twelve, Elder Thomas S. Monson of the Council of the Twelve, Presiding Bishop John H. Vandenberg, and Sister Belle S. Spafford, president of the Relief Society, form an advisory committee, with Elder Marion G. Romney of the Council of the Twelve as chairman. This committee provides me with help in guiding the program."[11]

Victor L. Brown Jr. became the first director (later commissioner) of the new social services entity.[12] In 1971, Social Services and Health Services were placed under the auspices of the Presiding Bishopric, and Unified Social Services was changed to LDS Social Services. Commissioner Brown shepherded LDS Social Services through the years when some members and leaders wondered whether or not there was a real need for professional counseling and other services when they felt most issues could be handled by local bishops. Bishop J. Richard Clarke clarified the role of LDS Social Services when he said,

> The purpose or mission of LDS Social Services is to assist priesthood leaders by providing quality licensed and clinical services to members of the Church. This is accomplished by using highly qualified staff members and volunteers whose values, knowledge, and professional skills are in harmony with the gospel and the order of the Church. We should remember that LDS Social Services exists . . . because our prophets were inspired to give local priesthood leaders a resource to meet social-emotional needs.

Bishop Clarke also quoted from the *Welfare Services Handbook*:

> The bishop and Melchizedek Priesthood quorum and group leaders are the Lord's ecclesiastical leaders. They cannot and

must not abdicate their responsibility to any agency. Social services agencies are established to be a resource to the ecclesiastical leaders. There is no substitute for the inspired counsel and
priesthood blessing by the bishop or quorum or group leader.[13]

In 1973, Church leaders saw the wisdom of making LDS Social
Services a corporate entity separate from the Church. Human problems being what they were, it was only natural that some legal issues
arose which made the creation of a separate corporation a wise move.
This choice protected the financial resources of the Church and the
workload of Church leaders and allowed worldwide membership to
grow unhindered by the possibility of lawsuits that would require inor-
dinate use of Church funds.

The period between 1969 and 1976 became a unification period
for LDS Social Services. Bringing together and organizing the three
main branches of the Church's social services efforts—Adoption, Youth
Guidance, and Indian Placement—necessarily meant trying to join
efforts, programs, and personalities that were originally very independent. It took some effort to figure things out and determine responsibilities. The three main facets of Church social services merged into
one organization to help ecclesiastical leaders and members deal with
serious human problems in clinically appropriate ways. Skilled professionals helped priesthood leaders by assisting with issues beyond the
scope and time constraints of most lay leaders.

The Road Widens: Social Services Encircled by Church Welfare

Harold C. Brown succeeded Victor Brown as commissioner of LDS
Social Services in the fall of 1976 and served in that capacity until
1981.[14] Victor went on to work for Brigham Young University and
helped establish the Comprehensive Clinic. This clinic offered counseling services to the community at discounted rates by employing graduate students from the various Brigham Young University mental health

Elder Harold C. Brown, longtime commissioner of LDS Social Services. (© Intellectual Reserve, Inc.)

programs who worked under their professors' supervision.[15]

Early in his career, Harold was assigned to develop and upgrade policies and procedures for case workers, and in 1973 he was promoted to coordinate all licensed service for LDS Social Services. By 1974, he and William E. Bush supervised all of the sixteen agencies under Oliver McPherson, the assistant commissioner under Victor Brown. Harold became commissioner of LDS Social Services in September of 1976. From 1976 to 1981, LDS Social Services was to some extent reintegrated into the administration of Welfare Services. In 1981, Harold left his assignment as commissioner to become the director of field operations under the managing director of Welfare Services. Later, from 1985 to 1996, Harold returned and again served as commissioner of LDS Social Services. His influence would continue when he later became chairman of the Board of Trustees of LDS Family Services while serving as managing director of Church Welfare. The influence of Harold C. Brown's influence may well be called the most important force in the modern history of LDS Family Services.

The period of 1976 to 1985 saw LDS Social Services taking its rightful place alongside other branches of the Church's welfare efforts (such as Deseret Industries, Church farms, and bishops' storehouses). Welfare Services covered all aspects of welfare concerns within the Church in an organized, correlated fashion. It became clear to Church leaders and members that LDS Social Services fit within Welfare Services in a way that made intuitive sense and seemed to indicate divine intervention within Church correlation efforts.

William S. Bush followed Harold Brown as commissioner in 1981 and served for the next two years.[16] Bush was disturbed by accounts of child abuse that seemed to be prevalent in the early 1980s not only among the general public but among Church members as well. It seemed to him that priesthood leaders needed some support in this area. He began to consider what could be done, especially for women affected by sexual abuse in their early years. He could also see that the placement program was becoming less and less necessary as an alternative to disappearing boarding schools on reservations throughout the United States and Canada. Though the program would continue throughout his time as commissioner, he could clearly see the end was near. As the Church Educational System (CES) began to reduce their involvement on reservations throughout the country and lose connections with reservation families, the influence of LDS Social Services diminished as well. During Bush's time as commissioner, adoption services went national, and LDS Social Services was represented on the National Council for Adoption.

Bush was succeeded by Larry L. Whiting in September of 1984. Whiting remembered stepping into this new assignment:

This was a time when child sexual abuse issues were surfacing (even possibly in a few cases with an exaggerated emphasis). Alert bishops were finding that some adult women had been sexually abused as children and young children currently were also suffering from abuse. Somewhat of froth was in the making as increasing numbers of women were being helped by professionals to "remember" abusive activities involving priesthood leaders and satanic perpetrations. Some were encouraged by misguided therapists to "create recollections" . . . where all manner of bizarre activities were allegedly being perpetrated on unsuspecting victims. Needless to say I was skeptical of such stories.[17]

Whiting and his administrative team began to craft a response to these serious issues in an effort to help Church leaders respond to matters such as these. Many laws were being passed around the country requiring citizens and professionals to report abuse cases to authorities. It became necessary for Church leaders to address issues of priest-penitent concern for both the victims and, in some cases, repentant perpetrators. It became clear that Church leaders were greatly benefited by being able to consult with both mental health professionals as well as legal counsel. An abuse help line was established to help local priesthood leaders proceed wisely and within legal limits where necessary. This timely help made a crucial difference for priesthood leaders and helped them offer sensitive and accurate assistance to members. Whiting's team also printed a Churchwide publication discussing abuse.

The Indian Placement Service faded away during Whiting's service as commissioner. Earlier, an official Church announcement said:

> The First Presidency has announced changes that will eventually shape the Indian Student Placement Program into an experience for high-school-age students only.
>
> Beginning with the 1985–86 school year, the program will be limited to students in grades six through twelve, and the entry age will be raised one level each year until the 1988–89 school year, when the program will be limited to those in grades nine through twelve.
>
> The announcement follows a change in 1984 that made only students in grades five through twelve eligible for the program.
>
> "In addition to the age change," the First Presidency said in a letter to General Authorities and to priesthood leaders in the western United States, "enrollment standards will be raised. Information regarding specific eligibility requirements will be available through LDS Social Services agencies. Current participants, regardless of their age, may continue to participate as long

as they meet the higher standards and their parents desire them to continue.

"These changes should not be viewed as a phaseout, but as a refinement of this program. The purpose of these modifications is to provide students with experiences that will promote spirituality, leadership, and academic excellence, and, therefore, strengthen the family, Church, and community."[18]

Notwithstanding the comment about a "phaseout" of the Indian Placement Program, it was reduced to the point of elimination later on. Ironically, Clarence R. Bishop, who was involved in some of the earliest days of the formalized Indian Placement Program, was present when arrangements were made regarding activities that would continue until the last students graduated from the program.

Thousands of Native American students had lived in Latter-day Saint homes from the early 1950s through the late 1980s. Most lost their fear of the dominant culture around them, while many Latter-day Saint families lost their fear of minorities. While arrangements were far from perfect, sacrifices were made, learning occurred, and barriers fell. Indian Placement students found employment all over the United States, many in responsible positions on and off their reservations. When the "fade-away" decision was made, Whiting said, "I lost control and wept."[19] The caseworkers who had supervised the children loved them. Most caseworkers made the transition other areas of the corporation, while some took early retirement.[20]

In 1985, Harold Brown again became the commissioner of LDS Social Services and served for an additional ten years. Policies and procedures were developed that represented a significant coming of age in the preparation of workers helping with the treatment of family and mental health problems. The adoption program was strengthened as well, even though the number of babies available for adoption decreased somewhat.

A very strong refinement and expansion era occurred between 1985 and 1995. Training was always an important element in LDS Social Services. In 1976 there was a major effort to increase the professional skills of staff. Val McMurray was hired to help develop and carry out this training initiative. The updated training after 1985 helped to significantly increase the skills of already competent caseworkers and prepared the way for an effective expansion of LDS Social Services throughout the United States and eventually internationally.[21] During this time there was a strong effort to learn more about common social problems and confront especially difficult issues, such as sexual abuse, by focusing on helping victims. A telephone help line for priesthood leaders provided direct consultation with professionals who could help handle challenging personal issues appropriately.

Paving the Road:
Social Services becomes Family Services

In February of 1996, LDS Social Services became LDS Family Services. "This name change will help us emphasize our goal to strengthen families through our adoption and family counseling programs," said managing director Harold Brown. "The name LDS Family Services is more descriptive of the services we deliver and the philosophy we embrace as we work with ecclesiastical leaders and members. More important, it furthers our focus on helping clients adhere to gospel principles and covenants that pertain to the eternal nature of the family."[22]

The new title reflected the very personal and family nature of the organization. It underscored the focus on the family that the social workers and other professionals employed by the organization were supposed to remember. It also mirrored the Church's strong family message by pointing to the most basic of social units emphasized by modern prophets.

Fred M. Riley, who became the commissioner in 1995, tried to maintain the core values of LDS Family Services while at the same making significant strides in the human resources side of the organization.[23] Many part-time personnel were hired to increase the number of hours of service that could be offered to Church members. Full-time practitioners took supervisory roles over the part-time therapists, which saved money and time and thus augmented Church financial and personnel resources. These part-time personnel participated in distance training via satellite, as did full-time workers. A weekly commissioner's chat highlighted issues and kept all personnel in touch with the head office in Salt Lake City.

The establishment of addiction recovery groups was a vital help to priesthood leaders and members who struggled to overcome addictions. LDS Family Services arranged with Alcoholics Anonymous to customize their twelve-step material as a basis for a Latter-day Saint addiction recovery program that has grown to help thousands work their way out of addiction. While sobriety was a desired outcome of the program, full Church activation was the goal.

Pornography addiction groups were added later, and they became a helpful weapon against this particularly difficult personal, marriage, and family problem. By 2008, over half of the participants were there to deal with pornography addiction.

Marriage and parenting manuals were also updated. The ongoing abuse help line, booklets, and videos greatly helped priesthood leaders, who could not be expected to be fully conversant in some of these serious problems. An adoptive parent group called Families Supporting Adoption was also organized. It was made up of couples hoping to adopt as well as couples who had already adopted and could serve as mentors to those either going through adoption or hoping to do so in the future. This group may well be the largest of its kind in the world. A website titled "It's about Love" was created to help promote adoptions services within LDS Family Services. Adoption efforts were further modified to allow a more open relationship between birth mothers and adoptive parents. This allowed birth mothers to play a role in choosing their child's parents and eventually placing their child in the open arms of eager adoptive parents.

The Internet Highway:
Faster, Leaner Services and Technology Enhances

Larry D. Crenshaw became commissioner in April of 2008.[24] Under his leadership, the organization has further increased its worldwide influence by more fully utilizing technology. This technology, rather than an increase in staff, helps deliver services to all Church leaders and members globally. Developing preeminent web-based services to help Church leaders better serve the social-emotional needs of their members is a major focus. For example, the website combatingpornography.org received thousands of hits through the corporation's efforts to reach strugglers and their loved ones by making the dangers of pornographic addiction understandable and offering guidelines for successfully overcoming this challenge. Individuals and their loved ones, along with Church leaders, can go online and access speeches, presentations, and scriptures to help them understand and overcome the evil effects of pornography. When fully developed, it will be much more interactive and provide more help. Indeed, using the computer to combat a problem that is usually exacerbated by computer use is a unique strategy for overcoming a very tenacious addiction that afflicts many individuals and families today.

Beginning in January 2008, a Presiding Bishopric study of LDS Family Services provided a broad analysis of the organization—including its strengths and weaknesses. This effort has resulted in several substantial changes to the organization. Some have been implemented already, others will be forthcoming. First, the hierarchy has been significantly flattened. The former director system has been eliminated, and most billing and financial functions have been outsourced to Church headquarters. Today, a new hire out of graduate school begins as a counselor, then becomes a specialist, and, with further certification, may become a supervisor or field manager. Competency-based training, testing, and compensation would facilitate promotion without requiring employees to be transferred from place to place. The savings from avoiding costly moves for workers and their families makes additional training opportunities possible.

Modern technology has also facilitated audiovisual training from headquarters to any employee with a computer, thus saving travel funds. LDS Family Services will now focus on four core services delivered through personal and web-based methods:

1. *Ecclesiastical Consultation*, providing bishops with 24/7 consultation services in multiple languages, including online consultation.
2. *Community Resource Development*, establishing a network that identifies preferred local providers (mental health professionals cleared by LDSFS) in a database accessible through an Internet portal to Church headquarters.
3. *Counseling Services*, assisting Church leaders, who are the primary source of counseling, by offering counseling mainly to those with social, emotional, or psychological issues that interfere with living gospel principles and covenant keeping.
4. *Services for Children*, helping with adoption, foster care, and birth parent support and related issues.[25]

All bishops and other leaders cannot be expected to have degrees in counseling but can access technical counseling help via phone or the Internet. The Lord has said, "I will hasten my work in its time" (D&C 88:73), and LDS Family Services is helping fulfill that scriptural mandate by addressing serious personal and social problems by assisting Church leaders worldwide.

Perhaps Amy Brown Lyman could not have foreseen the modern training, clinical tools, and technology that are fulfilling her vision of helping with personal and family problems. LDS Family Services has continually branched out, reaching more and more Church members throughout the world. What must have seemed to some priesthood leaders in the early years as a "nice" program has now become an essential tool in the Church, helping thousands who would otherwise remain roadside, disabled by their problems to instead face their issues, overcome their challenges, and take a higher road through mortality.

Notes

1. Loretta L. Hefner, "This Decade Was Different: Relief Society's Social Services Department, 1919–1929," *Dialogue* 15 (Fall 1982): 65.

2. Hefner, "This Decade Was Different," 66.

3. *History of Relief Society* (Salt Lake City: Deseret News Press, 1966), 64.

4. *History of Relief Society*, 94. There have been eleven other directors over the Relief Society Social Services Department: Amy W. Evans, Ora W. Chipman, Marie Tanner, Ruth P. Lohmoelder, Elizabeth K. Ryser, Mary Dillman, Lauramay Nebeker Baxter, Margaret Keller, Josephine Scott Patterson, Mayola R. Miltenberger, and Helen H. Evans. Josephine Scott Patterson, "Social Services in the LDS Church as I Have Known Them from 1955 through 1974," 3, Church History Library, The Church of Jesus Christ of Latter-day Saints, Salt Lake City.

5. Patterson, "Social Services in the LDS Church," 5.

6. Clarence R. Bishop, interview by author, September 10, 2010, Salt Lake City.

7. Bishop interview.

8. Patterson, "Social Services in the LDS Church," 13–14. An initial youth guidance advisory committee was organized with Spencer W. Kimball as chairman and Alvin R. Dyer, Bishop Robert L. Simpson, President Belle S. Spafford, and Sister Florence Jacobsen as members. Thomas S. Monson was added to the committee later. Youth guidance was then made a division of LDS Family Services in 1964, with Charlie Stewart as executive director. The program was moved to 50 Richards Street and then to Old Veteran's Hospital on Twelfth Avenue and E Street in 1966.

9. Allen J. Proctor, interview by author, September 10, 2010, Salt Lake City.

10. Proctor, interview.

11. "When You Need Help," *New Era*, March 1971, 4.

12. Victor L. Brown Jr. had formerly served in the Nevada agency of the Relief Society Social Services Department. Clarence R. Bishop had been responsible for the Indian Placement Program and Charlie Stewart supervised the Youth Guidance Program. Victor Brown's administration would serve from David O. McKay's presidency in 1969 until Ezra Taft Benson's.

13. In J. Richard Clarke, "Ministering to Needs through LDS Social Services," *Ensign*, May 1977, 85.

14. As a young missionary, Harold Brown had served in the northern division of the Southwest Indian Mission, beginning in November 1962, before the creation of the Northern Indian Mission in 1964. President Spencer W. Kimball visited that mission often and encouraged the missionaries to consider working with "Lamanites" after their missions if they were so inclined. Harold found employment with the Church Educational System teaching seminary to Native American students in Brigham City, Utah, for a short time, and then was invited by Clarence R. Bishop to join the Indian Placement Program as a local worker from January 1969 to June 1970 in Preston, Idaho. At the latter end of this assignment, he was assigned to go to Bismarck, North Dakota, to see if help could be offered to Native Americans on their reservations as opposed to interacting with students primarily in their foster homes. This effort became the precursor for Indian Placement offices to be opened in Rapid City, South Dakota, and Chinle, Arizona. One day, someone said to him, "Did you know you are a social worker?" That label had not occurred to him, but when he was transferred to Salt Lake City in June 1970, while still working full time he began graduate school in social work, finishing a master's degree in 1972. By the time he finished his master of social work degree, Harold was also responsible for the Indian Placement Program in Utah. He also worked later with urban Native Americans with Stewart Durrant, who served with the Lamanite committee, trying to create walk-in centers where Native Americans could access Church social services.

15. Initially, this clinic was to fall under the direction of the commissioner of LDS Social Services, but by 1981, it seemed apparent that the clinic might be better administered by Brigham Young University educators.

16. William S. Bush had come from a small town in Idaho, where he herded sheep as a teenager, and worked his way through Brigham Young University and the University of Utah. He began employment with Relief Society Social Services Department on June 10, 1963. He had not yet finished his bachelor's degree but was hired with the proviso that he would finish his degree soon after beginning as a caseworker with the Indian Student Placement Program. It seems that the early placement caseworkers loved serving among Native Americans and became a very cohesive group within LDS Social Services. In the early 1970s, Bush served as the very first assistant commissioner under Victor L. Brown as commissioner and Glen VanWagonen as associate commissioner. This new system of associate and assistant commissioners ended a system of division directors in which certain agency directors were designated as supervisors over the rest of the agency directors and were known as division directors. Bush was serving as a division director from the Phoenix agency when he was called to move to Salt Lake City to become the assistant commissioner.

17. Larry L. Whiting, "A Few Thoughts from Personal History of Larry L. Whiting While Serving as Commissioner of LDS Social Services" (unpublished manuscript in author's possession, 2010), 1.

18. "Indian Placement Modified," *Ensign*, February 1985, 80.

19. Whiting, "A Few Thoughts," 5.

20. Larry L. Whiting currently serves on the Board of Trustees of LDS Family Services.

21. Patterson, "Social Services in the LDS Church," 20. A Refinements Committee had been organized in 1973 with Art Finch, Juel Gregerson, and Brent Frazier. It was later enlarged and became the Planning and Training Committee (developing training materials) and was further enlarged to include William Bush and Rollin Davis. Eventually, Harold C. Brown, Victor L. Brown Jr., Glen E. VanWagenen, Lynn Marriott, and Charles Woodworth were added with Bill Bush serving as chairman.

22. "Policies and Announcements," *Ensign*, February 2000, 80.

23. Fred M. Riley joined LDS Social Services in Denver in February 1979, serving there for six years until the spring of 1985, when he was asked to move to Seattle to become the director of that office. In 1990 he became an assistant commissioner of the corporation, but remained in the Seattle area. About a year later, the Rileys moved to Salt Lake City. He became the commissioner five years later.

24. Larry D. Crenshaw was a Kentucky-born-and-raised descendant of Daniel Boone. His family joined the Church when he was a young man and he later served a mission in Denmark. He had received a master's degree from the Kent School of Social Work at the University of Louisville. He began work with LDS Family Services in Chicago, then was moved to Florida and ultimately to Utah.

25. Larry D. Crenshaw, interview by author, September 29, 2010, Provo, UT.

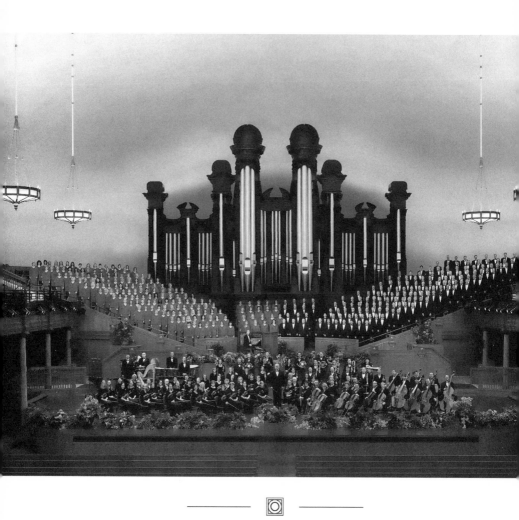

Mormon Tabernacle Choir and Orchestra at Temple Square in the Salt Lake Tabernacle.
(© Intellectual Reserve, Inc.)

Chapter 15

"From the Crossroads of the West": Eight Decades of *Music and the Spoken Word*

Lloyd D. Newell

We have in our home a gift from my mother, an old upright Philco radio that she listened to as a young girl on the family farm in Central, Idaho. It belonged to her parents, my grandpa and grandma Lloyd, and is a cherished heirloom. Even with its antique tubes and wiring, it still works. Its wooden frame is smooth and surprisingly unmarked for all the history it embodies. Only the station identifier for Salt Lake City radio station KSL is missing, perhaps from repeated use. Today the radio is prominently displayed in our home. For me, it is a visual and aural link between the early years of *Music and the Spoken Word* and today.

My mother told me that on Sundays her family would tune in to KSL and the Tabernacle Choir broadcast of *Music and the Spoken Word*. In my mind's eye, I can see my grandparents, my mother, and her siblings gathered around the Philco in their clapboard farmhouse. The

Lloyd D. Newell is a professor of Church history and doctrine at Brigham Young University.

305

tiny town of Central was far from everything except the slightly larger towns of Grace and Soda Springs, and even they seemed worlds away. So on Sundays, when they could listen to the Tabernacle Choir from Salt Lake City, it was a small miracle. Week after week they invited the familiar strains of *Music and the Spoken Word* into their home like a trusted friend.

"From the Crossroads of the West, we welcome you to Temple Square in Salt Lake City for *Music and the Spoken Word* with the Mormon Tabernacle Choir." These opening words of the broadcast go out today not only to farmhouses in southeastern Idaho but to a weekly audience that numbers in the millions. Some two thousand television, radio, and cable stations in many parts of the world carry *Music and the Spoken Word*, which has become the longest continuously broadcast program in the world. Besides bringing this little taste of Salt Lake City into living rooms throughout the world, the broadcast has also brought the world to Salt Lake City. Every week, thousands come to see and hear the choir live and in person, helping make Temple Square the most visited place in Utah and one of the most visited places in the United States. President Gordon B. Hinckley, whose involvement with the broadcast lasted nearly forty years, said, "No medium has touched the lives of so many for so long as has the weekly broadcast of *Music and the Spoken Word*."[1] As one of Salt Lake's most recognizable institutions, the broadcast has been touching lives now for more than eight decades, and it still does so today.

The Beginnings

Radio was a new medium and nationwide phenomenon that fascinated the public during the 1920s and 1930s, broadcasting music, variety, and comedy shows to an audience hungry for entertainment. During the Depression, radio became more than an amusement; it was a source of solace and relief from everyday troubles, if only for a few minutes. Radio also reflected the political and economic tensions of

306

the day. For example, Franklin D. Roosevelt periodically reassured the nation by radio during "fireside chats" in the 1930s and '40s. Radio was truly in its golden age and at the center of American culture.

In the early 1920s, approximately five hundred radio stations were established by various individuals, businesses, and organizations, creating a "broadcasting boom."[2] All across the country, people began to recognize radio's tremendous possibilities—and Salt Lake City was no exception. Leaders of The Church of Jesus Christ of Latter-day Saints saw radio's potential and encouraged the creation of a Salt Lake City station that today has become a recognized national broadcasting leader.

KSL began in 1922 as a tiny station that broadcast from a tin shed on the roof of a building in downtown Salt Lake. Known then as KZN, an NBC radio affiliate, it was an offshoot of the Church-owned newspaper, the *Deseret News*. The initial broadcast, which took place at 8:00 p.m. on May 6, 1922, was a message from President Heber J. Grant. President Grant's counselor, Anthony W. Ivins, said on that occasion, "When the 'Mormon' pioneers entered the Salt Lake Valley, in 1847, at which time the Pony Express was the most rapid means of communicated news from one point to another, they little dreamed that before a period of seventy-five years has passed, their children would talk to the world by wireless."[3] Two years later, thousands of faithful members listened to the first radio broadcast of general conference. The next year, radio listeners in Salt Lake City could tune in to a local program that showcased the Mormon Tabernacle Choir's Thursday night rehearsals.

It was about this time that KSL station manager and pioneer broadcaster Earl J. Glade had a brilliant idea—a nationwide, weekly broadcast of the Mormon Tabernacle Choir.[4] He first had to convince the choir that it could be done, and then he convinced the management of NBC. It was an ambitious plan to originate a national radio program from a remote and virtually unknown western outpost. Even choir conductor Anthony Lund had his reservations: "We can't sing with this great choir and have it come over a little kitchen radio." His concerns about the acoustics were legitimate—how would the choir's unique sound, which reverberates so beautifully in the cavernous Tabernacle, come across on radio speakers? To address these concerns, KSL's technicians hung a massive red curtain in the Tabernacle and covered the first ten rows of benches with old carpet from the station's offices.[5] With those audio problems addressed, KSL's newest radio program was ready to begin, though it is unlikely that anyone with KSL or the choir foresaw the magnitude of what they were starting.

First Broadcast, July 1929

The first broadcast of what would become known as *Music and the Spoken Word* took place on Monday, July 15, 1929, at 3:00 p.m. in the Tabernacle on Temple Square. On that hot summer afternoon, KSL ran a wire from its control room to an amplifier more than a block away in the Tabernacle, where the only microphone KSL owned had been suspended from the Tabernacle ceiling to capture the sound of the choir and organ. Nineteen-year-old Ted Kimball, son of organist Edward P. Kimball, climbed a fifteen-foot stepladder to speak into the microphone and announce the songs. NBC headquarters informed a KSL engineer by telegraph when to start the program. Hand signals to Ted Kimball marked the cue to begin. The microphone was live throughout the broadcast, and Ted stayed perched on the ladder for the duration of the broadcast. Ted approached the task "with some trepidation." He later recalled, "[My father] was more concerned with the job that I would do than he was with his own part [as organist] in the broadcast."[6]

The choir began its broadcast with "Gently Raise the Sacred Strain," a hymn written in 1835 that still opens the broadcast today. The first program included six selections:

Chorus from *Die Meistersinger*, by Richard Wagner
Sonata in B-flat Minor, first movement, by Boslip
"The Morning Breaks," by George Careless

"An Old Melody," arranged by Edward Kimball
The finale from *Elijah*, by Felix Mendelssohn
"The Pilgrim's Chorus" from *Tannhäuser*, by Richard Wagner

From the first time *Music and the Spoken Word* was sent out over NBC's thirty-station network, the program was favorably received, although some technical difficulties and a line hum caused some of the stations to cut off the debut broadcast early. By the next week, the technical problems had been resolved, and the program was on its way to making broadcasting history. On July 23, 1929, a telegram was received from M. H. Aylsworth, president of NBC: "Your wonderful Tabernacle program is making great impression in New York. Have heard from leading ministers. All impressed by program. Eagerly awaiting your next." The program was off and running. The *New York City Telegraph* gave this praise: "Somewhere in the world there may be more than one brilliant choral organization other than the Mormon Tabernacle Choir, but there is no broadcasting in America today to equal the one that comes from the air over the National Broadcasting System."[7]

The broadcast continued for three years on the NBC network, with the time and day varying from week to week. In 1932, despite efforts by NBC to retain *Music and the Spoken Word*, KSL switched to the new CBS Radio Network when CBS President William Paley offered to carry the weekly nationwide broadcasts of the Tabernacle Choir on a regular Sunday morning time slot.[8] On September 4, 1933, the broadcast began its Sunday morning run and remains to this day the longest continuous network broadcast in history.

Ted Kimball announced the first few broadcasts and then left to serve a full-time mission. Several other announcers followed until June of 1930, when a twenty-four-year-old announcer from KSL, Richard L. Evans, was chosen to announce the music for the program. Over the next forty-one years, he and the choir would bring unprecedented fame to both *Music and the Spoken Word* and its home—Salt Lake City, the "Crossroads of the West."[9]

Richard L. Evans Era, 1930–71

When he began as announcer, Evans simply announced the titles of compositions and gave the station identification, as his predecessors had done. In time, he began to relate the title of a song to some point of philosophy or moral profundity. These short thoughts flowed from the music and evolved into two- to three-minute nondenominational sermonettes. Listeners were so pleased with the additions he made that he began crafting weekly inspirational messages. His trademark sermonettes were known for their simple eloquence and uncommon wisdom.

Evans served as announcer, writer, and producer of *Music and the Spoken Word* through four decades. His name and voice are forever linked to the broadcast. Truly, he was the individual who created *Music and the Spoken Word* as we know it today. His indelible contribution is still imprinted on each broadcast. The closing words he wrote many decades ago remain unchanged today: "Again we leave you from within the shadows of the everlasting hills. May peace be with you this day and always."[10]

Born in Salt Lake City on March 23, 1906, Richard L. Evans was raised by a single mother, his father having died when Richard was just ten weeks old. At his mother's knee, Richard was taught the principles of the gospel and the importance of strong faith. When he was sixteen years old, an inspired patriarch blessed him that he would have a "bright career," that he would "stand in holy places and mingle with many of the best men and women upon the earth," and that he would serve the Lord in "distant lands, travel much and see many wonderful things." The patriarch also blessed him that his "tongue [would] be loosened and become as the pen of a ready writer in dispensing the word of God and in preaching the gospel to [his] fellow men."[11] He excelled in school and was the editor of his high school newspaper and yearbook, a champion debater, and recipient of the Heber J. Grant scholarship award.

Richard L. Evans standing in front of a microphone
with the Mormon Tabernacle Choir in the background.
(© Intellectual Reserve, Inc.)

At twenty years of age, Evans was called to the British Mission, where he served as associate editor of the *Millennial Star* and wrote the centennial history of the mission.[12] Not long after his mission, he got a job as an announcer with KSL Radio and began announcing the Tabernacle Choir broadcast.

These assignments allowed him to develop a close relationship with President Heber J. Grant. On one occasion, Richard spoke with President Grant about his desire to work on a doctorate degree and possibly to pursue broadcasting job opportunities that had opened up to him in several large eastern cities. When he asked President Grant's advice, the prophet "looked at him with a twinkle in his eye and said, 'I think I'd stick around if I were you.'" And so he remained in Salt Lake City.[13] Richard's brother commented that "as his life unfolded,

Richard L. Evans outside the Salt Lake Tabernacle. (© Intellectual Reserve, Inc.)

Richard recognized that . . . the President's advice had changed his whole life—and for the better."[14]

At age thirty-two, Evans was called by President Grant to become a member of the First Council of Seventy. After Elder Evans had served in that position for fifteen years, President David O. McKay announced Richard's name at the October 1953 general conference as the newest member of the Quorum of the Twelve. After a sustaining vote, President McKay introduced Richard by saying, "Elder Evans whom you know and have known because of his work on the radio and his service in the stakes, and whom the entire nation knows,— Richard L. Evans,—will now speak to us."[15]

As a special witness of Jesus Christ to the world, Elder Evans would take on new and demanding activities and assignments. All the while, he would remain the voice of *Music and the Spoken Word*, rarely missing a broadcast, still producing it, and writing and announcing its weekly message.

A year after Evans call to the Twelve, to commemorate the choir's twenty-fifth year of weekly broadcasts, *Life* magazine summarized the program's legacy with these words:

> Those who know this program . . . need no arguments for listening to it, or no introduction to its producer and commentator, Richard L. Evans . . . or to the disciplined voices. . . . Millions have heard them, and more millions, we hope, will hear

them in years to come. It is a national institution to be proud of, but what matters more is that Americans can be linked from ocean to ocean and year to year by the same brief respite from the world's week, and by a great chord of common thoughts on God and love and the everlasting things.[16]

In 1959, *Music and the Spoken Word* was voted America's most popular classical and religious program in a national listeners' poll. Elder Evans understood the tremendous power of broadcasting and other media to shape opinions and spread goodwill, so he worked tirelessly to share these gifts with a broader audience. With others, he was instrumental in bringing *Music and the Spoken Word* to a television audience in 1962.

Elder Evans was also busy with civic affairs, most notably with the Rotary Club. Over three decades, he rose from local offices to become president of Rotary International in 1966. During that year, he and his wife addressed audiences in sixty countries and in twenty-five states in the United States. It would be impossible to calculate the goodwill he generated as he traveled, spoke, and met with dignitaries and officials from around the world. Elder Evans's service in Rotary International helped countless individuals become better acquainted with the Church, with Salt Lake City, and with the choir's broadcast. In 2006, Rotary International held its annual worldwide convention in Salt Lake City, bringing many thousands of visitors to Utah. Several speakers mentioned Richard L. Evans, and the president of Rotary International told me personally that many members still have fond memories of Richard L. Evans and his distinguished service to Rotary.[17]

Elder Evans's death was unexpected. He was only sixty-five years old when he died just after midnight on November 1, 1971, in Salt Lake City. Elder Evans worked vigorously, as usual, up to his final days, when he became ill from a viral infection. Just before he died, he lay in his hospital bed when the Sunday morning broadcast of *Music and the Spoken Word*, which had been recorded previously, began. His voice and words, on nationwide broadcast, encouraged faith in the future: "There are times when we feel that we can't endure—that we can't face what's ahead of us . . . that we can't carry the heavy load. But these times come and go . . . and in the low times we have to endure; we have to hold on until the shadows brighten, until the load lifts. . . . There is more built-in strength in all of us than we sometimes suppose."[18]

Upon his death, the Quorum of the Twelve Apostles issued a statement to commemorate his life and contributions:

> Numerous people the world over have happily boasted that "Richard Evans is my church." For forty-two years, under intense pressures, Elder Evans has returned to the microphone nearly every week with a message of depth and faith and freshness and inspiration.
>
> As limitless approaches are made with the people all over the world by missionaries and others of us, we are greeted with the statement: "I listen every Sunday morning to Richard L. Evans." This apostle touched the hearts of millions.[19]

At the opening of the April 1972 general conference, President Harold B. Lee, First Counselor in the First Presidency, extended cordial greetings and then spoke of one who was missing:

> It is with subdued hearts that we remember our beloved Richard L. Evans. His voice, his spirit, and his admonitions and counsel were one of the highlights of his association as a General Authority of the Church. Richard L. Evans didn't just belong to the Church; he belonged to the world, and they claimed him as such. We know that there are heavenly choirs, and maybe they needed an announcer, and one to give the Spoken Word. If so, maybe the need was so great that he is called to a higher service in that place where time is no more.[20]

President Lee's words must have comforted those who had been mourning the death of this remarkable man. They also highlight the breadth of his influence. Salt Lake City claimed him as its own, but he truly belonged to the world. Through his church, civic, and broadcast work, he brought the world to the Crossroads of the West. Now, decades later, people from around the world continue to visit Salt Lake City each Sunday morning, and some of this can be traced back to the extraordinary work of Richard L. Evans.

Spencer Kinard and the Spoken Word, 1971–90

As a reporter for KSL Television, in November 1971, J. Spencer (Spence) Kinard was assigned to cover the funeral of Richard L. Evans. Ironically, he was also determined to break the story of who was going to replace Richard L. Evans as announcer of *Music and the Spoken Word*. Several months earlier, Spence Kinard had moved to Salt Lake City after working with CBS in New York. Meanwhile, Alan Jensen, a man who had substituted for Richard L. Evans from time to time, continued to announce the weekly broadcast on a temporary basis.

In February 1972, President N. Eldon Tanner called Spence Kinard to be the new announcer for *Music and the Spoken Word*. The following Sunday, Kinard received a blessing from President Tanner, was introduced to the choir, and began the weekly

Spencer Kinard served as announcer for eighteen years. (© Intellectual Reserve, Inc.)

315

announcing assignment. President Tanner encouraged him with these words: "Spence, we don't want you to start over; we want you to pick up where Richard Evans left off."[21] It was a frightening thought for the thirty-one-year-old announcer. He knew he could not fill Richard L. Evans's shoes; he could only do his personal best, relying on inspiration and divine help.

Kinard recalls, "I was reporting murder and mayhem Monday through Friday and preaching peace and love on Sunday." That changed a few months later as Kinard was promoted to be news director of the ever-growing KSL television station. The daunting part of the choir broadcast, he soon realized, was "not the delivery, but the content. What to prepare? What to write? What to say?"[22] For the first few years, Kinard, like his predecessor, continued to write the spoken word message every week, and then the inspired idea was born to invite other writers into a rotation and to turn production over to Bonneville Communications.[23]

As broadcast outlets expanded across the country during Spence Kinard's eighteen years of service, more stations began to carry *Music and the Spoken Word*. Meanwhile, the program continued to receive awards and strengthen its reputation as a national treasure.

Lloyd D. Newell and the Choir Today, 1990–Present

In October 1990, Spence Kinard resigned from his position as announcer of *Music and the Spoken Word,* and I was asked by choir president Wendell Smoot to fill in for him "until further notice." In the meantime, the position was opened for Churchwide auditions. Hundreds of people applied, and more than seventy-five formally auditioned in front of the camera in the Tabernacle. All the while, I continued to do the weekly announcing. In January 1992, based on the recommendation of the search committee and a final decision by President Hinckley, I was officially called and set apart as the "voice of the Spoken Word and announcer for the Tabernacle Choir."

Lloyd Newell speaking at the microphone, Pioneer Day Commemoration Concert, July 2008. (© Intellectual Reserve, Inc.)

People both within and outside the Church are often surprised to find out that this is not my full-time job—it's my Church calling. I occasionally receive letters to "Reverend Newell" at addresses such as "Church of the Crossroads of the West"—and my two predecessors received similar letters. I explain that, like members of the choir, I serve as an unpaid volunteer and that our program is meant to inspire and uplift through music and message. This is not our "worship service"; it's not a sacrament meeting. It's an inspirational program of music and message to feed a spiritually hungry world. Frequently, it prompts a desire for more information about who we are and what the teachings of the Church are; always, it creates goodwill and builds bridges of understanding, respect, and appreciation.

In addition to the weekly broadcasts, I accompany the choir as it travels to sing in concert halls throughout the world, as my predecessors did. Although Salt Lake City is the home of the broadcast, *Music and the Spoken Word* has also been broadcast from various other halls at locations from San Diego to New York City and more than a score of US cities in between. The broadcast has also originated from World Fairs around the world, including Montreal, Toronto, San Antonio, Seattle, and Chicago. It has even been sent over satellite from many locations outside the United States, including Mexico, Germany, Canada, England, New Zealand, Australia, Hungary, Austria, and Israel. I will never forget delivering the spoken word from the BYU Jerusalem Center on Mount Scopus, overlooking the Mount of Olives;

from Royal Albert Hall in London; from the Kennedy Center in Washington DC; or from the spectacular Palau de la Música Catalana in Barcelona, Spain—to name just a few.

Since its first broadcast, the program has run continually for more than eighty years, nearly the lifetime of radio, and has been broadcast well over four thousand times. The choir continues to receive more and more recognition, and has won countless awards. In November 2003, the choir received the National Medal of Arts (the nation's highest award for the arts) from President George W. Bush in an Oval Office ceremony. In April 2004, in conjunction with its seventy-fifth anniversary, *Music and the Spoken Word* was inducted into the National Association of Broadcasters Hall of Fame, joining broadcasting legends Bob Hope, Edward R. Morrow, Bing Crosby, Benny Goodman, and Paul Harvey. It is one of only two radio programs to be so inducted, the other being the *Grand Ole Opry*. It received two Peabody Awards for service to American Broadcasting in 1944 and 1962, and was twice awarded the Freedom Foundation's "George Washington Award" (in 1981 and 1988). In 1960, the choir won the Grammy Award for Best Performance by a Vocal Group or Chorus with a recording of "The Battle Hymn of the Republic." In 2006, the choir was honored as a Laureate of the Mother Teresa. In late 2007, *Spirit of the Season*, a Christmas album recorded by the Mormon Tabernacle Choir and the Orchestra at Temple Square, was nominated for two Grammy Awards: Best Classical Crossover Album and Best Engineered Album, Classical. And in November 2010, by a vote of the American listening public, *Music and the Spoken Word* was inducted into the National Radio Hall of Fame in the "National Pioneer" category.[24]

But perhaps its most remarkable accomplishment is its longevity. In a world so noisy and full of distraction, *Music and the Spoken Word* is a welcome reprieve, a faithful companion, a trusted friend. This program of music and message "from within the shadows of the everlasting hills" gently reminds its listeners of life's purposes and the everlasting things.

From the Crossroads

Central to the broadcast, from its earliest days, is the city from whence it originates. Salt Lake City is the home of the choir; it is the home of most of the members of the choir; it is the place where each week thousands gather to see and hear the choir live and in person. Each week I open the broadcast with the words "We welcome you to Temple Square in Salt Lake City" and close it with "Originating with station KSL in Salt Lake City." It is reasonable to assume that when countless people across the globe think of Salt Lake City, they think of the Mormon Tabernacle Choir, and when the people think of the choir, they think of Salt Lake City. When we are on tour outside Utah, everyone in attendance at the concert knows (or learns) that we come from Salt Lake City. For many years, some in the media even referred to the choir as the "Salt Lake Tabernacle Choir." Indeed, the choir and the broadcast, in a real way, are ambassadors that represent Salt Lake City and the Church to the world.

Each week, before *Music and the Spoken Word* begins, I ask the live audience, "Who is here for the first time?" About two-thirds of the audience—which numbers in the thousands—raise their hands. Week after week, people gather from far and wide to Salt Lake City to see and hear this beloved program live. Through all the ups and downs and twists and turns of the past eighty years, the essence of this beloved broadcast remains the same: inspirational music and messages that lift hearts, comfort souls, and bring us closer to the divine. Listeners who experience this inspiration in their homes around the world feel drawn to "the Crossroads of the West" to experience it in person. Truly, *Music and the Spoken Word* not only brings Salt Lake City to the world, it also brings the world to Salt Lake City.

Notes

I acknowledge my use of the following books in the preparation of this article: Charles J. Calman, *The Mormon Tabernacle Choir* (New York: Harper and Row,

1979); Richard L. Evans Jr., *Richard L. Evans: The Man and the Message* (Salt Lake City: Bookcraft, 1973); and Heidi S. Swinton, *America's Choir* (Salt Lake City: Shadow Mountain, 2004). Portions of this article were published previously in Richard L. Evans, J. Spencer Kinard, and Lloyd D. Newell, *Messages from Music and the Spoken Word* (Salt Lake City: Shadow Mountain and Mormon Tabernacle Choir, 2003). This article is a revised treatment of an earlier article: Lloyd D. Newell, "Seventy-Five Years of the Mormon Tabernacle Choir's Music and the Spoken Word, 1929–2004: A History of the Broadcast of America's Choir," *Mormon Historical Studies* 5, no. 1 (Spring 2004): 127–42.

1. Swinton, *America's Choir*, 101.

2. Swinton, *America's Choir*, 103.

3. Quoted in Swinton, *America's Choir*, 102. See also http://historytogo.utah.gov/utah_chapters/from_war_to_war/radioinutahbeganinmay1922onstationkzn.html; http://en.wikipedia.org/wiki/KSL_(radio).

4. KSL (originally designated KZN) began life as the radio arm of the LDS-owned newspaper *Deseret News*. It is Utah's oldest radio station. KZN's first broadcast came on May 6, 1922, in the form of a talk by then-LDS Church president Heber J. Grant. In 1924, it changed its call letters to KFPT, and then adopted its current call letters, with their association to Salt Lake, in 1925 after they became available (they had previously been used by an early radio station in Alaska). Earl J. Glade (later a four-term Salt Lake City mayor) joined the station in 1925 and guided KSL's operations for the next fourteen years. Power boosts over the next decade brought the station to its current 50,000 watts (daytime broadcast power) in 1932. It broadcast at several frequencies over the years before settling at 1160 kHz in 1941.

5. Earl Glade was the moving force behind getting the program started and served as its first producer.

6. See Swinton, *America's Choir*, 103.

7. Quoted in *America's Choir*, 102. "The Choir's 300 members practiced for a month before the first live broadcast, holding a final 'radio dress rehearsal' the week before. The chief divisional engineer of NBC called it an 'epic' event, with 10,000 radio fans eagerly awaiting the program. In the early broadcasts, the announcer

would aim the one microphone in the direction of whichever section was singing at the moment."

8. In July of 1999, when we celebrated the seventieth anniversary of *Music and the Spoken Word*, we used an early microphone much like the one used during the first broadcast. Speaking into this mike—one that was used by Richard L. Evans for many years—was a thrill I will not soon forget. As it turned out, television personality Oprah Winfrey was in the audience that Sunday and came up after the broadcast to speak briefly to the choir. She thanked them for inspiring her and said that she grew up listening to the choir. Having a famous broadcast personality in the Tabernacle, in awe of the choir, on the Sunday we were commemorating seventy years, is a memory to long cherish.

9. Quoted in Swinton, *America's Choir*, 104.

10. The CBS radio network and its affiliates began to air various choirs over the radio airwaves in the 1930s, among them the "Wings Over Jordan" choir. In addition, other radio stations began to air the Metropolitan Opera, the Grand Ole Opry, and other musical programming. *Music and the Spoken Word* began as a CBS network broadcast and is still carried over the network today, making it the longest network broadcast in the world.

11. The Salt Lake City area became known as the Crossroads of the West after the transcontinental railroad connected the Central Pacific and Union Pacific railroads on May 10, 1869, at Promontory Summit, Utah Territory.

12. The epitaph on Richard L. Evans's tombstone in the Salt Lake City Cemetery reads, "May Peace Be With You . . . This Day and Always."

13. Evans, *Richard L. Evans*, 23.

14. The history was subsequently published in 1937 under the title *A Century of Mormonism in Great Britain* (Salt Lake City: Deseret News).

15. Evans, *Richard L. Evans*, 45–46.

16. David W. Evans, *My Brother Richard L.*, ed. Bruce B. Clark (Salt Lake City: Beatrice Cannon Evans, 1984), 27.

17. David O. McKay, in Conference Report, October 1953, 128.

18. In Richard L. Evans, *From the Crossroads* (New York: Harper and Brothers, 1955), 14

19. One of Elder Evans's fellow Rotarians, Lowell Berry, led the push to endow a professorship in Elder Evans's honor when the Apostle passed way. The Richard L.

Evans Chair of Religious Understanding has played a significant role in improving interfaith relationships and reflects the type of outreach that Elder Evans and the Choir have been known for around the world.

20. In Evans, *Richard L. Evans*, 85.

21. "Statements from the Leading Councils of the Church," *Ensign*, December 1971, 11.

22. Harold B. Lee, in Conference Report, April 1972, 3.

23. Quoted in *America's Choir*, 109–10.

24. Quoted in *America's Choir*, 109–10.

25. Since the 1970s, *Music and the Spoken Word* has been produced by Bonneville Communications, a division of Bonneville International Corporation, and distributed internationally as a public service broadcast. Bonneville International Corporation is a holding company for numerous broadcast properties and has supported the broadcast since 1964. A wonderful, synergistic teamwork occurs as the choir leadership and Bonneville work together in the production and distribution of the program. Today a few writers are used on a rotating basis once or twice a month; I write the remaining messages, then I oversee and edit each message with the excellent assistance of Ted Barnes of Church editing.

26. For more information on the choir's history and accolades, see Lisa Ann Jackson, "From the Crossroads of the West," *Ensign*, July 2004, 68–73. See also Terryl L. Givens, *People of Paradox* (New York: Oxford University Press, 2007), chapter 13, which situates the choir in the context of both LDS culture and the broader culture and discusses the public perception and national appeal of the choir.

Chapter 16

Salt Lake City: An International Center for Family History

Kip Sperry

What Latter-day Saints now understand as "the mission of Elijah" was first suggested to the Prophet Joseph Smith when the angel Moroni appeared to him on September 21, 1823, at his parents' home in Palmyra (near Manchester), New York. Among other things, Moroni quoted, in modified form, the words of the prophet Malachi: "Behold, I will reveal unto you the Priesthood, by the hand of Elijah the prophet, before the coming of the great and dreadful day of the Lord. And he shall plant in the hearts of the children the promises made to the fathers, and the hearts of the children shall turn to their fathers. If it were not so, the whole earth would be utterly wasted at his coming" (D&C 2:1–3; compare Malachi 4:5–6).

Twelve and a half years later, on April 3, 1836, Elijah appeared to Joseph Smith and Oliver Cowdery in the Kirtland Temple, thus fulfilling Malachi's prophecy and promise that Elijah would return with priesthood keys (see D&C 110:13–16).[1]

Kip Sperry is a professor of Church history and doctrine at Brigham Young University.

An epistle from Joseph Smith to the Latter-day Saints, recorded in Nauvoo, Illinois, on September 1, 1842, gave directions and emphasized the importance of keeping proper temple records: "And again, let all the records be had in order, that they may be put in the archives of my holy temple, to be held in remembrance from generation to generation, saith the Lord of Hosts" (D&C 127:9). A second epistle included this important charge: "Let us, therefore, as a church and a people, and as Latter-day Saints, offer unto the Lord an offering in righteousness; and let us present in his holy temple, when it is finished, a book containing the records of our dead, which shall be worthy of all acceptation" (D&C 128:24). These two passages of scripture are significant for a better understanding regarding Latter-day Saint interest and emphasis on record keeping and family history research.

While these revelations provided some guidance, additional clarification regarding work for the dead was necessary. Wilford Woodruff, fourth President of The Church of Jesus Christ of Latter-day Saints, received a revelation in April 1894 that Church members should be sealed to their fathers and mothers—that is, their ancestors. His announcement in general conference in Salt Lake City ended the "law of adoption," a practice whereby some Church members were sealed by proxy in Latter-day Saint temples to prominent Church leaders instead of to their direct-line ancestors.[2] In making this important announcement, President Woodruff reemphasized the need for genealogical research and historical record keeping among the Latter-day Saints. Latter-day Saints who "seek out their ancestry have the spirit of Elijah as they turn their hearts to their ancestors and seal children to their parents. Thus, Elijah's mission is fulfilled through the temple ordinances and priesthood authority to do this work."[3]

Genealogical Society of Utah

Following this announcement in general conference, and with his emphasis on sealing families in Latter-day Saint temples, President

Woodruff oversaw the organization of the Genealogical Society of Utah on November 13, 1894, emphasizing the value of genealogical research and historical record keeping.[4] The society's stated purpose was to gather genealogical records and assist members of the Church with their family history and genealogical research.[5] Many members of other faiths have also used the Church's family history facilities for tracing their own family trees.

The purposes and functions of the Genealogical Society of Utah have changed over the years. The official organizational meeting was held in the Church Historian's Office in Salt Lake City on November 13, 1894. "The Articles of Association of the Genealogical Society of Utah announced three types of purposes for the organization: benevolent, educational, and religious. The benevolent goal was to be met by establishing and maintaining a genealogical library for the benefit of Society members and others; the educational purpose was to disseminate information regarding genealogical matters; and the religious goal was to acquire records of the dead in order to enable the performance of Church ordinances on their behalf."[6] To assist in this effort, the Genealogical Society of Utah published a quarterly for many years, the *Utah Genealogical and Historical Magazine*, which included doctrinal and religious articles, biographies, compiled genealogies, extracts of records, research methodology, and other news regarding genealogical research of particular interest to Latter-day Saints.[7]

The Church has made a major commitment to collecting genealogical and historical records and making them available to the public. The Genealogical Society of Utah is now known as FamilySearch, a nonprofit international organization sponsored by the Church.[8] Goals of FamilySearch are to gather, preserve, and share genealogical information throughout the world. FamilySearch is known worldwide for its microfilming, digitizing, and records preservation programs. Some of the services offered to archivists and other record custodians include image capturing, digital conversion, records preservation, online personal name indexing, and access to online family history and historical resources.

Family History Library

Soon after the organization of the Genealogical Society of Utah in 1894, the Church organized a research library to assist Church members and others in identifying their ancestors. The Genealogical Society Library, along with its book and periodical collection, initially shared space in the Church Historian's Office at 58 East South Temple Street in Salt Lake City. The Genealogical Society was housed on the upper floor with a reading room, classroom, and temple recording areas. The fifth floor was primarily designed to store records and files of both the Church historian and the society.

With the 1917 completion of the Church Administration Building at 47 East South Temple Street, the society relocated to occupy the fourth floor of the new building, separating its activities from the Church Historian's Office. The society remained in the Administration Building for nearly two decades until it was moved to the Joseph F. Smith Memorial Building at 80 North Main Street in 1934. This edifice had been part of the LDS College located near the former Hotel Utah.

The library's transient history continued when its large collection of books, periodicals, microfilms, family group records, and index cards (including the Temple Records Index Bureau) were again relocated in 1962 into the abandoned Montgomery Ward building at 107 South Main Street. Some administrative offices were also housed in the Beehive Bank Building on State Street. With the 1972 completion of the Church Office Building at 50 East North Temple, the Genealogical Society Library, later known as the Genealogical Department Library, moved again, occupying all four floors of the building's west wing, with administrative offices on several floors of the structure's center tower.[9]

Finally, after over ninety years of serving family history patrons, the Genealogical Department found a home of its own when its present building was dedicated on October 23, 1985.[10] Located west of Temple Square at 35 North West Temple Street, the magnificent facility contains research space divided among five floors. It was renamed the Family History Library in 1987, but it is now known as the

326

Original Genealogical Society of Utah office, located in the upper floor of the Church Historian's office (pre-1917). Individuals pictured are (left to right) Nephi Anderson, Lillian Cameron, Joseph Christensen, Joseph Fielding Smith, and Bertha Emery. (© Intellectual Reserve, Inc.)

FamilySearch Family History Library (hereafter referred to as Family History Library).[11]

The Family History Library in downtown Salt Lake City is regarded as the largest, and frequently as the best, genealogical research library in the world, primarily because of its extensive microfilm collection.[12]

The Family History Library is part of the Family History Department, also known as FamilySearch. A summary of name changes of the Genealogical Society are[13]

- 1894–1944, Genealogical Society of Utah
- 1944–75, Genealogical Society

- 1975–87, Genealogical Department
- 1987–2000, Family History Department[14]
- 2000–2008, Family and Church History Department[15]
- 2008 to present, Family History Department[16]

The five-story Family History Library houses its collection in 142,000 square feet. Humidity, temperature, and lighting are controlled to protect the collection from deterioration. There, professional consultants, library attendants, and volunteers serve approximately 1,500 patrons each day.[17] Library orientation and specialized classes are offered regularly, and research consultation is available from experienced staff members and volunteers.

Although the initial library collection included mostly books and periodicals, the growth of materials greatly expanded when the Genealogical Society of Utah began microfilming and preserving genealogical and historical records in 1938. Original records were first microfilmed in Utah (1938), Tennessee (1939), New York (1940), North Carolina (1941), Hawaii (1942), California (1945), Pennsylvania and Georgia (1946), and Connecticut, Delaware, Maryland, New Jersey, Ohio, Virginia, and other states beginning in 1947, while other family history records on microfilm were purchased.[18] By 1954, the collection exceeded one hundred thousand microfilm reels.[19]

In 1965, Elder Theodore M. Burton (1907–89), then vice president of the Genealogical Society, inquired about whether the First Presidency thought Genealogical Society microfilming should continue. Their response was that "the Society should continue as it has been doing, and concentrate its efforts in the records of the United States, British Isles, and northern European countries and then spread into those areas in which there is the greatest number of new converts and where it can be done most economically and the data obtained most readily."[20] Microfilming projects expanded internationally, first to Canada and then to European countries including Belgium, France, the Netherlands, Scandinavia, and West Germany; at the same time microfilming also expanded in the British Isles, Latin America, and the

United States.[21] Since 1998, FamilySearch has been digitizing, rather than microfilming, genealogical and historical records in the United States and internationally.

As the world's premier genealogical research library, the Family History Library includes millions of rolls of microfilm, microfiche, 350,000 books, 4,500 periodicals, maps and atlases, reference sources, and 3,700 electronic resources. It is estimated that the names of over 3 billion deceased people are included in this extensive collection. The online Library Catalog describes the library's collections.[22] Library resources may be searched at no charge and the library is open to the public. The collection represents records from over 105 countries, territories, and possessions. Genealogical and historical records are primarily from the United States, Canada, British Isles and other European countries, Latin America, Asia, and Africa. A majority of the records contain information about individuals who lived from the sixteenth century to 1950, although some records are earlier while others are from a later time period. Records are preserved in their original language and the collection contains an estimated 12 billion individual names.

The FamilySearch Center in the Joseph Smith Memorial Building, located east of Temple Square in downtown Salt Lake City, is an extension of the Family History Library and has access to genealogical databases and family history resources.[23] Access to individual computer stations is provided, and staff and volunteers are available to assist patrons with FamilySearch, especially those beginning their family history research, free of charge. Family history centers, now known as FamilySearch Centers, are satellite facilities of the main Family History Library. Initiated in 1963, FamilySearch Centers are located throughout the United States and in over 127 other countries. The largest regional center in the Salt Lake Valley is the FamilySearch Library in Riverton, Utah.[24] Other FamilySearch Centers are located in affiliate libraries, such as public libraries.

In addition to the Family History Library, other major research facilities located in Salt Lake City house family and local history materials. These include the Church History Library, International Society Daughters of Utah Pioneers Library, National Society of the Sons of Utah Pioneers Library, Utah State Archives and Records Service, Utah State Historical Society Library, and the University of Utah J. Willard Marriott Library.

FamilySearch

The Church introduced a free family history website known as FamilySearch.org on May 24, 1999.[25] FamilySearch is a nonprofit organization sponsored by the Church and today has over one billion searchable names in its online databases. With over fifteen billion hits since its launch in 1999, it is one of the most popular family history sites on the Internet.[26] The site receives over ten million hits per day. Popular websites associated with FamilySearch.org include FamilySearch, FamilySearch Blog, FamilySearch Centers (family history centers), FamilySearch Forums, FamilySearch Indexing (also known as Worldwide Indexing), FamilySearch Labs, FamilySearch Research Wiki, Family History Archives, Family History Library, Family Trees, Historical Records, Library Catalog (Family History Library), FamilySearch Community Trees, and online research courses and learning resources.[27]

Granite Mountain Records Vault

In addition to sponsoring public records, the Church also stores the world's largest collection of microfilmed and digitized genealogical and historical records in the Granite Mountain Records Vault. Construction of the vaults, which were tunneled into a mountainside, began in 1960. The vaults were completed in 1965 and dedicated in 1966. This long-term records storage facility lies beneath seven hundred feet of solid granite and consists of a series of tunnels containing over sixty-five thousand square feet. Constructed to safeguard master copies of microfilmed records, the vaults are located in

Interior of one of the vaults in the Granite Mountain Records Vault. (© Intellectual Reserve, Inc.)

Little Cottonwood Canyon, about twenty-five miles southeast of Salt Lake City. The vaults contain negative copies of original 16 mm and 35 mm microfilms, microfiche, digital masters of digitized records, and other valuable records, which are stored in a climate-controlled fifty-five-degree environment that maintains constant humidity and temperature.[28] Behind a fourteen-ton main door, the vaults are designed to protect the collection from natural disasters and calamities. Two videos that describe the construction and holdings of the Granite Mountain Records Vault were introduced at the National Genealogical Society's annual conference held in Salt Lake City on April 28 through May 1, 2010.[29]

The Granite Mountain Records Vault houses over 2.4 million rolls of microfilm masters and 1 million microfiche from more than 110 countries, territories, and possessions. The vaults contain over 3.3 billion significant genealogical and historical record images, such as cemetery records, census returns, church records, court records, emigration and immigration lists, family histories (compiled genealogies), land and property records, local histories, military records, naturalization records, vital records (births, marriages, and deaths), wills, probate records, and many others—in all containing over 20 billion names.[30] It is estimated that the microfilm masters could survive more than two hundred years because of the vault's ideal preservation environment.

The goals of FamilySearch and the Genealogical Society of Utah are to digitize, preserve, and share its genealogical records. Approximately two hundred cameras are currently capturing genealogical and historical records in over forty-five countries. To preserve these records, four key processes are associated with the Granite Mountain Records Vault: (1) microfilm and digital masters are preserved and safeguarded; (2) duplicate copies of microfilm are created and made available to over 4,600 FamilySearch Centers in over 127 countries worldwide; (3) microfilmed records are converted to digital images in archives, courthouses, historical societies, libraries, and other record repositories throughout the world; and (4) quality digital image masters are preserved where images are captured using digital scanning technologies. "FamilySearch and the record custodians benefit from the record preservation and access services accompanying these camera operations, making more records available to more people faster."[31]

Conclusion

Since 1894, the Genealogical Society of Utah, the Family History Department, and FamilySearch have grown into the largest genealogical organization in the world. They have provided over one hundred years of service preserving genealogical and historical records and lineage-linked genealogies throughout the world and for various time periods. Supported by a major research library in Salt Lake City, they have made their services and resources available to millions of people at no charge—including online personal name indexes created by over 125,000 volunteers, publications and finding aids, online research

Family History Library in Salt Lake City. (Courtesy of Woody Johnson.)

courses, and worldwide FamilySearch Centers.[32] Records are preserved for long-term storage in the Granite Mountain Records Vault, and are also made available online at no charge to a global community. For many years FamilySearch has assisted churches, commercial companies, genealogical organizations, governments, libraries, record custodians, societies, and software developers in helping thousands of people search for their ancestors, thus fulfilling Malachi's ancient prophecy that the prophet Elijah would "turn the heart of the fathers to the children, and the heart of the children to their fathers" (Malachi 4:6).

Computer and digital technology and personal name indexes have revolutionized genealogical record keeping and access. Today more people are interested in tracing their ancestry than ever before. Advancements in computer technology and the Internet continue to make family history research easier, available to more people, and more rewarding.[33] FamilySearch is helping people achieve their family history goals. Salt Lake City is truly the world's international center for family history.

Notes

1. See Karl Ricks Anderson, *Joseph Smith's Kirtland: Eyewitness Accounts* (Salt Lake City: Deseret Book, 1989); and Milton V. Backman Jr., *The Heavens Resound: A History of the Latter-day Saints in Ohio, 1830–1838* (Salt Lake City: Deseret Book, 1983).

2. *Deseret News 2011 Church Almanac* (Salt Lake City: Deseret News, 2011), 287. For additional information regarding the law of adoption, see Gordon Irving, "The Law of Adoption: One Phase of the Development of the Mormon Concept of Salvation, 1830–1900," *BYU Studies* 14, no. 3 (1974): 291–314.

3. Kip Sperry, "From Kirtland to Computers: The Growth of Family History Record Keeping," in *The Heavens Are Open: The 1992 Sperry Symposium on the Doctrine and Covenants and Church History* (Salt Lake City: Deseret Book, 1993), 291.

4. James B. Allen, Jessie L. Embry, and Kahlile B. Mehr, *Hearts Turned to the Fathers: A History of the Genealogical Society of Utah, 1894–1994* (Provo, UT: BYU Studies, Brigham Young University, 1995), 44–47; see also *2011 Church Almanac*, 84, 287.

5. The Genealogical Society of Utah is an incorporated, nonprofit educational institution funded by the Church.

6. Allen, Embry, and Mehr, *Hearts Turned to the Fathers*, 45–46.

7. The *Utah Genealogical and Historical Magazine* was first published in 1910 and discontinued in 1940.

8. Consult the Genealogical Society of Utah website (www.gensocietyofutah.org) for more details. The Genealogical Society of Utah does business as FamilySearch International, especially when dealing with international record custodians, and is the genealogical arm of The Church of Jesus Christ of Latter-day Saints. FamilySearch International is usually shortened to FamilySearch. The name of the Genealogical Society of Utah was changed in 1944; however, the incorporated name of the society is still used today and appears on the entrance to the Family History Library in Salt Lake City. FamilySearch is the consumer brand name for the Family History Department for a variety of products and services, including the FamilySearch.org website, Family History Library, and the FamilySearch Centers. FamilySearch is an umbrella term representing all of the Genealogical

Society's facilities and services. FamilySearch International is used in legal documents and contracts.

9. Allen, Embry, and Mehr, *Hearts Turned to the Fathers*, 45–49, 84–86, 123–24, 195–98, 295–98.

10. Elder Richard G. Scott, then executive director of the Genealogical Department, conducted the dedicatory service and delivered the opening address. See "Memorandum," Family History Department, November 1985.

11. Family History Library, 35 North West Temple Street, Salt Lake City, UT 84150-3440. Telephone (801) 240-2584, (800) 346-6044, or (866) 406-1830 (www.familysearch.org). Research assistance is available in person, by mail, telephone, e-mail (fhl@familysearch.org), or fax (801) 240-5551. The library is located directly west of Temple Square.

12. Consult the library's website for more details (www.familysearch.org).

13. Historical background courtesy of Christine Cox, director, and Sherry Smith, Church History Customer Services, Church History Library, The Church of Jesus Christ of Latter-day Saints, Salt Lake City; and Paul Nauta, FamilySearch Public Affairs Manager, FamilySearch, Salt Lake City; see also Allen, Embry, and Mehr, *Hearts Turned to the Fathers*; George D. Durrant, "Genealogical Society of Utah," in *Encyclopedia of Mormonism*, ed. Daniel H. Ludlow (New York: Macmillan, 1992), 2:537–38; and *Welcome to the Family History Library* (Salt Lake City: Intellectual Reserve, 2005). Kahlile B. Mehr and D. Merrill White of FamilySearch provided additional details.

14. In 1987, Church leaders announced the Genealogical Library would be renamed Family History Library.

15. On June 1, 2000, the Family History Department and the Historical Department of the Church merged into the Family and Church History Department, which included the Family History Library.

16. On April 7, 2008, the Family and Church History Department separated functions and became the Family History Department and the Church History Department.

17. Raymond S. Wright, "Family History Library," in *Encyclopedia of Mormonism*, 2:495.

18. Microfilm operator reports by James M. Black (1914–93), former North American Microfilming Supervisor. See also James M. Black, "Microfilming

Experiences of James M. Black, 1938–1972, in Service with the Genealogical Society," typescript, January 1972 (Family History Library microfilm 1313899).

19. David Ouimette, "Digitizing the Records in the Granite Mountain," FamilySearch Research Wiki (https://wiki.familysearch.org/en/Digitizing_the_Records_in_ the_Granite_Mountain). See also Ouimette, "The Vault: A Mountain of Granite and Gold," *Ancestry Magazine* 23 (March/April 2005): 32–37.

20. Genealogical Society Minutes, January 21, 1965, quoted in Allen, Embry, and Mehr, *Hearts Turned to the Fathers*, 233–34.

21. Kahlile B. Mehr, "Acquisitions, 1950–1970" (unpublished paper, manuscript).

22. See the FamilySearch Library Catalog online (http://www.familysearch.org/eng/ Library/FHLC/frameset_fnlc.asp).

23. FamilySearch Center, Joseph Smith Memorial Building, 15 East South Temple, Salt Lake City, UT 84150-3460. Telephone (801) 240-4085 (familysearch@ ldschurch.org).

24. See Riverton FamilySearch Library, FamilySearch Research Wiki (https://wiki. familysearch.org/en/Riverton_FamilySearch_Library).

25. The library's catalog and automated databases were made available on the Internet in 1999, originally known as FamilySearch Internet Genealogy Service. See FamilySearch Facts and Statistics (http://www.familysearch.org/Eng/Home/ News/home_facts.asp?ActiveTab=2).

26. There are four versions of FamilySearch: (1) the original version, available in DOS format in FamilySearch Centers, which still has several useful genealogical databases, (2) the first Internet version, sometimes known as the "classic" version of FamilySearch, (3) New FamilySearch containing compiled lineages, and (4) FamilySearch.org (www.familysearch.org).

27. Eventually these separate FamilySearch links, databases, and indexes will be included as part of FamilySearch.org. FamilySearch will also maintain FamilySearch Labs (https://labs.familysearch.org) as a separate website.

28. The first digital images from documents in local archives arrived in the Granite Mountain Records Vault in 1998.

29. Granite Mountain Records Vault videos are available online (http://newsroom. lds.org/article/familysearch-shares-plans-to-digitize-billions-of-records-stored -at-granite-mountain-records-vault) and on DVD (Salt Lake City: Intellectual Reserve, 2010).

30. Thousands of original images of indexed and unindexed digitized records (such as census returns, vital records, and many others), are available online as Historical Records in FamilySearch.org. Thousands of these digitized images have been indexed by volunteers using the Church program known as FamilySearch Indexing. Indexing is the transcription of the key fields in a record, such as personal names, dates of events, birthplace, other place names, and so forth.

31. Ouimette, "Digitizing the Records in the Granite Mountain."

32. Branch libraries were formerly known as family history centers, now FamilySearch Centers.

33. It is necessary to note that not all original records and printed sources are digitized, indexed, and available on the Internet. It is also necessary to stress the importance of using original records and primary sources whenever possible when performing genealogical and historical research and always citing the source where the information was found. An encyclopedic and comprehensive guidebook is Elizabeth Shown Mills, *Evidence Explained: Citing History Sources from Artifacts to Cyberspace*, 2nd ed. (Baltimore: Genealogical Publishing, 2009), which serves as an illustrated guide to the fundamentals of evidence analysis and source citation. See also Elizabeth Shown Mills, *Evidence! Citation & Analysis for the Family Historian* (Baltimore: Genealogical Publishing, 1997).

A view of the temple and severeal other important Church properties in downtown Salt Lake City. (© Intellectual Reserve, Inc.)

Chapter 17

Salt Lake City:
City Stake of Zion

Craig James Ostler

President Brigham Young's first matter of business upon entering the Salt Lake Valley in July 1847 was to locate the place to build a temple in which the Saints could make sacred covenants with God. Once the site for the temple had been designated, Church leaders proceeded to lay out the city plat of streets and city blocks, with the temple block as the starting point. Today, Temple Square and the bordering blocks in each direction exhibit care for the sacred nature of the heart of a city stake of Zion.

The concept of Zion has several meanings and the idea of Zion being a city laid out in a specific pattern is somewhat unique to Latter-day Saints. For example, Zion may refer to Jerusalem or specifically Mount Zion, a location in the southwest of the city of Old Jerusalem. It also refers to a people, such as the people of Enoch, whom the Lord called Zion because they were of one heart and one mind (see Moses 7:18),

Craig James Ostler is a professor of Church history and doctrine at Brigham Young University.

339

or to any group of people that are pure in heart (see D&C 97:21). On the other hand, the Lord revealed that the city of the New Jerusalem would be called Zion (see D&C 45:65–67), which city was later identified to be built specifically in Independence, Missouri (see D&C 57:1–3; 84:2–4). To describe Zion, Latter-day Saints have used the image of a tent whose curtains stretch out from the center place and are secured by stakes driven in the ground (see Isaiah 54:2). The Lord refers to stakes of Zion (see D&C 68:25–26) or stakes to Zion (see D&C 82:13), which are large ecclesiastical units, today composed of individual congregations called wards. Unique among the many perspectives of Zion is that of a city with a specific plat or layout for the city. Further, this plan for the city of Zion provided a guide for planning other cities settled by the Latter-day Saints. The Lord designated a city laid out in the same pattern as a "city of a stake of Zion" (see D&C 94:1), or what is referred to as a city stake of Zion.

The Prophet Joseph Smith laid out a distinctive city plat for the New Jerusalem or center place of Zion, and for the cities that formed the stakes of Zion.[1] Originally, he directed that once one plot of one mile square was laid off with surrounding acreage for barns, stables, and plated fields, "lay off another in the same way, and so fill up the world in these last days; and let every man live in the city, for this is the city of Zion."[2] The surrounding city plots were referred to as stakes to Zion. The movement of the Saints required that a continuous adding of city stakes adjacent to the center could not be implemented. Rather, city stakes adopting these original instructions were established in Kirtland, Ohio; Far West and Adam-ondi-Ahman, Missouri; and Nauvoo, Illinois. After the exodus to the west, the Saints established Salt Lake City, which became one of the most conspicuous of those city stakes. Although there are many organized stakes of the Church in the city today, until 1904 there was one exceptionally large stake of the Church for the entire city.[3] The concept of a city stake of Zion is most clearly recognized during the single-stake time period before the massive growth of the city. Nevertheless, more than a century later, the heart of Salt Lake City has retained the pattern of a distinctive blueprint for a city stake of Zion. The following discussion provides an explanation of Salt Lake City as a city stake of Zion; it connects elements of the city to the directions given by the Prophet Joseph Smith for building up the New Jerusalem in Jackson County, Missouri. These directions in turn echo the divinely revealed order of the camp of ancient Israel as they journeyed in the wilderness.

Plot for the City of Zion and Her Stakes

The Prophet Joseph Smith sent instructions to the Saints in the area of Independence, Missouri, regarding the foundation for the city of Zion. This city plot placed schools and houses for worship in the center. Two blocks were set aside for sacred buildings, with twelve buildings, or temples, in each block. The block to the west of the center was set aside "for store-houses for the Bishop, and to be devoted to his use."[4] The remaining ten-acre blocks that spread out in straight lines running north to south and east to west from the city center were generally for residential lots. These lots were one-half acre each, with one home per lot, and the streets were 132 feet wide. "Farming areas were located on the outskirts of town, allowing the farmer and his family to enjoy all the urban advantages of schools, public lectures, and social gatherings."[5] This basic plat was implemented in other cities where Saints gathered to stakes of Zion. Regarding the similarities among the initial plot for the city of Zion and cities in the stakes of Zion, Lynn Rosenvall pointed out, "The similarities and differences between the basic plan and the actual cities have been pinpointed in an examination of more than five hundred settlements colonized by Church members between 1830 and 1900. . . . As each city developed, the basic features of 'Zion' were retained, even though exact amounts of land designated for each function varied in each settlement."[6]

It is evident that Salt Lake City was patterned after the plot for the New Jerusalem, or the city of Zion (see D&C 45: 66–67; 57:1–3), revealed to the Prophet Joseph Smith. President Brigham Young assigned Orson Pratt to design the future city of Salt Lake by drawing upon Joseph Smith's plan for the city of Zion. Orson went to work immediately, drawing the city plot with wide streets and large lots (see figure). By August 2, 1847, the base and meridian were established as the southeast corner of what was to become Temple Square. From there, he and Henry Sherwood began to survey the plat for Salt Lake City; streets were identified by the number of blocks east, west, north, and south of the meridian marker.[7] The city plat for Salt Lake was not exactly the same as the early Missouri plot. For example, rather than each lot size being a half acre, the early Salt Lake City lots were more often 1.25 acres each. In addition, the streets were forty feet wider, as they included twenty-foot-wide sidewalks on each side. Further, more than one house could be built per lot, and Salt Lake City residential lots included gardens, barns, and places for livestock.[8] Regarding these variations, Craig F. Galli noted, "Brigham's adaptation to the original City of Zion Plat to allow for extra-wide streets facilitated future urban design adaptations that enhanced the community in several ways as Salt Lake City's population grew."[9] The wider streets have allowed for easier transition to meet the needs of automobiles, street cars, and mass transit without disturbing existing buildings. In addition, "as the Saints surveyed the city, they constructed city blocks to be altered to fit the foothill terrain and allowed buildings to be structured where none had been planned."[10] Nevertheless, the plat of Salt Lake City generally followed that of the city of Zion in Missouri. Thus it is accurate to state that the Prophet Joseph Smith received the revelation for the planning of Salt Lake City and Brigham Young and other Church leaders based the city in revelation.[11] Indeed, the American Institute of Certified Planners posthumously recognized the Prophet Joseph Smith's influence on Salt Lake City, designating the plat for the city of Zion as a National Historic Planning Landmark.[12]

Within the city plat for Zion in Independence, Missouri, the Lord commanded that the "city shall be built, *beginning at the temple lot*"

Early pioneer leadership property map of downtown Salt Lake City showing ownership of the blocks surrounding Temple Square. (Courtesy of Harold B. Lee Library, Brigham Young University.)

(D&C 84:3; emphasis added). Later, this command was repeated in "laying out and preparing a beginning and foundation of the city of the stake of Zion, here in the land of Kirtland, *beginning at my house*. And behold, it must be done according to the pattern which I have given unto you" (D&C 94:1–2; emphasis added). The Lord reaffirmed this pattern of beginning, or centering, the plot of the city from the temple lot in a commandment to the Saints gathered to Far West, Missouri, itself a stake of Zion. He commanded, "Let the city, Far West, be a holy and consecrated land unto me . . . . I command you to build a house unto me, for the gathering of my saints, that they may worship me" (D&C 115:7–8).

343

Before Brigham Young and the pioneer company crossed the Midwestern plains to the Salt Lake Valley, the Lord clarified that they were to establish a stake upon arriving: "Let every man use all his influence and property to remove this people to the place where the Lord shall locate a stake of Zion" (D&C 136:10). It is most likely that the previously established pattern of beginning a city stake of Zion focused greater emphasis on the selection of the site for the Salt Lake Temple and the plotting of the city from that point. Moved by the Spirit of God, on Monday, July 26, President Young and other leaders climbed what is now called Ensign Peak, located in the foothills north of Temple Square. They viewed the valley from that elevated spot to select the site for the temple. From Ensign Peak, those leaders waved a banner or ensign, symbolically indicating that the Salt Lake Valley would be a latter-day gathering place.[13] "Late in the afternoon [of Wednesday, July 28], all the Apostles then in the valley, accompanied by Thomas Bullock, the president's secretary, Brigham Young designated the site for the temple block between the forks of City Creek."[14] They were accompanied by Elders Heber C. Kimball, Willard Richards, Orson Pratt, Wilford Woodruff, George A. Smith, Amasa Lyman, and Ezra T. Benson. "Waving his hands, Young said that they should reserve 40 acres at that site for the temple."[15]

Moses' Tabernacle and the City of Zion

The pattern of placing temples in the center of the Lord's people was implemented long before this dispensation.[16] The earliest recorded pattern is found in the Lord's instructions to Moses regarding the tabernacle and the organization of the camp of Israel. There are several similarities between the plat for Salt Lake City and the organization of the camp of ancient Israel as the Israelites traveled in the wilderness. For example, the center of the camp of Israel was the tent of the Lord, or the tabernacle, a type of portable temple. Whether the people camped for one night or several weeks or were on the march, the Lord specified a particular order and layout of the camp of the tribes of Israel. In the camp, the curtained gate and doors of the tabernacle faced east, toward the direction of the morning light. The Lord revealed that the tents of the prophet Moses and his brother Aaron, the high priest, were to be pitched on the immediate east side or entrance of the tabernacle, "keeping the charge of the sanctuary for the charge of the children of Israel" (Numbers 3:38). This position of the families and tents of Moses and Aaron, the presidents of the Melchizedek and Aaronic Priesthoods, may have represented their assignments as the sentinels placed to guard the entrance to the holy space of the tabernacle courtyard and to the tent of the Lord. Immediately to the west, north, and south, Aaron's sons were given their positions in the camp of Israel, essentially surrounding the tabernacle with the priesthood as they pitched their tents along the way (see Numbers 1–2). In Salt Lake City, President Young and members of the Quorum of the Twelve Apostles set up inheritances for the presiding officers, similar to Moses, Aaron, and Aaron's sons. The properties of President Young and Presiding Bishop Newel K. Whitney, like Moses and Aaron, were purposely located on the block directly east of the temple (see figure). Like their ancient counterparts, they were the presidents of the greater and lesser priesthoods respectively (D&C 84:6, 25–27; 107:13–16, 91).

The environs of the ancient tabernacle and the modern temple were designed to protect the holiness of the house of the Lord. The Lord instructed Moses to appoint the Levites to oversee and care for the tabernacle and the sacred vessels and furniture that belonged to it. As part of their ministry, they were also to "encamp round about the tabernacle" (Numbers 1:50). Likewise, Brigham Young extended the spirit of holiness to the area surrounding Temple Square in Salt Lake City by placing the inheritances of modern priesthood leaders nearby. The residential lots in the vicinity of Temple Square were given to Church leaders such as Heber C. Kimball and Willard Richards, both counselors in the First Presidency, and Orson Hyde, George A.

Smith, Wilford Woodruff, John Taylor, Orson Pratt, Parley P. Pratt, and Ezra T. Benson—all members of the Quorum of the Twelve Apostles (see figure).

Buildings and Businesses in the City of Zion

In accordance with this pattern, during the years that have followed the original laying out of the plot of Zion in Salt Lake City, Church buildings dedicated to the work of the Lord, have risen on the temple block, and a wall has been placed around it. Each of these edifices contributed to building up Zion in her beauty and to helping the Saints become a truly Zion people. Similar to the twenty-four houses of the Lord that the Prophet Joseph Smith indicated were to be at the center of Zion in Missouri, many other Zion-oriented buildings have been erected in the center of Salt Lake City. Many of the early structures included meeting places on Temple Square—first under a bowery, then in an early gable-roofed tabernacle building, and later in the famed elliptical roofed Salt Lake Tabernacle.[17] From 1879 to 1882, President John Taylor directed the building of the Assembly Hall on Temple Square as a smaller gathering place. In 1855, to meet the needs of the Saints to receive sacred ordinances as the temple was being built, they erected the Endowment House, a temporary temple, on the northwest corner of Temple Square, later adding an adjoining room that housed a font for baptisms for the dead. "When the temple was completed," noted President Gordon B. Hinckley, "a wall was constructed surrounding what has come to be known as Temple Square. The traffic outside the wall is frequently heavy and noisy. Within the wall, there is an environment of peace and beauty. The grounds with their artistic walkways, broad lawns, magnificent trees, and brightly colored flowers become a world apart from the outer surroundings."[18]

The principles of Zion extended beyond the walls of Temple Square and governed the Zion's Cooperative Mercantile Institution (ZCMI) and other businesses. For example, placards were placed above many businesses with the inscription "Holiness to the Lord." This same plat for the city of Zion extended into other settlements throughout the West. The early Saints planted seeds of the city of Zion in their various communities after the pattern found in Salt Lake City. These seeds included temples, bishops' storehouses, businesses associated with ZCMI, and the homes and farms of Saints.

To understand the desire to establish Zion among the early pioneers, one must appreciate the concerns President Young and other leaders expressed about commerce. For example, William S. Godbe, a wealthy businessman and eventual apostate, desecrated the spirit of Zion and looked to commercial and financial concerns apart from the purposes the Lord had revealed.[19] Further, whenever any Gentiles, or non-Latter-day Saints, sought to gain power and control of the city, of businesses or of the government, they were viewed as opponents to Zion and to the city of the stake of Zion. That perspective adds insight to modern renovation projects in and around Temple Square. Often, the intent of these projects is to protect the sacred environment of Temple Square and permit visitors to enjoy the Spirit of the Lord, unhindered by surroundings not conducive to contemplating the beauty of Zion.

The Mountain of the Lord within the City of Zion

While the plat for Salt Lake City definitely has practical advantages, it has philosophical underpinnings as well. The design of a city of Zion with a temple at its heart has its beginning long before the Mormon settlement of Salt Lake City. Laying out a city from the point of the temple follows the divine pattern of the creation of the earth, when land first came forth out of the waters, creating a place for humankind to live (see Genesis 1:9–10). Recognizing that the land above the waters was, in reality, the top of a mountain breaking the watery surface and that God's matchless power brought it forth, the resultant land is referred to as the mountain of the Lord.[20] Further, the concept of the mountain of the Lord is associated with the dwelling place or house of

God on earth. At the very least, the mountain of the Lord is the location where God meets with man on earth. For example, Moses saw the burning bush when he "came to the *mountain of God*, even Horeb" (see Exodus 3:1; emphasis added). Isaiah and Micah wrote of a future day in which many people will say, "Let us go up to the *mountain of the Lord*, to the house of the God of Jacob" (see Isaiah 2:3; Micah 4:2; emphasis added). Decades before the Restoration of the gospel, Michael Bruce (1746–67) penned the words to a hymn, "Behold, the Mountain of the Lord," later included in the Latter-day Saint hymnal. His words express awareness of Isaiah's symbolic reference:

> Behold, the mountain of the Lord
> In latter days shall rise
> On mountaintops, above the hills,
> And draw the wond'ring eyes.
> To this shall joyful nations come;
> All tribes and tongues shall flow.
> "Up to the hill of God," they'll say,
> "And to his house we'll go."[21]

In accordance with this symbolic perspective, the Salt Lake Temple is often referred to as the mountain of the Lord. Indeed, its walls are made from mountain granite.[22] This designation follows a pattern established earlier in this dispensation when the Lord called "the city of New Jerusalem," "Mount Zion" (see D&C 84:2–3; 133:18). The actual elevation of the city or of the temple site varies only a little from the surrounding area, but it is designated as a "mountain of the Lord" because of the temple to be built there.

Latter-day Saints are not unique in associating temples with the primordial mount of creation. Many cultures incorporate the concept of a mountain of the Lord into their sacred buildings and temples. William J. Hamblin and David Rolph Seeley point out that "many temples were considered embodiments of the cosmic mountain—a high place of universal preeminence—which connected the heavens with the earth and where the gods often dwelt. The idea of the cosmic mountain, a place where humans ascended and Gods descended to meet them, is often reflected in the names of such Mesopotamian temples as *E-kur* (mountain house), the name of Enlil's temple at Nippur, and *Dur-an-ki* (bond of heaven and earth)."[23] The architecture of many ancient temples such as the ziggurats of ancient Babylon, the pyramids in Mesoamerica, and temples in many other cultures represented sacred mountains. The temples and the mountains themselves often became associated with the dwelling place of God.

Ultimately, the primordial mountain, the mountain of the Lord, or the temple, represents the beginnings and center place of Zion. Isaiah explained, "And many people shall go and say, Come ye, let us go up to the mountain of the Lord, to the house of the God of Jacob; and he will teach us of his ways, and we will walk in his paths; for out of Zion shall go forth the law and the word of the Lord from Jerusalem" (see Isaiah 2:3). In latter days, the Lord explained that the Saints were to gather to build the city of Zion, "which city shall be built, beginning at the temple lot . . . that the city New Jerusalem shall be built by the gathering of the Saints, beginning at this place, even the place of the temple" (see D&C 84:3). Thus temples philosophically connect the creation of the earth with building the city of Zion—a city dedicated and consecrated to God (see D&C 57:1–3; 58:57; 103:35).[24]

Concluding Thoughts

Salt Lake City provides a glimpse into what the Prophet Joseph Smith intended for the future building up of the New Jerusalem in Jackson County, Missouri. Indeed, Salt Lake City serves as a vivid example of a city stake of Zion. The modern building up of Zion connects Latter-day Saints with peoples that had the same labor in former times, specifically to the children of Israel in the days of Moses. The pattern of beginning a city stake of Zion, with a center block set aside for the work of the Lord, may draw us to the very creation of the earth. In addition, as a city stake of Zion, Salt Lake City heralds another type of creation—that of the millennial earth. Revelations and efforts to build Zion, her city stakes, and temples may teach of a day when the Saints will welcome the Lamb of God, when he "shall stand upon Mount Zion, and with him a hundred and forty-four thousand, having his Father's name written on their foreheads" (D&C 133:18; see also Revelation 14:1). Granted, Salt Lake is but a glimpse of Zion, but it may allow us to better envision with John the Revelator as he testified, "And I John saw the holy city, new Jerusalem, coming down from God out of heaven, prepared as a bride adorned for her husband" (Revelation 21:2).

Notes

1. Richard H. Jackson, "The Mormon Village: Genesis and Antecedents of the City of Zion Plan," *BYU Studies* 17, no. 1 (Winter 1977): 223–40. Specifically, the plats for Kirtland, Ohio, Far West, Missouri, and Nauvoo, Illinois, follow the pattern for the City of Zion in Independence, Missouri. It is suspected that Adam-ondi-Ahman, Missouri, was also laid out according to the pattern of the plans for the City of Zion. The original plat of the city of Far West, discovered in 1990, offers a visual image of the four-square city plan. "The historic document, in near-perfect condition, is drawn with black ink on sheepskin. It is labeled 'Original Platte of Far West, Caldwell Co., Mo.' In August 1836, two counselors in the Missouri presidency, W. W. Phelps and John Whitmer, selected the 640-acre site for Far West. The town site was surveyed with the temple block in the center and public squares in each quadrant. Surveyors platted all of the streets 5 rods wide, except those adjacent to the temple block, which were 8 rods, or 132 feet across. The different street widths are clearly evident in the leather plat. The document appears to have been used to note the assignment of city lots. In more than 60 of the lots, including one of the public squares, someone has placed a firm dot with a pencil." Glen M. Leonard, "Far West Plat Reflects Inspired City Plan," *Church News*, April 28, 1990, 4.

2. *History of the Church of Jesus Christ of Latter-day Saints*, ed. B. H. Roberts, 2nd ed. rev. (Salt Lake City: Deseret Book, 1973), 1:358.

3. See Thomas G. Alexander, *Mormonism in Transition: A History of the Latter-day Saints, 1890–1930* (Urbana and Chicago: University of Illinois Press, 1986), 104.

4. *History of the Church*, 1:358.

5. John Livingstone, W. Jeffrey Marsh, Lloyd D. Newell, Craig James Ostler, John P. Starr, and David M. Whitchurch, *Salt Lake City: Ensign to the Nations* (Provo, UT: Religious Studies Center, Brigham Young University, 2008), 72; *History of the Church*, 1:357–59.

6. Lynn Rosenvall, "Joseph Smith's Influence on Mormon City Planning," *Ensign*, June 1974, 26.

7. Orson F. Whitney, "Orson Pratt: Apostle, Pioneer, Philosopher, Scientist and Historian," *Improvement Era*, January 1912, 201. Livingstone and others, *Salt Lake City: Ensign to the Nations*, 21.

8. See Richard Jackson, "The Mormon Village: Genesis and Antecedents of the City of Zion Plan," *BYU Studies* 17, no. 1 (Winter 1977): 223–40.

9. Craig D. Galli, "Building Zion: The Latter-day Saint Legacy of Urban Planning," *BYU Studies* 44, no. 1 (2005): 117.

10. Rosenvall, "Joseph Smith's Influence," 26.

11. In a note to his history of the Church, referring to the plat for Salt Lake City, B. H. Roberts wrote, "the reader will recognize that this plan of city-building is nearly identical with that given to Joseph Smith for the city of Zion in Jackson county, Mo." *A Comprehensive History of the Church of Jesus Christ of Latter-day Saints, Century 1* (Provo, UT: Brigham Young University Press, 1957), 3:280n27.

12. The award plaque is located inside the west wall of Brigham Young Historic Park (southeast corner of State Street and North Temple). The park also honors Brigham Young for carrying out the City of Zion plat in Salt Lake City.

13. See Dennis A. Wright and Rebekah E. Westrup, "Ensign Peak: A Historical Review," in this volume.

14. Roberts, *Comprehensive History*, 3:280.

15. Thomas G. Alexander, *Grace and Grandeur: A History of Salt Lake City* (Carlsbad, CA: Heritage Media Corporation, 2001), 19; see also Wilford Woodruff's journal entry for July 28, 1847.

16. Although Enoch "built a city that was called the City of Holiness, even Zion" (Moses 7:19), no mention is made in the scriptures of a temple in that city or the city plat. The same is true of other cities that might have been built after this pattern, such as Melchizedek's city of Salem (see Genesis 14:18).

17. Gordon B. Hinckley, "To All the World in Testimony," *Ensign*, May 2000, 4; see also Scott C. Esplin, "The Salt Lake Tabernacle," in this volume.

18. Gordon B. Hinckley, "The Salt Lake Temple," *Ensign*, March 1993, 5.

19. Roberts, *Comprehensive History*, 5:258–69.

20. William J. Hamblin and David Rolph Seely, *Solomon's Temple: Myth and History* (London: Thames and Hudson, 2007), 9–14. Sometimes this mount is also referred to as the primordial or cosmic mount, underscoring both its prominence as the most ancient mount and its association with the mystical or celestial nature attributed to the works of God.

21. Michael Bruce, "Behold, the Mountain of the Lord," *Hymns* (Salt Lake City: The Church of Jesus Christ of Latter-day Saints, 1985), no. 54.

22. Underscoring this concept, in 1993 a film entitled *The Mountain of the Lord* was produced under the direction of the First Presidency to commemorate the one hundredth anniversary of the dedication of the Salt Lake Temple. "The Mountain of the Lord," *Ensign*, March 1993, 10.

23. Hamblin and Seely, *Solomon's Temple*, 10.

24. It may have been with this in mind that the Psalmist declared of God, "His foundation is in the holy mountains" (Psalm 87:1).

Index

Italicized page numbers refer to images.